A
STATE
OF
FEAR

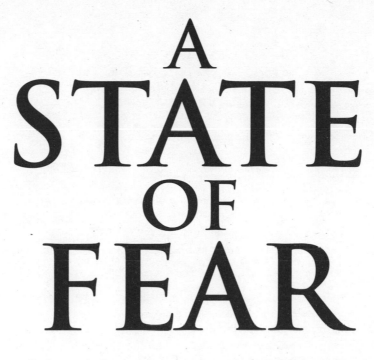

A STATE OF FEAR

My 10 years inside Iran's torture jails

DR REZA GHAFFARI

JOHN BLAKE

Published by Metro Publishing
an imprint of John Blake Publishing Ltd
3 Bramber Court, 2 Bramber Road,
London W14 9PB, England

www.johnblakepublishing.co.uk

www.facebook.com/Johnblakepub   facebook

twitter.com/johnblakepub   twitter

First published in hardback in 2012

ISBN: 978-1-84358-396-7

British Library Cataloguing-in-Publication Data:

A catalogue record for this book is available from the British Library.

Design by www.envydesign.co.uk

Printed in Great Britain by CPI Group (UK) Ltd

1 3 5 7 9 10 8 6 4 2

Papers used by John Blake Publishing are natural, recyclable products made
from wood grown in sustainable forests. The manufacturing processes
conform to the environmental regulations of the country of origin.

Every attempt has been made to contact the relevant copyright-holders,
but some were unobtainable. We would be grateful if the
appropriate people could contact us.

For my dear wife Firouzeh and my
children Sara, Zoher and Amir

Contents

FOREWORD

This is the story of my long and agonising journey through Iran's barbaric prison system, a network of institutions which created fear under the Shah and were maintained by the Islamic regime which overthrew him. The jails were designed to eliminate all opposition, to ruin health, to break minds. I spent six long years being shuttled from one hellhole to another, tortured, interrogated, abused and repeatedly broken.

Yet I had never been a man of violence myself. I was passionate about education and I was an active underground campaigner for resistance to both the Shah and the brutal regime that followed. It was because of my dedication to reform that I found myself caught up in the prison machine in 1983. My learning in itself was a threat which the authorities couldn't tolerate but I always loved reading. During my childhood and my time at Tehran University a great many books were deemed unsuitable by the authorities and therefore unavailable to me. Friends and colleagues would sometimes share stories and ideas from these banned works in hushed voices, like a nationwide version of Chinese whispers.

I had come from a poor family, my father was a carpenter. I was one of the first to be properly educated. Even as a young man I was already involved in organisations struggling to get rid of the Shah but I went on to study in America where I also lectured and was a journalist. The experience abroad was totally new. I will never forget the feeling of my first visit to the library in the US. Lines of bulging shelves seemed to stretch for miles. Here, rather than relying on a third- or fourth-hand retelling of a book, I could just go to the desk and ask for a copy. It was intoxicating.

I returned to my homeland to become a lecturer at the university in Tehran. After the Shah was at last overthrown in 1979 I was part of planning what should replace him. It didn't take long for me to realise that as a supporter of workers' rights, a passionate campaigner of the left, and as someone involved in the struggle of the Kurds I was seen as a dangerous criminal by the new Islamic regime. Our new rulers proved to be at the very least the equal of the Shah as a totalitarian government. For 15 years I had worked in secret for the left wing. But my struggle against what was called the Islamic 'revolution' led to long years of torture, degradation and imprisonment.

It was not until I had fled my native land and settled in England that I read a book that, above all others, encapsulated my experience of life in Iran, George Orwell's *1984*. With its dystopian vision, tales of surveillance, propaganda and torture it was, I know, often interpreted as a warning of the dangers of communism. But I have experienced the reality of life in a state of fear like the one imagined by Orwell.

And now I have a book of my own. It is a story that the Iranian authorities do not want you to read. It is not surprising they feel this way. What you are to read is a tale of brutality. Anyone who suspects that Iran is unfairly slandered in the West will have that scepticism dispelled.

This is not merely a catalogue of torture and prison massacres, it is also one of integrity and the triumph of the human spirit. I do not speak of myself, but rather of the thousands of my fellow prisoners – not just men but women and children – who did their best to hold on to their sanity and support each other. Few survivors are in a position to share their experiences and I feel compelled to share the stories of my fellow inmates as well as my own.

You will read of those on both sides of the struggle. Some stories I have chosen to tell are those of criminals in league with the worst elements of the Shah or the Islamic regime – in some cases, one after the other. And then there were those on the other side, whose idealism and honesty brought them to tragedy. I have painted as true a picture as I can of some of my comrades. Some of them are no longer around to have their own voices heard and mine is far from the only account of sustained torture and resistance which deserves to be recorded. Among the fallen is student Firooz Alvandi, whose life story best illustrates how the Islamic revolution sucked in and destroyed whole families and their young people who were bright and keen to make a significant contribution to their country. And I have carefully compiled the results of my own interviews with women who were shown no mercy in prison, even those who were heavily pregnant. Life in Islamic prison was unbearable for the men. For women it was much worse.

My role as unofficial spokesperson for the forgotten prisoners of Iran has led to threats. After my son and his wife, a poet, were terrorised in London, I was moved to a safe house by MI6. I was there for almost a year and only saw my family twice. After I was allowed back to my home it was kept under surveillance.

These days I live a quiet life. The years of torture have taken their toll on my health. There is a mixture of yellow, white and purple pills I must now take every day; regular, lengthy stays in hospital are just a part of my life.

The fatwah imposed by Ayatollah Khomeini against Salman Rushdie for writing *The Satanic Verses* made it difficult to find a publisher for this book in English. Versions were first published in Turkish, German and Persian for people of the Iranian diaspora and these led to me giving talks in America and Europe. So you will understand that it is a great relief to me personally that a version of my book is now available in English. It might not be an easy read but it is a book that I believe should be read.

Dr Reza Ghaffari
London, 2012

CHAPTER 1

WHEN DAWN'S LEFT HAND WAS IN THE SKY

'Don't move! Keep your hands in view'.

I opened my bleary eyes to find a circle of ten bearded faces surrounding my bed, scowling down at me. Just below each beard hovered the muzzle of a gun.

One, whose facial hair was flecked with grey, shouted at my startled wife. 'Don't just lie there, sister – cover yourself, put on your chador!' before throwing her from the room. In hindsight it was a ridiculous thing to say, like bursting in on someone in the toilet and reprimanding them for urinating in front of them. At the time, of course, it was terrifying. My wife returned with my pyjamas, as I was naked, before being bundled out once more.

They cuffed my hands tightly behind my back and blind-folded me with a piece of white cloth snatched from the floor. While this was being done, the others ransacked the room.

'Where have you put the gun?' one of them screamed.

I could hear a second group wreaking havoc throughout the

1

rest of the house. Our possessions were thrown into plastic sacks – books, tapes, the music centre, anything that would fit. It was as if these men were burglars, desperate to make a swift exit. But I already knew I couldn't call the police; the Hezbollahi were the police.

My family huddled together in the hallway: my wife, two daughters aged 10 and 12, my four-year-old son and their nanny, the elderly Khaleh Ghezi (who we called 'Aunty'). They were terrified, shivering and crying. They watched helplessly as, all around them, their home was ripped to pieces. Then, as I was still trying to put on my pyjamas, I was pulled to my feet and led away.

'Sister, we're taking him for routine questioning,' the older Hezbollahi told my wife. 'You'll have him back in a couple of hours.'

Hands grasped my upper arms, roughly pulling me onwards. Still blindfolded, I was moving too fast to safely feel my way, and I stumbled down the stairs to the front door.

Thrust outside onto the street, I briefly felt the gentle warmth of Tehran's spring sun on the back of my neck. I was led across the pavement and was bundled into the back seat of a car. A hand grabbed the back of my head and pushed it down – perhaps so I wouldn't try to see from under the blindfold or, more likely, to prevent anybody from noticing me. We pulled out. To where, I did not know. I could feel the coldness of a gun barrel against the back of my head.

I soon registered that another man was hunched beside me. Through a small space at the top of the cloth tied over my eyes I could see that he, too, was blindfolded. He seemed wholly subdued, a condition I would later recognise as a result of torture. He very deliberately hit his leg against mine. I didn't respond, but he nudged me again, this time with his elbow. This seemed strange. Who was this man? Was he the reason these thugs had come to my house? I was still in shock, my guard was up and I was too horrified to consider trusting anybody. I did not respond.

It was early and the streets were empty and silent. We were driving very fast and every time we turned I was thrown from side to side. Each minute felt like an hour but, finally, we came to an abrupt stop. The driver beeped the horn, and I heard the screeching of iron on iron. A heavy gate was opening. Sure enough, when the screeching stopped, we drove on.

Minutes later we stopped again. The door opened, rough hands grabbed my arms and I was hauled out of the car. Then, flanked by two guards, I was frogmarched to a nearby building and led to a room on the ground floor. As soon as we were inside my handcuffs were removed, although the blindfold remained. I was asked my name and the name of my father, my occupation, address and date of birth.

I was instructed to undress and I removed my pyjamas. A guard approached and checked inside the waistband of my underpants to see if I had anything concealed there. I was handed some clothes and a pair of black plastic slippers and ordered to put them on. They didn't even slightly fit me.

Finally the makeshift blindfold was removed and, blinking into the light, I nervously surveyed my captors and surroundings. A battered wooden desk stood in the right corner of the room, behind which was a stocky man in his thirties with a heavy black beard that covered his entire face apart from his nose and eyes. Above him hung a huge poster, almost two metres high, of the very familiar face of the Ayatollah Khomeini. Three or four young men, all sporting beards, stood along one side of the room. They were cradling Uzis and Kalashnikovs, and wearing pistols at their sides. On the other side there was a pile of worn plastic slippers, another of worn-out uniforms and a smaller one of what must have been blindfolds. I looked down to see that I was wearing a threadbare prison uniform with faded vertical stripes.

All this I glimpsed in a second. I didn't get any chance to see more as my eyes and nose were covered by a standard issue black prison blindfold, stiff with sweat, dirt and dried blood. It smelt of faeces.

'How long have you been a counter-revolutionary?'

I hesitantly replied, 'Brother, there must be some mistake. I have never been a counter-revolutionary. I have always supported the revolution.'

'What revolution?'

'The revolution that overthrew the Shah.'

'When did you become a counter-revolutionary American leftist?'

'I have always despised intervention by any foreign power, especially American intervention in the internal affairs of my country.'

'Which counter-revolutionary group do you belong to?'

'None whatsoever,' I said.

A grunt signalled that the interview was over. Hands seized me, pulling me through the door leading to the bowels of the jail.

Welcome to hell.

CHAPTER 2

THE NARROW
GATE TO HELL

I could hear a terrible sound. As I stepped into the open prison yard, I realised what it was: the sound of torture. Once you hear those screams they stay with you forever. They penetrated the walls and echoed down the corridors and inside my skull. I can still hear those echoes today. I particularly remember the sickening sound of a woman screaming out for help. These hellish sounds grew louder and more piercing as we ventured inside.

I was hurried along a long corridor. As we came to some steps I stumbled and fell to my knees, almost smashing my head on the ground. A guard grabbed my sleeve and pulled me back on my feet. I already knew why he had grabbed my sleeve rather than my arm: I was considered 'untouchable' by my devout captors. Further inside the prison I hit my forehead against what must have been a low ceiling. It made a sickening, dull thud and I collapsed for a second time.

This corridor was the narrow gate to hell. Every 'untouchable' would have walked along it. Every prisoner would have fallen on that step and hit their head on that ceiling. This journey was a blunt and somehow fitting introduction to a world of psychological disorientation. We came to a room and I was pushed down into a chair. I could just make out a simple desk standing in front of me. I heard men filing in.

'We've captured all of you bastards now,' someone said. 'You can die together.'

'Brother Rahman, hand him to me,' another of them shouted. 'I'll send him straight to hell.'

They began incessantly cursing me and members of my family. It almost sounded like an incantation, a ritual they repeated for every new prisoner. I tried to convince myself that these taunts were the punishment, but inside I knew that they were just psyching themselves up before they began. Eventually, it started.

'Tell me, which organisation do you belong to?'

'Brother, there has been a mistake. I'm not a member of any organisation.' I was in fact a member of an underground workers' organisation called Rahe Kargar, which literally means 'Workers' Way'. Trades unions were banned, so secret cells of Rahe Kargar sprang up around the country.

He struck the back of my neck with the edge of his hand. It was followed by a wild flurry of punches to my head and face.

I was taken to an adjoining room. Still reeling from this initial beating, I was pushed into a corner. I was so close to the walls that I could feel the concrete against my nose. With my eyes still covered, I was now seriously disorientated. I tried to keep calm and not think about what was going to happen next. It emerged that I did not have to wait long to find out.

Something struck from behind – not a fist, it was far too powerful for that – and my face and chest smashed against the walls in the corner where I stood. Badly winded and unable to breathe, I collapsed to my knees. I desperately fought for air but, like a fish on a slate, I was helpless. It was agony, like sharp bolts of electricity were being passed through my body. Someone tried to pull me to my feet but my legs wouldn't support me.

Once my system allowed me to swallow air again I saw, through the small slit above my blindfold, what had hit me. It was swinging from the ceiling and looked a bit like a punch bag, but bigger and filled with gravel. It was about a half a metre in diameter and a metre in length. When it slammed into you it felt like a train. While I was still on my knees, a heavy boot of one of the Hezbollahi delivered a swift kick to my head, then another to my back. The man grabbed my hand, pulled me up, and I was dragged, staggering and breathless, to another room.

From beneath my blindfold I saw the feet of my torturers. From what I could make out there were at least four men in the room with me. I also saw an iron bed frame, covered with what would have been a mattress if it wasn't made of wood. They forced me onto it, face down.

One interrogator sat on my back, firmly placed a hand on the back of my head and forced my face into the wooden board. Two others strapped my ankles to the crosspiece of the frame and my wrists to the top. My arms were stretched out straight. Then they began their 'holy duty', lashing the soles of my feet with a length of thick, insulated cable. The pain was indescribable. It tore through every inch of me. I screamed like never before, all the while anger growing inside me. The guard on my back only pushed down harder, grinding my face into the wood. As the flogging intensified, so did my screams. One of the men pushed torn pieces of blanket covered with dirt, blood, dust and hair into my mouth to gag me.

Throughout the ordeal the interrogator demanded names, times, places and houses of my 'comrades'. He was fixated on the times and places of alleged secret meetings. I couldn't have answered even if I had wanted to; with my mouth stuffed with rags it was difficult to breathe, let alone speak. The pain from the lashing was almost obscured by the feeling of blind panic that I was going to choke to death. Focusing what little energy I had, I was able to dislodge the rags in my mouth. They were trying to break me mentally as well as physically, claiming they knew the time and place of a certain meeting and demanded that I confirm it. I knew they were bluffing. What they really expected from me was detailed information leading to the capture and arrest of my comrades. Mercifully, I passed out.

My body was covered with a cold sweat. It felt like I had been soaked in icy water. From under the blindfold I could see a narrow beam of light shining through a hole in the door of the torture room. The rags had been removed from my mouth. The chief interrogator told me that Haji Aghah – a priest and representative of the Ayatollah Khomeini in the prisons – gave him written permission to torture me to death.

'Now, what are you going to do? Do you talk, or should I ask our brothers to make you talk? We have forced central committee members to talk. Do you want to be a hero? You're a fool. No hero will emerge from this cell alive. Do you know where we'll take your corpse? To a cursed hole where dogs will tear you apart.'

'Brother,' I said, sobbing, 'I swear by Imam Khomeini that you have made a mistake, I know nothing about these names and addresses.'

The chief interrogator and two others took the straps off and sat me up on the bed, still blindfolded, so that I was facing the door. I heard more people entering the room and four more boots appeared on the ground, along with someone wearing plastic prison slippers. I assumed he was another prisoner, but had no idea who he was. The chief interrogator spoke again. 'Farhad, take off your blindfold and tell us who this man sitting on the bed is.'

8

With some hesitation, the prisoner said, 'He is Karveh, a lecturer at the University of Tehran.' Karveh was the secret underground name I was known by for 20 years and more while in the Rahe Kargar movement. He gave a list of names of people supposedly working under me and recited a statement that had obviously been dictated by prison officials: 'My wife and I have both been captured. Our organisation has been attacked at the very top. We have given the brothers all the information that we have. You should do the same, otherwise you and your family will be destroyed.'

Farhad. I knew that name well. And that voice was familiar, too… it was that of a cadre in Rahe Kargar. It took me a second to place him as he sounded different, broken and desolate. It was a tone that I had never heard before, although I now understood the reason for it. I was aware that anyone I said I knew would share my fate. A name would mean a death. I would be helping to destroy the struggle of which I was a part; the struggle for workers' rights. Workers had no right of association, unions or bargaining power and it's the same now. Rahe Kargar was helping to organise secret cells inside factories to fight for these rights. There was only one way to respond.

'Why are you lying?' I said, furiously. 'Who are these people you are talking about? Why are you accusing me of having contact with them? Have you ever introduced any of them to me? I have never met any of these people.'

'You are lying,' the interrogator snapped. A fist connected squarely with my head. I heard Farhad being taken away. The torture was about to begin again. From under the blindfold, I glimpsed a deep pile of dried scraps of flesh and pools of blood. The macabre remains of those who had been tortured before me, who had died or were imprisoned in this hellhole. I knew that some of these 'untouchables' would have been no more than children: only 12 years old, boys and girls. Some would have been as old as 80. Yet the flesh was not so much revolting as inspiring: a testimony to those who, in the name of justice, had refused to break.

'I must make a decision,' I thought. 'Should I give up all the values of democracy, freedom and justice that I have held for so long? Or should my blood join that of the others who resisted and remained firm in their commitment?' I knew then that I would not jeopardise the lives or activities of my comrades. I would not be helping myself even if I did talk. Anyone brought in because of my confession would only be tortured until they produced more evidence against me. But would my silence protect me? Perhaps. Only if Farhad had not disclosed anything else about me and no other comrades from our organisation – especially those from the *Rahe Kargar* newspaper – were arrested.

The interrogators worked for Savama, the Ministry of Intelligence and National Security. This was the secret police and they were experienced. Some had been employed in the time of the Shah and when he was overthrown in the Islamic revolution of 1979 they discovered their skills were still much in demand. The one the others called Haji Rahman shouted at me: 'Motherfucker, we caught you red-handed in one big net. We'll hang you all.'

'Give this motherfucker to me,' screamed another. 'I will kill him and send him to hell right now.'

'Hey, let's hear from your own fucking mouth which counter-revolutionary group you belong to,' said one more.

'Brothers,' I said, 'I swear by Imam Khomeini, there is a mistake here. I have never been a member of any organisation.'

Someone punched me again. Haji Rahman shouted, 'I swear by Imam Khomeini's glorious spirit that if any of the information is withheld and if any of them get away, I will kill you with my own hands.'

'We don't just want details of your underground activities, we need passwords too.'

'I swear I have no information or passwords to give!'

'We won't let you out of here alive. We have no time for heroes,' Haji Rahman said. 'Brothers, teach him how to talk.'

The torture began. With each blow I screamed clear and loud. I blacked out and awoke to find myself in an infirmary, tubes attached to my body. The doctor – a prisoner from the Blaoch region – came to my bedside when he saw that my eyes were open. 'God has had mercy upon you. You have had a stroke due to the trauma to your head. You've been unconscious for three days, very close to death. The right side of your body has been affected.'

My first thought was that they could not push me further. I was relieved. They didn't want to kill me… not yet, anyway. I was in the infirmary for days. I began to feel a little better and my wounds began to heal but I knew that it was only a matter of time before the interrogators returned. They still wanted information. Sure enough, at about three o'clock in the afternoon, the one they called Haji Samad, the chief interrogator, returned me to the cells. 'The original information we wanted from you is useless. All the meetings will have taken place by now, and they'll know that we have you,' he said coldly. He threatened to take me to Lanat-Abad, the infamous mass graves for communist victims, where he would finish me 'with one shot'.

'Haji,' I cried, 'I beg you to kill me. What you've done to me is unbearable. I'm blind in my right eye, my right arm and foot have lost their power to move, my feet are covered in scabs and open sores. My bladder is bleeding and my urine is full of blood. Living like this is worthless. Kill me then I'll feel relief from the pain and wounds you've inflicted on me. At least I know I'll be remembered by our people for resisting.'

'You think the people support you?' he scoffed. 'You're nothing. All of our people are Hezbollah. They despise you. If we handed you to them they'd tear you apart.' He removed the blindfold and handed me a pen and stack of paper with a list of questions. 'Answer all these questions and anything else you know. I'll be back.'

It was not until around midnight, nine hours later, that an interrogator entered and asked me if I had finished writing. 'No,' I replied, taking the opportunity to add, 'My medicine is still in the infirmary. I have to take it every three hours. Now nine have passed. Would you please take me to the infirmary?'

He reluctantly agreed and, after reapplying the blindfold, led me away.

Every two or three days, Haji Samad or another of the interrogators would demand information. One day, while I was sitting on that now familiar bed frame, a Hezbollahi came over and whispered in my ear. He knew my name and talked about where I used to work. 'I know you weren't a bad guy,' he said, 'but I warn you, if you don't co-operate, you won't get out of here alive.'

I never saw that man again. Or if I did, I was not aware of it. But then I never actually saw the faces of my interrogators, as my time with them was spent blindfolded and turned against the cold prison walls. Not long after that strange encounter the Hezbollahis tried a new approach. I was taken to the torture rooms as usual, then Haji Samad entered with two others. 'The information you've given us is rubbish,' he said. 'Are you going to tell us what we need to know, or not?'

'Haji,' I replied, 'you have all the information I've got.'

'Hang him from the meat hook.' he ordered, 'and keep him there until he's more talkative.'

The two men bound my wrists together behind my back with one elbow behind my head pointing up and the other pointing downwards. They picked me up and hung my wrists over a meat hook fastened to the ceiling. My entire body weight was now supported by my shoulder joints at an agonising angle and my toes barely scraped the floor. Ribs, spine and shoulder joints were instantly put under enormous stress. This is a form of crucifixion and it severely restricts breathing. I could only prevent asphyxiation by making my legs rigid and standing on tiptoes. But I couldn't take this forced position for long and my legs soon started shaking with exhaustion. I was forced to take the stress back on my chest and shoulders. I alternated from one agonising position to the other. They took me off the hook for short periods, during which I was fed and taken to the toilet.

This torture is known as ghapani after the system used to weigh lamb carcasses. It was used as far back as the Shah's reign and many of the unfortunates who are hung up in this way would lose all sensitivity around their shoulders. They are left with great pain in their neck and back which persists for years. My own time on the ghapani only ended because I could no longer be kept conscious long enough to be tortured. On the third day the stress on my body caused my left collar bone to snap. I screamed in agony, again and again. I couldn't breathe. I couldn't stand. At last I couldn't get any more air into my lungs and, thankfully, passed out.

The Hezbollahis had at last seen there was little point in probing my immediate political activities and moved onto broader issues. 'We understand you teach at the university.'

'That is correct.'

'There are lots of pretty girls there. Did you have sex with them?'

'My job is to educate our youth. It's to enrich our country through its people. It pays peanuts for what it is but it's a job I'm honoured to do. When I enter a lecture room, it's like entering a mosque. The youth before me are like a congregation to whom I have responsibility, every bit as strong as to my own children. I have a part in moulding our people's future for the better in what I can teach. Do you think I'd abuse that? If you need a straighter answer than that for your records: no, I don't sleep with them.'

It was important to give an unambiguously negative answer to this line of questioning as unapproved sexual relations in Iran can be punishable by death. They changed tack. Had I smoked dope? Tried opium? Drank alcohol? All carried heavy sentences and every prisoner was asked these questions. Extensive background enquiries would be made in which the authorities would look at intelligence computer files dating back to the time of the Shah.

If anything, my interrogators were less interested in political questions than they were in morality. They were obsessed with the sexual habits of all us prisoners. One 75-year-old woman that I spoke to was pressed to confess the misdemeanours of her youth to the eager listeners. They got a licentious kick from forcing our peccadilloes from us.

The various lines of questioning seemed to go on without end. How long had I been here? It was difficult to tell, but I reckoned about three months. Three months... and already I was a wreck. During the rare moments of peace, I thought of my wife and children, wondered what had happened to them and tried to recall the events leading up to my arrest.

The Hezbollahi first raided my home some two months before I was eventually taken away. My family were sitting on the floor, enjoying the evening meal and watching one of Ayatollah Khomeini's speeches on television (an attack on 'leftist stooges of American imperialism', I think). Aunty went to see who it was. Before the lock was properly off the latch, the door was flung open, trapping her against the wall. There was a clatter of boots. One man began shouting orders.

I was taken to my study by two armed guards, the older of the two clearly the leader. He started firing questions at me, making notes of my answers. The questions were textbook secret police: 'What's your contact with the left, counter-revolutionary organisations?'; 'Are you a member or sympathiser?'; 'Do you know anyone who is?'; 'Have you ever read their papers?' I was also asked broader questions about what I thought about the nature of the Islamic regime and the war with Iraq.

While I played safe with non-committal answers, the younger man began rifling through my bookshelves and the notes I prepared for the following day's lectures while others ransacked the rest of the house. As the search proceeded their disappointment became evident. Someone had obviously led them to believe that this was a safe house, brimming with wanted activists from clandestine organisations and everything from left-wing pamphlets to missile launchers. They were not in luck.

This was early 1981, a period marked by regular clashes in the streets that frequently led to the indiscriminate killing of demonstrators. Raids on private houses were commonplace and I had taken the precaution of getting rid of anything that could be deemed counter-revolutionary. On the wall of my study there had once been posters supporting workers' rights and the Kurdish national struggle. There was now a banner supporting the taking of American hostages in the US embassy in Tehran. I had made a small bonfire on the roof several days earlier and ashes were all that remained of my piles of left-wing pamphlets, papers and books. It had not been easy to burn 15 years of agitation, propaganda and debate.

The police finally gave up at 11pm. According to their warrant they were looking for material linking me to specific organisations; a printing machine, and evidence that the flat was used as a safe house. Instead, they found a family sitting down to tea, watching Khomeini on television. The oldest Hezbollahi went outside to radio in his report and wait for instructions before the police finally left with the house a mess – but still standing. After my arrest the whole house – and some of the homes of my relatives – would be stripped bare. This was common. Confiscating 'evidence' – which included everything from money and jewellery to TVs, stereos and cars – and selling it on was highly profitable.

The oldest raider turned to me as they left and said, 'We're sorry about this, brother. Our information is normally accurate. After all, it was one of your relatives we heard it from.' It was certainly an inconvenience but it was also a warning that my name was on the Hezbollahi's list. I told comrades from my organisation not to come to the house. I was torn: should I flee the country or await arrest? I decided to sit tight and see what would happen. Back then I thought that going to prison for my political convictions at this time was the right thing to do. Sitting in my cell, looking back, it seemed like a very long time ago. A different world.

I still had no idea which prison I was in, but I guessed it was the country's main interrogation centre, known as Evin. I was mistaken. I found out about four months later that I had been held in Komiteh Moshterak (Centre for the Committee of Anti-Subversive Activities). It had been established by the Shah's Savak – which was later replaced by the Savama – as a special complex for the interrogation of political dissidents. The majority of its inmates were members of the Fedayeen and Mojahedin, the two guerrilla organisations fighting against the Shah. Under the new regime Komiteh Moshterak and other prisons continued to exact a terrible revenge on political prisoners. Reports filtered out that made the persecution of political prisoners under the Shah look tame by comparison.

Komiteh Moshterak had been built by the last Shah's father, Reza Shah and it once held hundreds of fighters for freedom, democracy and socialism. Although prisoners were allowed deliveries of home-cooked food, conditions were generally far from humane. A revolutionary poet named Farokhi was put to death by having air injected into a vein. His executioner was Pezeshk Ahmadi, a veterinary appointed the position of prison doctor. The Shah's father also imprisoned those responsible for establishing the Group of 53, the first communist party of Iran.

Just as they did with almost everything else in Iran, Khomeini's regime Islamicised the names of the prisons. Mine became known as The Centre for the Islamic Revolutionary Guard. It was supposed to hold a hundred maximum security prisoners at a time but now packed in around 2,500. They occupied every conceivable space available: lavatories, yards, balconies of upper floors and hallways. There were queues everywhere. Prisoners lined the corridors. On each side of every passageway they laid head to foot, blindfolded and facing the wall. I lay like this for a period of four months, only moving to be taken for torture and interrogation or to the bathroom. On these breaks we would be taken, perhaps ten at a time, and given one or two minutes despite there being only three or four cubicles. This happened three times a day, once after each meal. If we had time and could get to one of the sinks, we could use this short visit for washing dishes, hands, faces, and even our prison uniform.

As long as a prisoner was under intense interrogation, he or she would be kept inside the torture room and witness others being tortured or outside waiting their turn or in the yard adjoining the torture block. Those who survived with terrible wounds would be taken to the cramped, crowded hallways or balconies. If they were lucky, they might end up on a more spacious corridor if other prisoners were taken away to other jails – or taken away to be shot. There was absolutely no information – written or otherwise – from the outside world and communication between prisoners was risky. Once I was approached by a man who stood behind me and whispered in my ear.

'Would you like to read the Koran?'

'Brother, I can't read Arabic.'

'I can help you to read it,' he said.

'I'm bleeding internally. I can't keep my mind focused.'

'Those who have not repented,' he hissed, 'will be wiped out from the face of this earth!' With this sweet thought he departed, thankfully never to be encountered again.

It was during a break, after six months of imprisonment, that I first discovered where I was being held. Usually the guards hurried us along, but on this occasion we were left to ourselves. A young man called Adel helped me get onto his shoulders so I could look through a small window. I immediately recognised the main communications tower in central Tehran and, from this, we figured out where we were.

We were permitted a quick shower only every two or three weeks. First the prisoners in the so-called 'solitary' cells were taken. After they had been it was the turn of those in the corridors, balconies and hallways. Each prisoner was given a piece of black, dried-out, stony soap. Between three to five prisoners would huddle under each of the five showerheads. The shower also served as a laundry and we would wash our uniforms as best we could. Under the showers we could take our blindfolds off, allowing a rare chance to see the faces of our fellow prisoners. In truth, these were my happiest moments in prison. Of course, the guards were always watching, making sure that we did not try and communicate. When 20 minutes were up, we would put on our dripping clothes and leave.

Mealtimes were not so much of a relief. We ate every eight hours, sitting down facing the wall and remained blindfolded. The prison food was tasteless, colourless and meagre. The heat was sometimes unbearable – the temperature can hit 44 degrees celsius in Tehran – and the thick grey walls were dank from sweat. Cigarettes were, of course, not permitted although we were given one cup of what resembled tea every 24 hours. This was between three and five o'clock in the morning, depending on the time of morning prayer. The yellow and foul-smelling drink was accompanied by between two and four cubes of sugar to last the whole day.

The prison had only one doctor, himself a prisoner, and once a week he was allowed to administer nothing more powerful than painkillers under the watchful eyes of the guards. Any smile or kind word would lead to severe repercussions. Prisoners in great pain would have to plead for medicine but unless they were dying the guards would often stop the doctor. 'We need the medicine for the Islamic devotees fighting a holy war against Iraq,' they would say.

Many prisoners had vicious wounds on the soles of their feet and contracted infections so severe that some of them died. Others were bleeding and in constant pain from broken bones. A few had even lost their sight in one eye. There were few who did not have some form of skin infection. Unsurprisingly, there was an ever-present stench from untreated wounds. Some of my fellow prisoners caught severe fevers, chest infections and tuberculosis. Lice were everywhere.

The warmth of the sun, the smell of trees, the stars at night… all were distant memories. Each of our movements was calculated to form part of our torture. You might think that going to the bathroom would bring some relief to the prisoner who had been lying on a floor, blindfolded, facing the wall for ten hours. But not when one had to urinate or defecate in a matter of minutes surrounded by people in severe pain, many bleeding. I had blood in my urine for a long time. Others were affected by stomach disorders and needed more time than we were allowed.

All our activities were accompanied by an orchestra of horrifying noises. The most disturbing was the sound of cars stopping at the entrance late at night and in the early morning. They were bringing more victims. The main door would screech open and, within ten or twenty minutes, the prison would be filled with the chilling sound of someone experiencing the torture room for the first time. Each scream reminded me of the torture I experienced. It was impossible to block that sound out, let alone sleep through it. Listening to others being tortured was more demoralising for us than experiencing it personally.

Then there was the prison tannoy system. The authorities subjected prisoners to a constant barrage of readings from the Koran and other religious texts. They relayed speeches by leading clerics and government officials, from Khomeini downwards. Sometimes they played military marches or entreaties to support the regime's war with Iraq, accompanied by constant bulletins crowing about the defeat of Iraqi forces and the supposed advance along the road to Baghdad and Jerusalem. Guards ran down the corridors while the reports blared, kicking us in the back indiscriminately and shouting, 'You have turned your backs on God, Islam and Khomeini! You must repent or die!' Some guards had themselves come from the frontline and were shell-shocked and unhinged. They were deliberately chosen to 'guard' their enemy. Mainly young, illiterate peasants, they were fooled into accepting the hell of the here and now by the promise of the next world.

There were just three sounds that were welcome: the food trolley, birdsong – a rarity in this urban prison – and the whirr of the overhead fans. I would breathe a sigh of relief when I heard one of those old fans spinning, heralding a much-needed breeze.

We never knew how long we had before torture began again. Day and night the guards would go back and forth, picking on prisoners. We were kept in a state of fear; a blow from a fist, clubs or boot could come at any time. You could be beaten for anything: putting your hands over your head, scratching your nose, touching your blindfold. An attack frequently resulted in bleeding ears, eyes and noses, or broken teeth and jaws.

On one occasion after torture I was taken back to the corridor where I was ordered to lie down. I was exhausted. My feet were bleeding and I was completely unable to hold myself up. No sooner had the guards bundled me into a corner than a boot smashed into my back.

'Leave me alone!' I screamed. 'Let me die!'

'You son of a bitch!' the guard yelled back. 'You're trying to identify me by looking underneath your blindfold! I'll kill you!'

'Why have you attacked me?'

I was too drained to even think. I knew this guard, and had suffered at his hands before. He was universally feared. As he was shouting at me, a religious figure who was one of the prison directors was passing by. He stepped in.

'Haji Johary [the guard] has lost four of his children fighting the Great Satan [America],' the director said. 'Two of them in Kurdistan fighting the communists, the other two were just 14 and 16 when they gave their lives on the front against Iraq. Haji Johary himself continuously visits the front, where he is directing groups of Khomeini fedais. He lost his dearest brother during one such operation and was himself injured in an explosion.

'We're fighting America and Israel, and you counter-revolutionaries say that the Islamic Republic is importing guns and ammunition from them! Our great Imam and his children the Hezbollahis are fighting against American imperialism and Soviet atheists and communists and you accuse us of trading oil for guns with them! You had better open your eyes and ears. This war is not against Iraq but, as Imam Khomeini has said, against the superpowers and that is the secret of the holy war which is being supervised by the Imam on Allah's behalf. That's the important point that you unbelievers have missed.

'Our brother Haji Johary is still carrying shrapnel fragments from the Iraqi missile that hit his bunker. It has affected his mental balance. When he gets angry with you, he cannot control himself. Haji Johary is the ears and eyes of the great Khomeini here.'

I made no response and my wounds went untreated as normal. Like all of the political prisoners who populated the corridors, I made almost no contact with my neighbours. At most, you could glance under your blindfold at those lying either side of you, or count the feet of those passing by on their way to the showers or the bathroom. But trying to distinguish your comrades from the guards and torturers by their shoes was dangerous. Some guards would sneak up on us wearing black plastic prison sandals. At night, when there were fewer guards moving back and forth, it was a little easier to see comrades lying across from you.

If the hands and feet of the man next to you were not bruised or bleeding, you were suspicious. This mistrust was necessary as you had to identify those you could trust. An index of this was how many wounds they bore. This told you how resilient they had been under torture. A man with smooth hands had been no trouble for the torturer.

It did not take long for me to decide that I needed to keep my mind active. I organised court proceedings in my head, in which I was the defendant. Each day I would present a very strong clear defence of freedom, democracy and social justice, explaining my reasons for participating in political activity and my struggle against the Islamic Republic. I repeated these court proceedings and each time I made them longer, until I fell asleep. But before long the cries of someone being tortured, my own pain, or a kick from a guard, would wake me.

Another pastime was following beams of light shining underneath cell doors late at night or rays of the sun glimmering through the doors to the balcony. But these distractions could do nothing to alleviate the mental effects of imprisonment and there can be no surprise in learning that in my corridor alone,

22

some prisoners lost their minds completely. Their madness compounded the horror with their wailing, their banging of their heads against the walls, their tearing at their blindfolds, their cries for their mothers and fathers or their curses of Khomeini, God and Islam.

After about five months I was moved to what was called a solitary cell on the fourth floor. I pulled off my blindfold, expecting to find myself alone in a dark cell. But this three-by-three metre cell already contained more than 15 other prisoners. They sat, backs to the wall with their feet stretched out. After the soul-destroying isolation of the corridors, it almost felt like returning home to find a welcome party had been organised. But there were still drawbacks to life here. We frequently weren't even given the chance to use the lavatory and we would have to use a plastic bag in the corner of the cell.

The inmates moved around to make room for me to sit and the introductions began. As I was clearly injured – the wounds on my feet were quite visible – I was given the best position. Once my back was propped up in a corner I was handed some blankets. I was given some biscuits that came from the families of prisoners who had been in the cell for over a year.

I was asked for my story and what I was charged with. I was wary in case there were any collaborators among my new cell mates. Some of them had not been tortured, though they were clearly shocked by my condition. I told them what I knew and I had some questions of my own. It emerged that ten of my cellmates were accused of membership of the Tudeh (Party of the Masses, a communist organisation). Five were there as a result of association with other left organisations: Rahe Kargar, Fedayeen Minority and Peykar (a Maoist organisation). There was also a young man from Kurdistan who was a former member of the Islamic Revolutionary Guard. He had been accused of infiltration and treason and had been in the cell for around two years. He couldn't have been more than 20 years old. His beard was long and matted, and his face so pale and grey that it appeared that there was no blood in his veins. I was told that he continued to protest his innocence with unshakeable faith in the regime. Like so many of us, he was being held indefinitely without trial. He constantly exercised in his corner of the cell and made little effort to interact with the rest of us.

The ten Tudeh members had been captured through information given by their own leadership. General secretary Nooredin Kianoori announced the dissolution of the party on his own arrest and told members to give themselves up. Many did hand themselves over to Islamic prosecutors in Evin, Komiteh, or elsewhere. The party surrendered its membership lists with details of its structure throughout the country. In my cell the former Tudeh members had consensus on three points. Firstly, that the war with Iraq had been imposed on the regime by an imperialist conspiracy. Secondly, the regime was genuinely anti-imperialist. And thirdly, that it enjoyed mass popular support.

None of these ten men had been tortured… not yet, at least. They were mostly middle-class university students or professionals and I listened to their stories with great interest. Parvis used to work for an Iranian television station; Adel Zahmatkesh was a fourth-year dental student at the university of Tehran and had been Kianoori's personal chauffeur for a time; another student, Mohsen, had been in his fourth year on an engineering degree; Shafagh was a doctor who told me that he had run a successful practice before he was arrested.

Parvis was adamant in his support for the regime's war against Iraq, its genocidal policy against the Kurds, and the annihilation of left wing opposition – which stuck me as bizarre, since he himself was a victim of this. 'If Imam Khomeini's line is really a revolutionary one, why is it that the Islamic regime has arrested hundreds of thousands of the democratic and revolutionary forces, and killed and destroyed tens of thousands of them?' I asked.

'You people deserve what you get!' said Parvis. 'You have risen up against a popular revolutionary and anti-imperialist regime which is also an ally of the Soviet Union. Your politics does not support our people or any revolutionary cause – it only serves the interests of American imperialism.' We hunched together for such discussions, speaking in hushed voices. Our exchanges became sharper rather than louder and other cellmates shuffled closer to hear. Tudeh members supported Parvis with their contributions. The others listened too, nodding and grunting as we spoke. They were more hesitant about expressing their own opinions, perhaps because they were more conscious of the danger we were in. The pro-Khomeini Tudeh members were, after all, an unknown quantity.

'What about the genocide against minorities: the Kurds, the Bah'ais? The suppression of freedom and civil liberties? The subjugation of women under the veil?' I asked.

'Well,' he said, 'who are those women who came out and demonstrated against the Islamic government? Prostitutes, monarchists and those who sought sexual self-gratification. As for the Kurds and the Baha'is, the leaderships of these movements are part of the American imperialist conspiracy against the Islamic regime. The suppression of civil liberties is only a problem for a handful of intellectuals. The workers and peasants in the factories and fields throughout the country are concerned with improving their condition. The Islamic revolution works for their well-being. You oppositionalists are frustrating this process.'

I had heard these arguments before. Some of the academic staff at the university of Tehran who belonged to the Fedayeen Majority had replied in exactly the same way. Not even the brutality of this regime shook them out of their fantasy. 'How can a regime that has obtained weapons from America and Israel and their allies for use in the war with Iraq and the civil war against the democratic forces be described as a revolutionary regime?' I said.

'The Chinese received US aid against Japan in World War II. That did not make China counter-revolutionary.'

'Okay,' I said, 'but how can the regime be improving material conditions? It has wiped out the workers' councils which arose from the revolutionary overthrow of the Shah. Millions of hectares of land were liberated when the Shah was overthrown. Now they are being confiscated by the Pasdars and given back to feudal landlords.'

He answered, 'The Islamic shoras [people's councils] are the revolutionary answer to independent organisations. Anyway, they were being used as counter-revolutionary bases against the Islamic regime by the left. The Islamic regime will develop its own land reform programme which will lead to the orderly handing over of land to the peasants.' I ended our discussion. I could not yet trust everyone in the cell and, more importantly, I could tell that there was no way that he would see reality.

Adel, the dental student, was a young man with tremendous energy and vitality. By contrast with Parvis his own defence of the regime had become more qualified since his arrest. He was the one on whose shoulders I stood to look out of the window when we went to the bathroom. Now I knew where we were being held. I would have been more wary of this offer had it come from any other prisoner. None of the other Tudeh prisoners would have taken a risk like that.

Adel maintained a good relationship with all other left-leaning prisoners. His dental training came to good use too and he was always willing to examine the teeth of other prisoners, irrespective of their politics. A passionate figure, he participated in unified prison resistance movements and was killed in a mass execution of political prisoners in 1989. Parvis, on the other hand, refused to take part, even when other Tudeh members were involved. I later learned from some of the prisoners that served with him in Evin that he had been accused of co-operating with prison officials. I saw him again in another prison in 1987 and was warned to keep well clear. But we shared a history and I tried to maintain a cordial relationship. Whether he actually co-operated with the authorities or not, he also went to the gallows in 1989.

There was solidarity between the other four leftists in my cell. They, like me, strongly opposed the regime. None of them could have been described as middle class and they had all been tortured. Taregh, one of the two Fedayeen Minority members, was a high school student and only 16 years old. He was the most energetic of the four. Morad, the other Fedayeen, was a school teacher arrested after being informed on by Islamic students – 'the ears and eyes of Khomeini'. Ahmed was a worker from a factory in Karaj, an industrial city about 40 miles outside Tehran. He had been arrested as a result of a strike in his factory and was a member of Peykar. The fourth, Kaveh, was a member of Rahe Kargar and had been arrested due to his political work at a car plant. All kept their distance from their Tudeh cellmates.

Open political arguments were dangerous, but I couldn't stop myself from chipping in with references to the defeat of the 1979 revolution or to the nature of the regime. Yet there was little point. Everyone had very set positions in order to protect themselves.

CHAPTER 3

ROOTS

These days, as I stare up at the ceiling, unable to sleep because of constant nagging pains from my injuries, I sometimes ask myself how the hell I got into such a mess. My answer starts with the stories of Iran's own tragedies. It was once Britain's unofficial colony. During the 19th century it was strategically important but took on a new importance with oil. When BP moved in, the British government was not far behind. They began to buy off the backward tribal chiefs and destabilise the democratic government introduced after 1907.

In 1920 the British played a key part in installing Reza Shah as dictator – a man who had a nasty little habit of cutting out the tongues of those who criticised him openly – but he started paying court to the Nazis. While I was growing up in the early 1950s, the British were at it again. This time, under a Labour government, they didn't like a democratically-elected government wanting a fairer share of the oil riches.

Everyone in our family was kept informed about what was going on by my grandfather. He would come home each evening with a basket of food in one hand and a copy of the nationalist paper *Shouresh* (Rebellion) in the other. We would sit and listen to him reading the latest court intrigues. I sat close, keen to hear every word. In the paper I saw and liked a cartoon of Churchill, complete with dicky bow and tails, dancing cheek to cheek with the Shah's twin sister, Ashraf. The editor, Karimpur Shirazi, hammered the political point of the cartoon with an editorial raging against the monarchy's collaboration with imperialism, and in particular BP.

My father was a carpenter who left home around half past five every morning to work in a factory two miles away that produced doors and windows. I was the first born and, when I was six, I went to help my father at his work. I used to hold the end of the planks as my father fed them through the machines. He called me his right hand. The noise and smells, hustle and bustle of the workshop were captivating. I was very happy, playing with the piles of fine sawdust on the factory floor. It was official: I was a grown-up.

We used to get home at about six in in the evening, where our evening meal would be waiting. But not everyone was happy. When I was ten, my grandparents decided to have it out with my father and told him I was out of control and needed to go to school. In truth, when I watched my friends carrying their books to and from school, I did feel jealous. Even at that young age I knew that, without any real education, I faced a bleak future. My father could not read or write a word, even his own name. He agreed that education was essential if I was to avoid his fate and so I started school, albeit as a late developer. I realised from the outset that this was my only life-raft; the penalty for failure was to finish up like my father.

My mother was born in 1927, some two decades after the proclamation of the universal right to secular education. Nevertheless, like my father, she never learnt to read and

30

write. She was married at 11 and was 12 when I was born. By 20 she had given birth to no less than six children. She was dead by 35, totally exhausted by the birth of her tenth child. She was always a distant figure to me, having yet more children, suckling one baby from the breast, breaking ice during the freezing winter to get water to wash clothes for the others. She never had any opportunity to get to know any of us – that was the way things were in a society that saw child brides as perfectly normal. Her own mother died in her mid-40s of a heart attack while she was washing clothes by hand. The cycle went on, unfortunately. My sisters never had any education to speak of and Khomeini went on to 'turn back the clock' so women could be buried up to the neck and stoned to death for such crimes as adultery.

The years after World War II were a golden age by comparison. Ideas of all kinds were allowed to flourish. Britain had been seriously weakened and its grip on Iran had slackened. The introduction of Soviet troops in the north had inspired many and rocked the ruling class. The country was ripe for change. My grandfather was a simple working man who made quilts for a living – for the Shah's court – but rather than being a sycophantic flunkey, he somehow knew who his real friends and enemies were. Like millions of others, we were all strong supporters of Mohammad Mossadegh, the prime minister who was democratically elected in 1951.

He was overturned in 1953 with the help of the CIA and Britain's MI5. My family's favourite newspaper editor, Karimpur Shirazi, was murdered in prison and his charred remains displayed on posters to ensure that everyone got the message. Richard Nixon, the new vice president of the United States, came over to review the handiwork of the leaders of the new regime. He condemned Mossadegh as a communist and told the Shah that, 'the coup would establish an island of stability in the turbulent waters of the Persian Gulf.'

Massacres and persecutions were a feature of this new 'island of stability', including the arrest of 500 Tudeh sympathisers in the officer corps, most of whom were executed. Everyone kept their heads down. I buried myself in my studies but stayed true to my allegiance to Mossadegh's ideals, joining others to chant support for him during our 15-minute meal breaks, taking part in demonstrations, and distributing leaflets in support of his party, the National Front. There was no going back for me and I threw myself into the world of the political activist.

I was far to the right of the Tudeh party but I agreed to distribute their leaflets at the school. My luck ran out when, two months after the coup, a hostile teacher caught me and I was hauled before the military authorities and interned in an open air military camp in the centre of Tehran. I was badly beaten, once after my arrest and again after reaching the camp. My home was ransacked and the few books I had confiscated. My arrest even made the national news when they said that I had been arrested for failing to stand up in the cinema before a patriotic song for the Shah. I was eventually released after five months, but was barred from school for a year.

Years later I entered a military training college. The principal hauled me in and, after praising my grades, stated bluntly that I had no future in the armed forces as I would always be politically suspect. This had a devastating effect as my dream had been to work my way into the officer corps and to get rid of the Shah, opening the way back to democracy. But if I left now I would be required to pay back the entire cost of my education. I had to find a way to square the circle. Six months later, after I had passed all my examinations with distinction and moved to the officers training corps, I sneaked out of my barracks. My heart racing, I used a lamppost to clamber over the barbed wire perimeter.

After some time in hiding I was free to go to the University of Tehran. I passed the entrance examinations in five faculties but I still didn't feel safe. I qualified for a place at a foreign university, but was not granted a visa despite many applications. An exasperated official eventually whispered, 'You might have passed our exams but you have failed Savak's. Talk to them if you want to know.'

I finally got permission through my one and only contact with the intelligence services. My father was appalled at the astronomic costs of the US, but the family had a whip-round and, in 1961, I made my way to Wyoming. I took any job that would pay. My fellow students were convinced that I owned at least half a dozen oil wells in Iran and I gave them some cock and bull story about a delayed inheritance. College jobs and summer holiday work enabled me to pay my way to a degree at Brigham Young University in Utah. Initially, I studied petroleum engineering, but moved into economics. I did not forget the huge sacrifice the family had made and saved enough to send back $1,000.

After moving to New York I was able to combine my doctorate with covert campaigning against the Shah (I still have copies of my articles for *International* and the *American Militant*, credited to 'Kaveh Ahangar'). By 1974, the year I returned home to Iran, I had established a reputation as a young tenured lecturer.

Savak had not forgotten me and were unimpressed by the name I had made for myself in the US. With the temperature rising at home I found myself in the firing line once again. But by this time I had learned to box more cleverly, despite regular and extended chats with the secret police who watched my every move. I was a man with a mission. In Tehran I was working at one tenth of the salary I had been offered in the private sector. But money was not important. The real agenda was making contacts and building up influence as the regime moved inexorably into crisis. I accepted invitations to lecture at provincial universities throughout Iran to learn more about the people of my country, their problems and aspirations. It was also a useful method of familiarising myself with the geography of Iran as, after 12 years away, I was something of a stranger.

The 1953 coup had forced the left in Iran to reassess the future and take a long hard look at the nationalist politics of Mossadegh. Tudeh was discredited by failing to act to defend the gains made by the nationalisation movement. It then lost even more credibility when it appeared to subordinate itself to the foreign policy interests of the Soviet Union, which was trying to gain an economic foothold in Iran.

Young people in Tudeh and the National Front found alternative models in both the Cuban struggle as personified by Che Guevara and in the Vietcong's battle in Vietnam. Their revolutionary ideals led to the formation of a dizzying array of political and religious groups, determined to change the regime. The Fedayeen was one of these groups and they were set up in 1970. Out of this organisation emerged the Rahe Kargar, originally called the Prison Boys. These Marxists broke with the politics of Guevarism and identified the working class as the main agency of revolution. Other young people in the National Front and the religious movement formed the Mojahedin, committed to armed struggle and social change. They were linked with Islam and their secular equivalent was Peykar, a Maoist group with overtones of Marxism-Leninism. They considered Albania 'the most progressive socialist state in the universe'.

I had moved on too, politically. I still had a soft spot for Dr Mossadegh but now leaned towards some kind of socialism rather than nationalism. Yet the Soviet Union had shown itself to be repressive and China's Maoist quasi-religious dogma was equally unappetising. Vietnam had demonstrated that the Third World could buck the trend and Castro's Cuba seemed to offer the way out of tyranny. The Shah made his last visit to Washington to see President Carter in 1977 and we all seethed as he mouthed Nixon's monstrous phrase about Iran being an 'island of stability'. Could it be made to happen again? Could 1978 or 1979 be the year of another revolution... and more?

Chapter 4

Revolutionary Days

In the late 1970s the Iranian government faced an economic crisis and its counter-inflationary policies led to strikes and even uprisings. No one was left untouched. The millions that had been ruined by the Shah's policies and now lived in the shanty towns saw their squalid corrugated-iron shacks bulldozed. When they protested, guns were turned on them. But there were more protests, uprisings and massacres and each was larger and angrier than the last. The state response became bloodier, culminating in South Tehran in September 1977 with an outright massacre. Tanks and helicopter gunships tore through wide swathes of Tehran's poor and hungry.

The world of academia was not left untouched. The university of Tehran sat in the centre of the city. To the north of the campus lay the villas of the rich and to the south were the shanty towns. From the top floor of the main block, you could – and still can – see the rift through Iranian society expressed in that division through its capital. My colleagues at the university saw the tanks roll through the city centre and heard the whirr of the helicopters overhead. Every day the papers brought further reports of repression. When I say we saw blood in the streets, I am not speaking metaphorically. On that terrible day when the Shah's troops slaughtered thousands in Tehran, there were rivers of red flowing across the pavements and down the gutters.

After each massacre there was a shocked silence. A small group of us at the university decided we would speak out. Out of a staff of three thousand, a hundred of us signed an open letter of condemnation. It was a small voice circulated and republished by the opposition press, read in the factories, the bazaar, and even at prayer in the mosques. It spread far and wide.

The confidence of the people was growing. In the middle of the government campaign against rising prices, oil workers actually secured a wage increase of 20 per cent. Their success spearheaded a wave of brave strikes at a time when some shopkeepers were actually jailed for raising prices by the equivalent of one tenth of a penny.

Although there were no legal unions, Iranian workers came together to use their new-found strength. They extended their demands to include freedom of the press, breaking the state monopoly on television and releasing thousands of political prisoners. In late 1978 student activists held a university-wide sit-in. Their demands echoed those of other workers and it did not take long for the Shah's minions to identify this centre for education as a hotspot of trouble. All universities were closed. But this just spread the opposition further afield as students took their demands to factories and shanty towns.

University staff were barred from entering the empty buildings and began a process of consultation. I was elected as one of the two representatives from the Economics faculty. We decided that an occupation of the university was the most appropriate response to the Shah's actions. Around 30 of us – one from each department – walked through the police cordon and went to see the chancellor. Filing into his room in the administration block at the centre of the campus, we demanded that the university be immediately reopened.

'It is not my decision,' he told us. 'His Majesty and the military governor of Tehran must decide that'.

For two hours we haggled. Things became heated. Some of my older colleagues even began brandished their walking sticks to emphasise their arguments. Eventually the chancellor stormed out, slamming the door behind him. We barred the doors and phoned the university faculties and student groups.

'The occupation's on!'

As others arrived, university officials cleaned their desks and left. Within just 24 hours we were in control of the entire administration block. The oil and electricity workers were out on strike again but we still had power. While the Shah ate cold chicken by candlelight, our five-storey block was a brilliantly illuminated watch-tower. It was an unforgettable symbol of solidarity. Looking out over the city we could see the pin-pricks of millions of candles in the blackness. Unfortunately, our privileged status also made us sitting ducks for soldiers squinting at us down their gunsights.

On the second day, lecturers from other colleges in Tehran occupied the Ministry of Science and Education. A Savak sharpshooter opened fire on them, killing one young lecturer. A crowd of hundreds of thousands gathered spontaneously to help carry his coffin from the hospital morgue for miles through the city, passing it from shoulder to shoulder to the university. The academic staff formed a single line along the front of the building with a eulogy written for the young martyr and all those murdered by the Shah. Just the other side of the square, we could see the crowd heading towards a large roundabout. Thousands of voices were chanting as one.

Tanks, mortars, machine-guns,
Bakhtiar and his cronies,
Will not stop the masses!

Then the roar of automatic fire ripped through the air. We stared with horror at the slaughter, frozen. A few people fainted. Suddenly the reality of the situation hit us and we bolted for cover. I ran, head down, as if all the hounds of hell were after me. From the echoes we believed we were being fired on – it later emerged the soldiers were on rooftops, firing down at the crowds – and we took refuge in the loft of the administration block. Between a hundred and two hundred people were killed, unarmed men and women, ambushed at Reza Shah Roundabout – later renamed, after the Shah's fall, Revolution Roundabout.

The university occupation became a potent symbol of the resistance. Each day, the latest news, along with political pamphlets and press releases, was discussed and formed the basis of our developing strategy. There was a small but active minority of lecturers – around ten – who were left-wing, alongside about 20 hardline Islamists. Although none of them spoke of 'Islamic universities' at this time, under Khomeini many of them were actively involved in purging the universities of every last vestige of secularism. The others – the majority – were liberals and democrats.

Some of the liberals continued to insist that our occupation was not political and that we had nothing to do with what went on outside. They argued that our only aim should be the reopening of the university. The minister for education had their ear and he used his influence to ensure that the occupation remained 'non-political'. As for me, I argued that we should hang banners from the balconies and windows. Given that there was strong anti-US sentiment and that the Shah's government was created and sustained by the CIA, I proposed that we hang a banner reading 'Down with US imperialism.' It took no less than 20 days of relentless discussion to get this accepted.

Ayatollah Talaghani, the most prominent figure in the Islamic opposition movement in the country at the time, sought to link his movement with us. The Islamists managed to jump on his bandwagon with the help of professors such as Dr Mohammed Malaki. The good doctor later became the head of the university of Tehran as a reward for obeying instructions until he fell from favour and was jailed for a total of seven years. He was even forced to participate in one of the humiliating show trials staged by the Islamic revolution's prosecutor Haji Lajiverdi.

Some of the other Islamicists were more fortunate. One of them – perhaps the quietest – became Minister of Agriculture. To this day, I honestly don't believe he knew one end of a turnip from another! Some of his fellows are now in the Iranian equivalent of government. As these committed academics came to learn, the wages of sin are not eternal damnation, but parliament.

We published a daily occupation news report which was pasted on the university walls. Discussions would begin with our immediate proposals for the reorganisation of the institution, aimed at making it more democratic and responsive to the needs of its students. But as our cause spread and became a movement of the masses – millions throughout the country – we were driven to consider a much wider and more fundamental problem: the total restructuring of Iran. It now seemed obvious that shoras composed of students, workers and lecturers should run the university. Some of us went further and believed that shoras should run the entire country. It sounded unrealistic to some, but this was no academic pipe dream. In early 1979 more workers were mobilising and testing their strength and ability.

We organised the distribution of press releases about our activities and in support of the strikes and demonstrations. These were relayed to the outside world by a network of student suppliers – a sort of pony express, but with motorbikes, though it was hard to find gas for the engines. Tehran was experiencing its coldest winter for years, and there was no fuel. The sight of a moving car became a rarity as petrol was nearly impossible to come by. With the streets almost devoid of traffic, sometimes the only sound you could hear throughout the sprawling city was the familiar crack of gunfire.

In total about 80 of us participated in the occupation. We took turns keeping guard, watching for signs of another attack by the riot squad. As our actions had become a focal point for the demonstrations which were now taking place all around the city, there were now rumours that the authorities wanted one of us shot dead to disperse the demonstrators.

Looking out of windows of the administration block over the main fifth floor balcony and across the square, we could see police barricades stretching 150 metres in all directions. At night, it was as quiet as a cemetery. We were all on edge, fearing a stealth attack by the Shah's crack troops. Sunrise could not come soon enough, when we would be greeted by the faces of family members, smiling and waving from the far side of the barricades. Later in the day demonstrators would arrive to show their support.

As the days became weeks, the crowd of demonstrators grew larger. Before long we found ourselves watching in amazement at the seemingly endless sea of people that would flood the barricades, waving banners and even trying to break through and join us. And, all too often, we would watch in horror as their efforts were met with gunfire. It was nothing short of murder.

On the 25th and final day of the occupation, after the regime conceded the demand to reopen the university, we marched at the head of a mass demonstration to celebrate our victory. We had issued a call for everyone to come with us to reopen the university. Shops and workplaces closed as around half a million people converged on the campus. A platform was erected in the university square and reporters from all political trends that had supported the occupation were invited to speak. Those of us that had been involved in the occupation were distinguished by armbands.

Because I could speak English I was the spokesperson for the world's press. One reporter from an American television network asked, 'What happens next?', and I remember telling him, 'When Khomeini arrives from Paris the masses will take over. The people will run the country in a democratic and just manner.' Unfortunately, like so many others, I misjudged Khomeini's intent, taking at face value his statement that he wanted no more to do with politics, but only to return to the holy city of Qum to take up his religious duties.

The journalist pressed me further: 'How will the people exercise this power?'

'Possibly through the shoras,' I said. I don't believe that, at the time, any of us had any more than a vague idea of the possibilities we were presented with… or of the dangers that we were walking towards.

With the reopening of the university and the fall of the Shah, we experienced a real sense of optimism as the snows in Tehran thawed and the winter passed. It was a period that was widely known as 'the spring of freedom'. The university came alive with a sort of joyous chaos. Its corridors teemed with all manner of people, eager to learn and teach. Everyone seemed to carry a book in their hand, if not a pile cradled in their arms and held in place by their chins. These books – untitled, plain, white – were budget editions of previously banned titles by authors including Marx, Engels and Lenin. They sold in huge numbers now they were freely available.

Every inch of available space at the university was used. You could find a corridor blocked by a crowd of oil refinery workers clustered round a young Fedaii, explaining the workings of the AK47 rifle he held in his hands. In another corner of the building, a group of Islamic students would be praying. Outside on the grass forecourt, there would be a lecture and discussion of what agricultural policy we should now adopt. It was an extraordinary and exciting time.

Revolutionary poet and dramatist Said Sultanpour led an ad hoc poetry circle which was highly political. He had just been released from prison and organised an agitprop street theatre group on the lawn. Dotted all around were speakers from different parties, each with a crowd of people around them, listening, murmuring their approval or heckling.

The arts faculty became a gallery of liberated arts. Artists commandeered corridors, lecture rooms, even broom cupboards. Walls were covered with paintings that had been previously banned. It was as if the university had been turned into an art gallery. All Iranian cultural life was here. And people flocked to it. Workers and peasants who had been denied access to this kind of creative expression in the past came to look, feel and understand art.

Every shade of opinion that had overthrown the Shah, from Islamists to communists, was represented in the university and on the shoras that ran it. This paralleled developments within Iran, as workers seized the factories and peasants the land, running the country democratically through their respective shoras.

Parts of the university were occupied by main political parties. The engineering faculty became the Fedayeen headquarters. The place thrummed with energy, young people came and went, armed with Kalashnikovs or carrying bundles of newspapers. It was to the Iranian revolution what the Smolny Institute in Saint Petersburg had been to the Soviets. These headquarters were still used as lecture theatres, however. Passing through one day, I happened upon a lecture by Houma Nategh, a professor at the department of Persian literature and a noted activist herself.

More than 500 people sat in rapt attention while she spoke about the contribution of women to the armed struggle.

In fact, the engineering faculty became something of a revolutionary tourist attraction, with workers and peasants coming to gawp at 'the kids with machine guns who have taken over the country'.

Our brand of open, libertarian education spread throughout the country. Once a week I would make the 100km drive to Ghazvin to lecture at the university. These lectures were open to anyone. They dealt with problems from the industrial shoras to the nature of the land reform. Hundreds of young people would turn up, most associated with the Fedayeen.

Khomeini himself returned in early 1979, two weeks after the Shah left for exile. On 1 April that year, the country voted to become an Islamic Republic. By the end of 1979, Khomeini had been declared supreme ruler. But it was soon felt that the revolution wasn't making progress and I began to focus my own criticism on the reluctance of the new Islamic regime to make any progressive concessions to the workers and peasants. Our revolution was being taken from us. The regime began to take action against the workers' and peasants' shoras. Khomeini declared a jihad – a holy war – against the Kurds and sided with the feudal and capitalist forces against the workers.

This assault was not confined to Kurdistan and the workplaces of Iran. It showed its ugly face in the attacks by Hezbollah thugs against the universities and other places of learning. Calling itself the Islamic Cultural Revolution, it spilled the blood of the students and professors who had fought so courageously against the Shah. This counter-revolution brought with it sexual apartheid and shackled all freedom of expression.

CHAPTER 5

THE HOUSE OF
REPENTANCE

The autumn after my arrest, guards came to the cell and told me to pack up what things I had and put my blindfold on. It came completely out of the blue and gave me no time to bid my farewells to my Komiteh Moshterak cellmates, most of whom I never saw again. It is a tragic certainty that the majority of them will have ended up in front of a firing squad or on the gallows.

I was escorted out of the cell and through the prison corridors. We descended the steps to the ground floor reception I had passed through over five months before. No words were exchanged during this walk. In silence, a guard passed me a plastic bag. It contained the pyjamas I had been arrested in. I was on the move – but where to, God only knew.

A guard led me through the yard and, for the first time in months, I briefly felt the sun on my face. We walked across the yard to a black Mercedes and I was pushed into the back seat. To one side sat a guard, cradling a Kalashnikov in his lap and on the other was someone I could not quite see. The passenger seat in the front next to our heavily bearded driver was not in my limited line of vision either.

A guard outside shouted, 'Do you have your guns and all your prisoners?' The guard beside me grunted confirmation. 'God be with you!' came the reply. 'Open the door and let them out'. Iron screeched on iron as the gate swung open. Once we were moving and swinging round the bends in the road, I took the opportunity to look at the person beside me. To my surprise I saw that it was Farhad, the man who I had sat next to the morning of my arrest, and who had been my reluctant accuser in my initial interrogation. He was wearing the same shirt, with a distinctive green stripe, that he had on when we used to meet. Then I caught sight of a woman in an Islamic black veil sitting in the front passenger seat. At one point she turned around enough for me to see that she wore a blindfold under her veil, so I assumed that it was Mariam, Farhad's wife. I was relieved to see them both alive.

I began to believe that we had left the brutal interrogations behind us. It was my understanding – or at least my hope – that they were taking us to the Islamic court. My mind was racing, but I kept thinking that whatever the outcome of the court proceedings, at least I would not have face torture again.

The side and rear windows of the vehicle we were in had been blacked out, so it was only possible to see what was directly in our path through the windscreen. I drank in the familiar sights of Tehran rushing by. Women, hidden under black veils and with children hanging from their necks, asked for money from passers-by in the street. Some even tried to run after the cars during the journey. At busy junctions, when cars were forced to stop, women, old men and small children begging would swarm around them.

Our driver drove like he owned the road, like everyone else should be subservient to him. I swear he tried to overtake every single car. It came as no real surprise when we had an accident, colliding with the back of a truck. Immediately, two escort vehicles accompanying us screeched to a halt. Our driver got out, approached the elderly driver of the truck and landed a swift punch on his nose. The old man staggered back, ran to the cab of his truck and pulled out an iron bar. A fight began and the guard inside our car leapt out and joined in.

I could hardly believe it: here was the opportunity I'd been waiting for and I turned to speak to Farhad. I was so frail and had lost so much weight through torture and my stroke that I only just had time enough to explain who I was before the guards returned. The poor old truck driver had worked out who his attackers were and had got away.

After another hour of driving through thick traffic in the streets of central Tehran, we reached the north of the city. We went through a large iron door and all three of us were hauled out of the car and handed over to a new set of guards. They were armed. Whatever this place was, it did not have the feel of a court. I could hear the voice of the muezzin from a loudspeaker in the building followed by the echo of evening prayers. Farhad and I were marched to the top of a staircase and they took his wife to the next landing.

'Don't move your head!' a guard shouted. 'Don't touch your blindfold, and keep quiet.'

They put me on one side of the landing and Farhad on the other, both facing the wall. After waiting around 15 minutes I guessed we might be able to talk quietly. 'Why did you give them information about my identity and whereabouts?' I asked. 'Don't tell them that I have been a member of the organisation, I've denied it.'

He said nothing. To be honest, I didn't really expect an answer. Just because we couldn't see or hear anyone, it didn't mean no one was listening. After about two hours, a guard returned, signed for us and took us to a new building. We were led to a large hall where many other prisoners sat facing the walls. I heard a familiar, frightful sound that confirmed my worst fears: the shrieks of a young man being tortured nearby. His voice sounded like it hadn't fully broken yet and I guessed he could not have been more than 14 or 15 years old. He repeatedly called out for his mother and father.

'You are in Evin,' a voice bellowed. 'Evin is the house of repentance. Talk! Tell us everything you know. This is your last chance to save yourself.'

'Brother,' he screamed, 'they just captured me in the street! I was on my way to play football with my cousins. I don't know what you want. This is a mistake. I am innocent, believe me. I swear to God, I am innocent. Let me go! My parents are waiting for me.'

'Speak or you will be sent to hell.'

The noise of the lashes and the screams of the boy echoed around the hall. It was sickening… but at least I now knew where I was.

Evin was synonymous with torture. It had a bloody 30-year history, from its construction with the help of Israeli experts as a maximum security prison to hold those who had escaped torture and interrogation during their stay in Komiteh Moshtarak. Evin was the Bastille for Iranian revolutionaries. They stormed it, the place that claimed many freedom fighters under the Shah's regime. Among the executed were seven leaders of the Fedayeen group led by the socialist Bihjan Jazani and two Mojahedin. In 1972 they were 'shot while attempting to escape' – i.e., taken to the top of a hill and machine-gunned. Between 1981 and 1982, more than 10,000 Iranian revolutionaries died either under torture or in front of the firing squad.

The guard in charge of this hall appeared to be in his 50s. He was called Sayed and was very diligent, making sure that prisoners did not talk to each another or touch their blindfolds.

He even asked each of us what we were charged with, in order to ensure that no two members of the same organisation or group were sitting near each other. I was made to sit in a different place from Farhad, who I had been hoping to communicate with. As the night drew on, I tried to think of a pretext to allow me to move closer as I thought that we would be moved to court the next day. I was desperate to tell him to deny any link between me and the organisation. When a hand went up from the other side of the hall requesting permission to go to the lavatory, I squinted under my blindfold and saw that it was Farhad. I got up and followed him, making out that it was an emergency, running doubled up across the hall with my hands over my groin.

I arrived at the toilet door at exactly the same time as Farhad did. Inside, we pushed up our blindfolds a little higher so that we could see. There were three or four cubicles and a sink. 'We need to talk,' I said. 'When we return to the hall I'll try and sit next to you.'

Back in the hall I followed him to his place. We stayed facing the wall in silence until lights out, when it was less dangerous to talk. Now Farad told me his whole story. One of the members of the organisation had 'repented' and gave information to Savama, the Ministry of Intelligence and National Security. This person had taken the security forces to where Farhad's parents lived and, after staking out the house for a week, the secret police told his elderly mother that her son and his comrades would be shot and she would be arrested and sent to Evin. The old woman was painfully aware that this was not an empty threat and made the leader of the security forces swear on the Koran that if she gave them the address he would spare Farhad's life. Very early the next morning she took dozens of Hezbollah gunmen to the safe house. They seized various documents, including a list of activists in the underground cells within the factories.

Farhad explained that, to save the leadership, he had to give up other comrades. He lamented a failure to destroy valuable information lying around the safe house which he said had greatly increased the pressure. Mariam, his wife, was harshly treated, not least because she was pregnant at the time and therefore identified as a soft target. She withheld essential information that, had it come to light, would have resulted in my death. Despite the shock and disorientation of their arrest, both Farhad and Mariam kept much from their interrogators. I was not only grateful but also impressed, even though my arrest had followed the raid on their safe house. Farhad went on to warn that the secret police were also being fed information by collaborators within the prison itself.

Our clandestine discussion in that dark and silent hall continued until almost 4am. I will never forget that night, it felt historic: the first meeting with a comrade since my arrest, the first chance to exchange information. The time passed so quickly and, before I knew it, it was 5am and the guards were filing in again. The day started with the muezzin calling us to the compulsory prayer session over the prison sound system. The guards then collected up the dirty blankets we had slept in, exchanging them for dirty red plastic cups filled with the traditional yellow, foul-smelling tea (with bromide that made the stench worse), sweetened with two cubes of sugar. This, with a piece of under-baked doughy bread and a small slice of stale cheese, was breakfast.

After eating we lined up in single file. Still blindfolded, each prisoner put their right hand on the shoulder of the one in front. At the front of the line a huge, bearded guard held a piece of cable attached to the first prisoner, thus avoiding physical contact with the 'untouchables'. Another guard, brandishing a stick, ran up and down the length of the queue. Every now and then he would start beating a prisoner on the head, shoulders and back and scream, 'Why were you speaking?' Bringing up the rear was a third guard.

I clasped Farhad's shoulder and hoped that we would be put in a cell together and therefore able to continue our discussion.

Some prisoners were left behind on the ground floor while the rest of us were taken to another secure area in the facility. Farhad and I were separated and he was put into another cell. I never saw him in that prison again. The guards handed us over and the prisoners had then to wait for hours in the corridor until new guards opened the door into another block. One by one each of us was forced to strip down to our underpants and then we were searched. There were a few prisoners who still had decent clothes and even watches, rings and money. Everything was taken. We dressed ourselves in new uniforms.

I was led down more corridors and witnessed some horrendous scenes from underneath my blindfold. Prisoners lined the walls on either side of me, some of them bleeding from fresh wounds on their heads, hands and feet. Some appeared to be dead, a dirty blanket as their shroud. A few men and women had been manacled and were hanging from doorframes or the bars of the windows. They looked like they had been there for some time; some showed no sign of life.

The corridor was about two metres wide and between 40 and 50 metres long. Every five or six steps I took, I saw another corridor intersect the main one at right angles – each of them was lined with more huddled inmates. The familiar sound of torture filled the air, the screams of young girls and boys mixing with those of the old. There was another sound, one that was new to me: the cries of children, some of them infants, looking for their mothers.

The despair I felt was almost overwhelming and questions flooded my brain. Why had they brought me here? I had been through all this before. Weren't those interrogations in the Komiteh enough? Was I going to be tortured again? What about those thick files that the guards had in their hands earlier were they related to my case?

My despair deepened when I discovered which section of Evin I had been moved to: block 209. This was a centre of torture. It was in the hands of the Islamic revolutionary prosecutor who worked closely with Savama and the information and security section of the Islamic committees. The committees, which were scattered throughout the different boroughs of Tehran and the provinces, sent all the reports they could gather on each suspicious case to the Islamic prosecutor. He could then give the order for further arrests.

Block 209 was run by a member of the Islamic Revolutionary Party who would later become Tehran's deputy to Iran's government, the Majles. His rise to power was not unusual. Many officials, deputies routinely among them, were involved in torture and massacres. He also later became managing director of the Al Hadi Foundation. Although 'charitable', it made large profits from many different companies – including one that produced women's underwear. His position came by way of a fatwa from Khomeini.

For five long days and nights I was a witness to torture. Then a guard arrived and, standing in the middle of the corridor, read out a long list of names. I heard him call out my first name, Reza, followed by my father's first name. Surnames were avoided so prisoners would not be able to identify one another.

I was taken into a room in which an interrogator was waiting. He was reading a file that I suspected was the same one prepared on me at the Komiteh prison. Looking up, he asked my name, political affiliation and charges. With the formalities over, he grabbed me by my uniform and pulled me out of the room, along the passageway, down a staircase leading to the basement and into another room. The first thing I noticed was the familiar sight of a metal bed frame. I was put face down and my outstretched wrists and ankles were secured with plastic ropes. Somebody sat on my neck and shoulders while two others beat me with cables on the soles of my feet and on my back. They took turns to flog me, all the time shouting '*Allahu Akbar*!' ('God is great'.)

I begged for them to stop, explaining that I had already been interrogated for six months in Komiteh and that I should be awaiting trial.

'We only rely on our own information, not anyone else's,' they said, as the beating continued. 'The information in this file is useless. Speak, or we will send you to hell.' This was my introduction to life on block 209.

The chief interrogator responsible for my questioning called himself Masoud. His underlings included two guards, Ghasem and Mojtabah, and two prisoners who were former members of the organisation I was accused of belonging to and had 'defected' to the regime. It was felt that they could add extra 'intelligence' to the interrogation, as well as four more fists and boots when called upon.

I at last passed out and was only pulled back to consciousness by the sharp pain from the lacerations on the soles of my feet but I could not physically speak for 48 hours. When the interrogators eventually came for me again I was handed a piece of paper with two questions written on it: what were the names and addresses of each and every person I had met in political circles? Would I give information on each of them?

After more beatings to my back and feet, I was again subject to the ghapani torture. My hands were chained together so that my forearms crossed diagonally behind my back. I was suspended by the chain at my wrists over a hook from the ceiling, my feet dangling in the air. My collar bone was still damaged from the last ghapani session and the agony was doubled. I was taken down when I passed out and my limp body was thrown back into the corridor.

The torture session continued every two or three days and I looked and felt like I had been pulled from a serious car wreck: both of my feet were bleeding; my collar bone had broken again;

a particularly vicious blow to the head had led to the loss of 95 per cent of vision in my right eye; both of my eardrums had ruptured; the vertebrae in my lower back were bruised and damaged from guards constantly kicking and stamping on me; teeth had been punched out. My back was incredibly painful; I would scream so loudly that other prisoners would carry me on their shoulders to the infirmary, pleading for injections of painkillers. To this day, loss of balance, constant tinnitus and back injuries continue to make my life miserable. The damage is irreversible.

Four months into my ordeal I was taken to a room where, under the blindfold, I could make out a large table around which a number of people were sitting. I could hear voices from different parts of the room – different accents and dialects including Azeri and refined Persian. I had a strong feeling that those around this table held my life in the balance. 'Is anyone else in your family involved in political activity against the Islamic Republic?' A lumpen southern Tehran accent, very coarse.

'No.'

'How about your in-laws? Weren't they helping you financially?'

'No. In fact, they've made a fortune as a result of their activity in the market in this war, so they wouldn't be interested in politics.'

'Lumpen' specifically asked if two of the named in-laws had helped me. He seemed to know them – and me – calling us by first names throughout.

'Do you believe the Islamic Republic is revolutionary?' A voice from my left side this time – a strong Arabic accent.

'The Islamic Republic came about as a result of a revolution against the Pahlavi regime, which was a stooge of American imperialism.' *Dodge the question altogether.*

'Do you believe the Islamic Republic is a stooge of imperialism.'

'The Islamic regime is acting independently from American influence.' I was phrasing my answers very carefully. Here I simply repeated the position of our organisation about the regime's foreign policy.

'Do you believe in the Islamic revolution? Are you ready to go to the front to fight Iraqi aggression?'

'I participated fully in the revolution which overthrew the Shah, and I am still a believer in those principles. As for going to the front, I can't stand on my feet. I'm old and frail. I don't have anything to contribute.'

Another question from another man, this time with a thick Azeri accent and an educated tone: 'What are your views on the Soviet Union?'

'I have always rejected any intervention and influence in my country's internal affairs by any foreign power, be it American imperialism or the Soviet Union.'

'If so, then why have you tried to raise discussions on socialism?'

'I am in favour of a balanced representation of all views,' I said, quickly adding, 'including the Islamic point of view.'

'What are your views on current developments in the Soviet Union, and the successes they have had so far?'

Tricky question. *Be careful.* 'You are asking me to talk about the successes of the Soviet Union. My understanding is that at this stage they themselves don't claim that they have achieved all their goals. In a country where you still have queues for essential goods, I can't see how you can claim they have succeeded.'

After more questions, accusations and abuse, they called in a guard who took me to an adjacent corridor, where another guard led me to a solitary cell.

Solitary was a relief because this was only the second period since my arrest that I was free to remove the rank prison blindfold. The first thing I saw was a big iron toilet and, to the left of the door, an iron sink. In the corner beyond it was a covering and behind that were a series of pipes and cables – the perfect hiding place for listening devices. I had to be wary of every word. There were three threadbare, woollen, military-issue blankets and, in one corner, a battered red plastic tea cup. When I lay down and stretched out to sleep, the top of my head touched one wall and the soles of my feet the other. I stared up at the lightbulb. It had a wire cover to prevent prisoners from removing the bulb and electrocuting themselves. I'd heard that some prisoners had attempted to do this by standing on the sink late at night when there were fewer guards around. If that didn't work, they had instead broken off jagged bits of the wire guard and slashed their throats or wrists and bled to death.

The walls in my new cell were grey concrete, so hard that you could not even scratch your name on them. In lieu of any graffiti were passages from the Koran and a portrait of Khomeini painted directly onto the concrete. Calls to repent and denunciations of America and Iraq faced you on every wall of the prison.

The door had a barred, oblong hole through which the guards could watch and I was never warned before this would be opened. Meagre meals were pushed through a hatch on the bottom of the door. Whenever it was opened, I had to put my blindfold back on and face the wall. There was also a very small window in the cell – barred, of course. It was positioned too high to look through, but it was appreciated nonetheless. Time passed painfully slowly in solitary and I used to follow the passage of the sunbeams as they made their journey from one corner of the cell to the other.

I tried to exercise and rebuild the strength I had lost over months of torture. Late at night and early in the morning I would stretch my muscles and run on the spot as slowly and as quietly as I could, so I could not be heard outside the cell. Any form of exercise was banned.

Just a few days had passed when the cell door was opened at around 10 o'clock one morning and a tall, bearded man wearing a blindfold was led in. The door was locked, the man removed his blindfold and he sat in the opposite corner of the cell to me. He looked to be between 35-40, his hair was light and brownish, his skin light and he had blue eyes and a bright face.

'What are you accused of?' I asked.

'I was a leader of a guerrilla organisation in Sanandaj, Kurdistan.' The city was the capital of the Kurdish province of Iran. 'I studied in America and graduated in engineering. You?'

At first I found it refreshing to have someone to talk with, but I soon got the feeling that something wasn't quite right. He kept asking me about the details of my case and my attitude toward the regime. 'They got me by mistake,' I insisted. 'They will soon let me out of here when they find out I am innocent.'

'This is the second time I have been captured,' he told me. 'The first time the Islamic regime exchanged me for a number of their guards held by our organisation. But now I have come to understand that the Islamic regime has the support of the masses and those who are fighting against the regime in Kurdistan are acting in America's interest. I have repented and become a Tavab [one who accepts Islam and becomes a collaborator with the prison officials], and I pray five times a day. I am working in prison to enhance the Islamic revolution's fight against subversives. What are you going to do? If you don't repent, you know they'll put you in front of the firing squad.' We called collaborators 'kapos'. Fortunately, I had been very careful what I told him.

'Who, me?' I said, trying to sound as indignant as I could. 'I have nothing to repent. If it wasn't for the likes of you, who took things into their own hands, rampaging through the streets, I wouldn't be here. As for praying, I'm an innocent man. If I start to pray now, the guards will think that I have done something wrong and am repenting. I've never prayed inside prison and I see no reason to start doing it now. They'd think I'm trying to fool them.'

Each morning at about three or four o'clock, when the guards hammered on the door and bellowed 'Prayer time!' the sound system relayed the wailing voices calling us to prayer. My cellmate would rise and put a large prayer mat in front of the small hole in the prison door so that if the guards looked in they could see him 'hard at it'.

Two weeks after the man had walked into the cell he was removed. Sure enough, after two more days, he reappeared at the cell door with a file in his hand. There was another Tavab with him, another former member of a Kurdish group. These two both had a long discussion about articles in an internal prison newsletter called The Tavabins ('The Repentants'), which they and others had put together to undermine prisoners' morale. From their discussion, I gathered that it contained articles directed against revolutionary organisations in Kurdistan and elsewhere in Iran, which they branded as anti-Islamic and pro-American. The man would arrive in the evening and work on the file he had with him until the early morning. Initially, I thought that this file contained his written answers to the interrogators' questions, much as I had been asked to write, but it seems that he was making comments on the files of other prisoners for the interrogators. He was in fact helping the interrogators in their persecution of the prisoners. It was clear he was evaluating me. A few days later they again took him out of the cell.

I remember him asking me about the films I liked which had affected me, ploys like this. So I would respond, giving him a synopsis of some films I had seen, with beautiful landscapes and mountain climbing – anything I could think of that didn't have any political connotations. He asked me if I'd seen a particular film about a peasant revolt in pre-revolutionary Russia. 'No', I lied. 'I don't go to political films.'

My time in solitary came to an end – finally – in the spring
of 1982. I was moved out of the hated block to a cell shared
with other prisoners. Outside the walls of Evin, there were now
constant clashes between the Islamic guards and the various
shades of opposition to the government. Whenever the guards
raided the underground organisations and killed some of their
members, they brought the corpses to Evin. Haji Lajiverdi,
Evin's revolutionary prosecutor, would force us prisoners out of
our cells to look at the bodies, supposedly to identify them. This
was only a pretext because they already had more than sufficient
information. This gruesome routine was really to break the
prisoners' resistance.

Early one cold morning, at about three or four, my cell door
was flung open. I had my uniform on and was blindfolded but
had no shoes. The guards took me down to the lower floor,
near the slaughter house used by the firing squad which
executed thousands of prisoners, often two or three hundred
at a time. I was marched along with about 80 other inmates.
This was a confusing moment. Prisoners had already been told
by Haji Lajiverdi that if the Islamic government was in any
danger of losing power, 'We will clean the prisons by putting
the lot of you in front of the firing squad'. My mind was
racing. I had the distinct feeling that my time had come and I
was to be executed.

One of the prisoners sung a revolutionary song, others
started to shout slogans: 'Long live the revolution!' and 'Down
with the counter-revolution!' We were ordered to remove our
blindfolds. I will never forget the horrific scene in front of me:
a line of corpses lay stretched out on the floor. Men and
women together. All had been shot. Some of the bodies were
missing feet, hands and entire limbs – their flesh ripped apart
by machine-gun bullets. Others, while intact, had been
mutilated beyond recognition by head shots. Prosecutor Haji
Lajiverdi was there. He ordered us to look closely at each

corpse, one by one. If we were able to recognise any, we should inform him of their identity.

Many of the people who had been killed were members of a group of Mojahedin militia, which had been active in the armed struggle against the Shah. Their leader was Mousa Khiabarni. Alongside his body were those of other central committee members, including the wife of Masoud Rajavi, another leader of the Mojahedin. Her body had been mutilated. Above them on the wall hung banners with a verse from the Koran. Haji was triumphant at having killed so many key figures. He carried a baby in his arms, which he said belonged to Ashraf, the dead woman. He gloated, 'These are your leaders' corpses. You will have the same fate.' He called on prisoners surveying the scene, 'Repeat loudly: "God's curse be upon them! Long live Khomeini!"'

Prisoners murmured the slogans and Haji wasn't satisfied. He wanted it loud and clear. Picking on one of the prisoners, he ordered, 'Repeat it, or do you want me to kill you in front of everybody here?' The poor prisoner shouted loudly, 'Long live Khomeini! God's curse be on them!' and saved his neck.

I later found out that this repulsive display had been going on for almost a week. All prisoners in Evin had been escorted to this horrifying scene and ordered to curse the corpses. An Armenian, Rafik, and his comrade Enayet, both of the left-wing group Rahe Kargar, were strung up from a tree in the prison yard after refusing to spit on the bodies. Prisoners from other cells and blocks were brought to watch and to curse their lifeless copses. Another young prisoner, a Mojahed named Habibalah Islami, was hanged in public. Hundreds of prisoners, both male and female, were assembled blindfolded before the tree and most believed they were in for another tedious lecture from a priest. Tavabs walked through the seated crowd, shouting slogans. The order came for all the prisoners to remove their blindfolds and they saw Habibalah standing on a plank between two step ladders. They were ordered to watch as a noose was placed around his neck and the ladders kicked away. A roar of disbelief erupted from the prisoners. Some cried out and fainted. Habibalah took minutes to die. As he struggled helplessly the guards ordered the crowd to shout, 'Down with America!', 'Down with the counter-revolution!', 'Long live Khomeini, the spirit of Allah!'

That was not the only display. Late one hot summer night, I was taken to a room where around 70 to 80 corpses were packed with ice. Congealed blood mixed with melt water to create an ugly, foul-smelling liquid. Some prisoners fainted, others vomited.

Prisoners were also forced to donate blood from time to time around this time. We would be led out of our cells to the infirmary to make 'a voluntary contribution to our Islamic war heroes fighting American imperialism'. Each prisoner would have to give half a litre, a considerable 'contribution' considering that many of us were already extremely weak, undernourished and suffering from internal bleeding, asthma, TB and the like.

Death could come at any time. In the toilet one morning I found the body of an old man, maybe 70 years old. Parchment white in death, he had obviously been squatting over the hole through which we defecated when life left him. He had collapsed back into the hole, so now the corpse was bent double: head, shoulders and legs splayed up and out, his backside and midriff lodged firmly in the hole, like a doll thrown into a bin. The corpse was locked in its undignified posture by rigor mortis. I fled from this macabre scene, shouting for help. A guard ordered me to return and pick up the body with another prisoner. I grasped the old man's shoulders, the other man took his ankles and the body was unceremoniously bundled out of the block. I could feel the ebbing warmth of the body as I clutched it.

'Just throw him outside the door' the guard said, as if he'd been a rat.

'Good,' commented another, 'one less mouth to feed.'

On 30 August 1981, Iranian president Mohammad-Ali Rajai and prime minister Mohammad Javad Bahonar were attending a meeting of the Supreme Defence Council in Tehran. An aide entered, put down a briefcase between the two men and left. When it was opened it triggered an explosive device which left five people dead, including the president, prime minister and the chief of police in Tehran. That night the guards rampaged throughout Evin. Prisoners were pulled out of their cells and herded into the yard. Those with glasses, moustaches, or anything that was seen as a sign of education, were selected for slaughter. That night approximately 400 of my fellow inmates were killed in retribution.

Mass executions again erupted less than a year after the assassinations. Night after night a noise would rumble across the surrounding valley like thunder. The first time I heard it I thought it was girders being unloaded for ongoing construction work. It didn't take me too long to find out that the thunder came from barrels of the automatic weapons of the firing squad. Five thousand rounds were fired in each instance. These were always followed by a pistol shot to the head of each victim. All of Evin's 10,000 inmates would sit and count the number of pistol shots: one, two, three… thirty, forty… the toll ran higher and higher. Our morbid arithmetic would tell us approximately how many of us had been shot at the back of the block that night. Some nights we would count up to 400 single shots. Still, we would hear on the prison broadcasting system's Friday morning prayers, one of the deputies complaining, 'We don't hear the sounds of machine guns from Evin enough!' In addition, the Hezbollah would chant 'Death to the hypocrites and the godless'; the hypocrites being the Mojahedin, the godless those with any communist or socialist orientation.

These mass executions went on every night for months, not only in Evin, but throughout all of the country's prisons. The period of most intense slaughter ran from June 1982 to February 1983. Around 8,000 were massacred in Evin alone. Conditions for the surviving prisoners at this time were unbearable. Between 80 and 120 inmates were packed into cells that, during the Shah's time, housed no more than ten. In the corner of every cell in the block there were single bunk beds stacked in threes and 12 people had to sleep in these three beds. As a result prisoners would occasionally fall out during their sleep, injuring both themselves and the unfortunate souls they landed on.

There was only enough room to lie on one side at night. If you changed position, you would lose your place and be forced to stand in a corner for the rest of the night. Trips to the lavatory were regulated: three visits every 24 hours and no more than two minutes to go to the toilet and wash. Because of various injuries, many prisoners could not hold on that long and would have to piss in the bowls we used to drink out of and leave them in a corner of the room. Then, when they got to go to the bathroom, these bowls would be emptied and cleaned. Prisoners who complained were sometimes forced to drink the urine by the guards as punishment.

Occasionally people would die of their injuries in these cells or individuals would be led away for 'block 4 treatment' – this was the area where the mass executions were carried out and we all knew those unfortunates were never coming back. Their places were quickly filled by new arrivals.

Evin was split into a number of sections. Members of various organisations were kept separately. One section was given over to Saghari – prisoners under 15. All were forced to pray five times a day. There were six blocks, each of which contained between 1–2,000 prisoners. In total, there were 200 cells in all blocks.

At night the guards descended upon the cells. They would look at each of the prisoners carefully, ask them a couple of questions about their activities outside prison, including what they were charged with. Then a handful would be picked out at random. Out in the corridor the Tavabs would write the name and date of birth on the inside of the right leg of the selected prisoner with large marker pens. None of these prisoners were ever seen again. All were shot. These were executions without even a show trial, in retaliation for the bombing campaign of the Mojahedin. During these raids, other prisoners were asked if they would participate in the execution of their comrades. Those who refused to do so often found themselves in front of the firing squad. The inmates who did assist were taken to the execution yard and told to shoot the wounded in the head. Others removed the bodies torn apart by machine gun and dumped them onto waiting trucks.

Many younger prisoners, especially those with religious backgrounds, capitulated and became Tavabs. Mojahedin militia members, up to and including leaders, gave information which led to the arrest of hundreds of girls and boys. One informant was known as Vali 300 – '300' because that was the number of people who were arrested as a result of the information he provided. The torturers in Evin and other prisons set comrade against comrade, children against parents, parents against children.

Within Evin's walls was a block that stood separate from the others. It was built by the prisoners themselves and called the 'resting place'. A thousand cells contained the leadership of various oppositional left groups, those who were active in organising resistance in other prisons, those whose case notes were incomplete and could not yet be sent to court and those who were thought to be potential troublemakers within the prison system. Inmates were kept in the small cells for three or four years in solitary confinement. 'Resting place' to the prisoner meant that you stayed there until you rot.

I came to know it from the inside in 1986. It all started when one of the guards came to the door of my block for me. 'Get your essentials together, but be quick – and get your blindfold on. You are coming with me. Don't try to talk to anyone.'

Hastily, I gathered up my toothbrush, toothpaste, soap and several items of prison clothing and put them into a plastic bag. As he hadn't told me to collect up all of my belongings, I felt fairly certain that I was off for just a short while. He stood over me as I grabbed my things to ensure that I made no verbal contact with any other prisoner. I followed him out of the block. He led me to a waiting vehicle. The guard helped me into the back of it, prodding my back to indicate that I should sit down on a bench inside. From behind my blindfold I could just see two guards, two women prisoners and three other male prisoners. Obviously, with these two guards looking over us, there was no way we could converse or try to establish our destination. The truck started up, and we drove off out of the prison perimeter.

After about an hour-and-a-half of driving, I could tell that at least we were not going to the prison of Gohardasht, as that was only 30 minutes' drive away. The vehicle eventually drew to a stop and we were all led out into the open. We were handed over to a new set of guards and led into a second vehicle, this one more like a minibus. From behind my blindfold I could just about see through the large glass windows. We were back at Evin! The minibus drove us from Evin's gates right into the prison complex.

Several short stops were made. Each time, one prisoner was taken out, then the minibus drove on again. The fourth stop was my turn. Once out of the minibus, I was led into the resting place. Still blindfolded and with plastic bag in hand I was taken through a corridor to a large staircase and up to the fourth floor. My guard handed me over to another and as I was led down a passageway, I could just about see that there were small cells on each side of the corridor. It was clear to me that I was to be a new guest of honour here. A large, strong hand clamped itself onto my right shoulder and brought me to a halt. Someone whispered into my ear.

'This is called the resting place. No one here makes a sound. You understand, yes?'

'Yes, brother, I understand', I replied, also in a whisper.

The hand moved to grab my sleeve. I was gently tugged along, though I could not hear a sound, not even the sound of my guard's shoes on the concrete floor. We stopped at the doorway to a cell. He asked me for my bag of belongings. He took it from me, sat down on the floor and started to rummage around inside it. I could see what he was doing as I was still standing and he had elected to squat just in front of me. He opened my medicine bottles to ensure I had nothing concealed in them. He looked carefully at my other items, even the toothpaste tube was 'frisked' and he searched through the few items of clothing I had managed to bring with me. He found nothing. He stood up and ordered me to remove my shoes and my clothing down to my underpants. He searched these items as well. Then he poked a finger inside the elastic of my pants and took a peek, front and back, then he let the elastic go with a snap. Once fully satisfied that I had nothing concealed anywhere, he opened the door of the cell in front of me.

'Go in. I will get you some prison clothing shortly. You cannot take anything with you inside the cell.'

'But what about my medicines? I need them to survive.'

'Anytime you need them,' he replied, 'just push a little piece of paper under your door – a guard will attend to you.'

The cell door was closed, and I turned to view my new home. *En-suite* facilities, I thought to myself upon seeing a grubby toilet and sink. Apart from that, there were four dirty, reeking blankets. This 'resting place' really was quiet. No one made a sound all day long. Obviously, I thought to myself, they use severe torture of some sort in order to ensure such quiet here. As a result of this absolute silence, it was very difficult to establish the number of other prisoners.

Three times a day a food trolley would be wheeled down the corridor. It would stop outside each cell. Each door had two slots, one at eye level, the other at the floor. Through the slot at the bottom of the door, our food ration arrived; a guard would slide a small plastic plate of food to each prisoner. By counting the number of stops the food trolley made, and listening out for the number of plates pushed under each cell door, I estimated the number of inhabitants.

Every week, we would be allowed one visit to the shower-room— a short ten minutes. Within these minutes you had to cram in not only a shower, but also a laundry service of your full wardrobe. Then, your time up, you would be whisked back to the cell and locked up safely again. Only then could another prisoner make his laundry visit. Once again, I used the sound of the activities to estimate the number of other prisoners. However, anyone who had not completed both the shower and laundry within his allotted ten minutes would be denied his visit the next week, so this second counting method proved not as accurate as the first. At least it helped me to pass away the long days of silence.

I had to take doses of my medicines on three occasions each day. Each time I had to attract the attention of a guard to open up my cell door. He would allow me just enough time to open the appropriate bottle and grab the dosage. Then he would quickly lock my cell again. Each time I performed this ritual, I made an effort to catch a glimpse of the corridor. I quickly established that I was the proud resident of cell no. 487. Additionally, I discovered that the neighbour to my left, 486, also had a supply of medicine outside his room. Over a period of several days, I managed to read the name on his bottles and from that I was able to establish his identity. He was one of the founders of a guerrilla movement in the mid-1960s who served part of a life sentence under the Shah. Freed by mass action during the revolution in 1979, my fellow prisoner had been re-arrested by the Islamic regime in 1983 as one of the leaders of a group critical of the newly-formed Islamic regime. His arrest had been used for propaganda in the war being waged against 'infidels'.

This purging of opposition had been particularly intense between the summer of 1981 to the end of 1982, when the Islamic regime legitimised itself by ratifying its constitution in the Majles Khebragan (Parliament of Islamic Experts). It tried to eradicate the class struggle in the cities, factories and countryside, reversing the peasants' seizure of land in Kurdistan, Baluchistan and Turkmenistan. All forms of working class organisation, including the workers' councils and peasants' councils, were viciously attacked by Islamic guards who carried a gun in one hand and the Koran in the other. Khomeini was intent on consolidating power. One such attack was organised in December 1981 against striking workers at the Iran National car assembly plant. Some 176 of the striking workers were arrested. A number of them were taken to Evin and put in front of the firing squad. Many revolutionaries were dragged out of factories, offices, schools and universities and killed on the spot, or beaten and then taken half dead to prisons, which ranged from government warehouses to unknown underground depots.

The clergy were planning to establish a reign of terror – the absolute rule of the religious authorities. And at the top sat Khomeini.

CHAPTER 6

AN ARTIST'S
IMPRESSION

A middle-aged prisoner named Parvis was a professional artist with left sympathies. He would take the trouble to speak to most prisoners who were considered to be part of the opposition and he was scrupulously polite. He was even courteous to the Tavabs, though cautious of them too.

During his torture, his interrogators learned of his artistic ability and in particular his painting skills. Parvis negotiated his way out of a quick execution by offering his services to 'the Imam's great revolution'. He agreed to paint a huge portrait of Khomeini in preparation for the anniversary of the Islamic seizure of power.

The portrait was to be a massive one, around three metres wide and six metres high. A thick, wooden frame would be built for it. It would be one of the centrepieces of the celebrations. It would be paraded all around the centre of Tehran and would be seen by hundreds of thousands of people: a great icon of Khomeini.

And so, the prison authorities rounded up the necessary materials so that Parvis could commence his great opus. Seemingly no expense was spared for this endeavour. First, a huge canvas was ordered, then paints, brushes and mixing pots. This project was seen as a great propaganda coup for the prison authorities. Khomeini often proclaimed the prisons in general and Evin in particular as the 'universities of Islam'. The production of this picture would help the regime disseminate the myth that, in fact, the prisons did 'cleanse' the opponents of Islam, rather than just physically eliminate them.

Parvis was given a large room in the block in which to produce this epic painting. Normally it would have held 60 or so prisoners, but for this project he had sole use of the room. It had even been cleaned spotlessly for him. The authorities kept it locked, but Parvis had his own key so no one else could get in.

Every morning at eight, Parvis would gather his paints and brushes and lock himself in the room for a 12-hour session at his canvas. Week after week, month after month this went on. After his 'day at the office' he would lock up, return to his cell for a meal, roll a cigarette and talk to one or two prisoners. Some would ask what he was doing all day long. All he would say was that he was keeping himself busy painting.

After some six or seven weeks, one of the other prisoners managed to catch a glimpse of the inside of Parvis' 'studio' as he locked up one night. All that was seen was the outline of a figure drawn roughly with charcoal. From then on, an attempt would be made to casually pass the door just as Parvis emerged each night. In this way, news emerged of the nature of his work.

Some prisoners took a rather dim view of the whole affair to start with; after all, would you have been happy knowing a grand portrait of the country's greatest hangman was being painted by one of your fellow inmates? So at the beginning he had quite some explaining to do, but after some weeks people generally left him alone to get on with it, though some leftists would mutter to themselves about him, belittling his personal character and mettle in resisting the regime.

No one would say much openly. We were all aware of the pressure that the regime could exert if he refused point-blank to co-operate with them. In fact, after some time, a gentle air of respect arose for him as a recognition of Parvis's dedication to his task. It was clear that the scale of the painting was so vast that it would take him almost a year to complete. But some of the Mojahedin's sympathisers and some other leftists speculated that Parvis had become a Tavab. I was certain this was not the case. After all, the job of the Tavabs was not to lock themselves away from everyone else, but to keep an eye on as many prisoners as possible. After some time, this conception of Parvis lost its attraction and the notion was forgotten.

One of the prison officials, Haji Reza, a small man aged about 35, would be escorted by a couple of Islamic guards to view the work in progress. Their visits were frequent but irregular. They would chide Parvis over the amount of materials that he was using, his lack of progress, the slowness and wastage of materials. 'You lazy bum!' they would shout at him. There was obviously some impatience developing – perhaps someone's promotion depended on the painting being completed quickly. Parvis would respond calmly each time, shrug his shoulders and laugh at them. 'You're all so impatient – I'm not a magician, you know!' he would reply in a slightly mocking tone. So they would leave the chamber and he would return to his task.

By the 11th month, January, panic set in among the prison authorities. The celebrations were due in just one month's time, and there were great expectations for the painting. Poor Parvis worked like a dog for those last four weeks. He often would not leave the painting chamber until well past midnight, often 3am or later. He was under tremendous pressure.

Over these eleven months, I had often passed Parvis after his sessions in the painting chamber and we had exchanged pleasantries, if not much more. But as the painting progressed, I got to speak to him more often. Personally, I would rather have done the painting than go to the firing squad, so I considered myself more on his side. Once or twice I relayed to him what was being said quietly behind his back, for which he was grateful. I must have gained a fair amount of his trust during these short exchanges because, on the day after he finally completed the painting, he came up to me.

'Come with me', he beckoned, 'I want to show you something'.

He took me to the door of the painting chamber and drew a long iron key from his pocket. He quickly unlocked the door to the room and motioned me to step inside. Then he closed the door and locked it behind me. Upon the wall I saw for the first time his huge portrait of Khomeini. 'Take a very close look, my friend, and tell me what you see'.

I took a long hard look at the massive image of the face of the Imam.

'The personification of our enemy!' I replied. These words alone could have got me instantly executed had I been overheard.

'Yes, yes. Look again, closer this time – what do you see?' Parvis asked again. I looked again, closer this time, but I could not discern anything but the face.

'All I can see is a huge Imam Khomeini, but with pursed lips – why are they like that?'

'Listen to me, I will tell you what I have painted in this huge portrait,' Parvis said. 'Look at the face – concentrate on the mouth, the nose, the two eyes, the brows and the forehead. Oh yes, and the beard, don't forget the beard!' Parvis' eyes had lit up by this time.

'I still don't see anything special, Parvis. What have you painted? What are you trying to say with this painting?'

'Listen, and look carefully. I have painted a portrait of Khomeini that will not only outlive Khomeini himself, but will also outlive this miserable Islamic regime! I'm not joking – this picture will see off the mullahs and will see their overthrow by the people. Then this painting will be viewed by very many people as a symbol of prison resistance to this regime.'

'Do you mean to say that you believe people will still want to look at a portrait of Khomeini even after the mullahs have been done away with? Surely not!'

'Yes comrade. This portrait will find itself a nice, quiet resting place in a gallery somewhere where art lovers and ordinary people will view it every day, after the fall of the Islamic regime.'

'I can't quite understand why this would be the case', I replied.

Parvis then said to me, rather more quietly than before, 'The facial features, you see them, yes? Look, I have painted a woman's genitalia, not Khomeini's features! You see? You see? His mouth is her vagina, the nose signifies the clitoris, the beard and eyebrows the hair and his forehead is the belly! Surely now you see? What I am saying in this picture is this: these mullahs, so sanctimonious, they represent the most depraved creatures imaginable. Yet they're so hung up, they're shocked by a woman's hair! I am showing their hypocrisy in this painting so that all can see! They're so obsessed with sex, they only see women as a sexual organ.'

'Yes, now I see it, Parvis. How did you paint this, though?'

'They forced me to paint this man, but I have added my own touch to it!'

Parvis's painting illustrated something most profound about the contradictory situation we found ourselves in. Firstly, there was the immense pressure from the interrogators, torturers and the guards to submit totally. Then there was the pressure within one's own self to resist, the basic, human instinct to survive as well as the drive to protect our own integrity. Then there was the expectation among prison colleagues not to succumb. Added to that was the expectation of colleagues outside of the prison that we would not 'go under' politically. All of these pressures manifested themselves in the way that each prisoner resisted and survived, in the routines that he devised and in the day to day battles he fought with himself and his surroundings. Parvis's painting was his own, unique expression of defiance and resistance to the prison regime in Evin. It was not only a depiction of Khomeini but was also a judgement on the Islamic republic itself.

Chapter 7

Writing on
the Wall

The guard was holding a piece of paper in his hand. I caught my breath and my heart sped. Guards carrying pieces of paper never brought good news. The paper would have a list of names handwritten on it. There were four possible fates for prisoners on these lists; execution, trial, removal for torture in block 209 or a transfer. It was 6am and everything pointed to it not being a good day.

For three years I had been in cells where guards had entered with such lists in their hands. I had seen many comrades and prisoners whose names had been on one of these lists leave, never to return. The guards would often come back for their belongings: a signal to us that they had been executed.

Hasan Ardin – who used to run Rahe Kargar's underground printshop before his arrest – was called from among us one day. He knew he would not be coming back. Calmly turning to me, he took off his glasses and held them out: 'Give these to my children, if you can. Tell them their father always stood firm.' I kept these glasses with me for years, from block to block, and one prison to another. Almost five years later, I sent them back to his family through a prisoner I trusted who was due for release.

The guard standing at the cell door started to call out the names on the list. He read out 15 names very quickly, mine was eighth. 'Pack up your stuff! Do not forget your blindfold! Leave the cell within five minutes'

What will happen to me next? I thought. Will it be the firing squad, another visit to 209, or a transfer? Please let it just be a transfer! Within this cell, 25 inmates will remain. I have less than five minutes to pack my things and say my farewells to them. Either I will be executed and I will never see any of them again, or they will have been executed themselves if ever I return.'

Panic prevented me from thinking clearly. Although I had become accustomed to the minute-to-minute unpredictability of prison life and had heard my name read out many times before, it was not possible to face this moment calmly. I embraced and said goodbye to all of the remaining prisoners except the two Tavabs, to whom I merely nodded.

The guard returned, opened the cell door and shouted, 'Out, get out now! Put your blindfolds on and get out!' Each of us pulled the blindfold over his eyes. We lined up in single file and were told to place our right hand on the shoulder of the person in front of us. The prisoner at the head of this line was led by the guard's stick. We filed out of the cell behind him, into the corridor and out through the iron door that led down a flight of stairs and into the prison yard. I sensed that we were walking towards a wall that ran to the left of the door that we had just emerged from. We were ordered to stop walking at this point. The guard then prodded each prisoner with his stick, urging us all to stand one metre apart from each other He turned us to face the wall and sat us down. I could just see the wall about 30 centimetres from my feet out of the bottom of my blindfold. He shouted again, 'Do not move your heads. Do not touch the blindfold! Don't talk to one another!'

This is not the procedure for executions, I thought to myself. And it's not the way to 209. So there must be something else in store for us – perhaps we will be transferred to some other prison. Panic ebbed away, and my thoughts moved to trying to work out what might happen next. I could sense the movements of the guard as he walked up and down behind the line of seated prisoners. As he moved away, towards one or other end of the line, I started to speak very quietly to myself so that the prisoners each side of me would be able to hear but the guard would not see any movement. I tried to convey my conclusions as to our fate. Others agreed under their breath. They also thought we might be transferred from Evin but they were cautious: it was not impossible that some prison official could change his mind.

For five hours we sat there, blindfolded, facing this wall. Anyone who moved or fidgeted was struck on the head by the guard's stick or kicked at the base of the spine. Another guard arrived who stood us all up and led us out of the yard on to one of the roads within the prison compound. A bus waited, its engine idling. As I boarded the bus, I raised my head slightly so that I could see if any other prisoners were already there. It was already almost half-full. There were four armed guards, one at the very back of the vehicle, one at the front and two towards the middle. Each one held a Kalashnikov pointed at the floor, but ready to be used in an instant. We filed into the bus, sitting on the two-seater benches. A further group of prisoners was led in after us. Now the bus was completely full. A guard ordered us to draw all of the curtains on the windows. Although we were still blindfolded, they did not want anyone outside to see us. The curtains did not completely cover the side windows so it was possible to catch a glimpse of what was going on outside. I could also see out of the front window by tipping my head back, pretending to sleep.

I remember feeling relieved, glad that I was leaving that place. Nothing can be as bad as what I've already been through, I thought; no more torture, no more interrogation. As we turned onto the main road, after leaving the long narrow track from Evin, from under my blindfold I could see young children walking home from school. Others were being driven by their parents in elegant Mercedes cars, while a few were being escorted by servants. Evin is situated in the northern part of Tehran. The houses there are owned, in the main, by the business associates of the regime, the clergy and prominent Hezbollahis. The Shah's lackeys had lived here and their abandoned Beverly Hills-style villas were confiscated, and the allies of the mullahs moved in. Some cunning individuals had, however, managed to switch allegiance in order to retain their marble villas, swimming pools and landscaped gardens.

We passed the spectacular Tehran Hilton, now renamed the Freedom Hotel by the mullahs and through Evin district's construction sites. Building workers passed by. In their hands they carried their meagre lunches, a loaf of bread and a soft drink, some also a half melon. The lowest paid section of the workforce, the most destitute peasants driven from the country into the towns, they sat down to consume their pitiful meal in the marble palaces. Their wage would have been less than £1 a day. One of those villas would have cost millions. Evin – the richest, the poorest and the most repressive elements of Iranian society, all in four square miles!

I strained to see how the real world outside the prison walls looked and worked. My first impression was of beggars, aged from three or four right up to over 70. They operated in groups of between five to 15. They would run to cars and vans stopped at traffic lights and plead for money or wipe the windscreens in the hope of a few Rials. Obviously the economic situation had worsened markedly for such poverty to be displayed so openly on the streets.

I could also see portable monuments to those killed in the war. These were erected on the pavement outside people's houses and trundled from one place to the next once a week. They were hollow wooden or steel structures, four feet in diameter and about five feet high, with a chandelier and lights hanging inside them. They bore pictures and inscriptions in gold letters: 'This is our fallen blossom, offered to our great leader Imam Khomeini'. There were an amazing number: down some small alleys you could hardly move for them. The monument would be hired from crooks in the bazaar for a fortnight at a time.

At the start of the Iraq war, the Islamic government paid for the costs of the funerals of those who fell on the battlefield for 'the cause of the Imam'. Each family would also receive a payment of 200,000 Touman (around $8,000 in 1981, dropping to about $2,000 at the end of the war because of the falling exchange rate). In the countryside, where the annual family income for many peasants might be less than 10,000 Touman, this seemed like a gift from God. The 'martyrs' were given a key to heaven, and their families access to cheap goods and a higher status. For some, it seemed a fair trade. The government was printing money to keep up with these payments, but it was necessary as a part of the war propaganda machine.

As the bus drove through Tehran I could see graffiti on the walls. Some was from before the revolution and was familiar. But many of those old slogans had been whitewashed or partly covered with paint. There were still inscriptions, political slogans, the insignia of the various opposition and left-wing organisations, but these had not been painted recently, though. I could just about see the remnants of some of the large but faded May Day slogans dating back to 1979–81: 'Long live May Day – International Workers' Day!', 'All power to the shoras!', 'For workers' control of the factories!', 'Long live proletarian internationalism'. There seemed to be no new graffiti by the opposition. They had been driven off the streets.

There were, however, areas with freshly painted slogans. The Tudeh Party and the Fedayeen Majority, who supported the Islamic regime, were still allowed to paint their slogans on the walls: 'Place heavy guns in the hands of the Islamic Revolutionary Guards!', 'Support the war effort!' and 'Khomeini's anti-imperialist line is the path to revolution!'

We joined the motorway that took us out of Tehran west towards the city of Karaj, 40 kilometres away. On each side of the road were endless large industrial complexes. I looked for left-wing graffiti on the factory walls. During the revolutionary period and immediately afterwards, left-wing organisations had tried to gain influence amongst the factory workers in this area but had not been very successful. Division among the left, their inability to establish a foothold within the factories, the presence of the Islamic shoras and associations and the strong presence of the Islamic Guards within these plants had ensured that their influence was negligible. These factory walls had been absolutely covered with graffiti and slogans, dating from the time of the Shah's white 'revolution' in 1960-3, throughout the 1970s, the revolution of 1979 which deposed him and up to the present day. Most of it was no longer legible – unlike the slogans in support of the Islamic regime. I saw 'The revolution was not for watermelons – economics is for the donkeys: Imam Khomeini', 'God himself is a worker – he takes no time off, he works all day, every day – he needs no May Day!: Imam Khomeini, 1 May, 1981', 'Death to communists and the hypocrites!'. Slogans such as theses were daubed in large bold letters through the streets. The regime had worked all out to direct their propaganda specifically at industrial workers to counter that of the left-wing organisations.

Once we were on the road to Karaj I calculated that there were two possible destinations and once we passed the Gohardasht jail I knew it had to be the prison they called the Golden Fortress (Ghezel Hesar). This was on the outskirts of

Karaj, around 25 miles from Tehran. Like the other prisons I had been held in, the Golden Fortress was built during the Shah's regime, and had held many political prisoners – not a few of whom went back into jail under Khomeini.

The complex rose out of the barren plain as our bus rattled its way towards it. Putting my head back, feigning sleep, I watched my destination loom larger and larger still from under my blindfold, until its dark grey mass towered over our little bus. Thick concrete walls of up to 12 metres rose vertically up from the dusty earth. Each one sprouted barbed wire from the top.

The Golden Fortress sprawls over a vast flat wasteland. There is no chance of escape: The guard towers rise up like huge forbidding minarets, giving an uninterrupted view for miles all around. There is not even so much as a bush to hide behind on the plain. The electrified, powered gates were opened – sometimes prisoners' relatives were crushed when these gates were deliberately closed on them.

A number of armed guards marched over to our bus as it came to a halt. They boarded and spoke to the guards from Evin, who handed over the paperwork. The new guards quickly counted how many of us there were to ensure no one had managed to get off on the way. The bus started up again. We drove for about one kilometre through this grey, soulless complex. Then the bus stopped abruptly. A second set of guards led us into the main building of the prison. Our 'guides' from Evin went to a rest area where they could eat before shuttling a group of prisoners back to Evin.

There was to be no relaxation and food for us. We were pushed down so that we were all sitting on the floor, still blindfolded, facing the wall in the reception area of the main building. Guards were running back and forth with sticks in their hands to ensure no one spoke to anyone else, or passed on any information. Some prisoners I travelled with were sick and they complained to the guards; they asked for some scraps of bread as none of us had yet eaten – without any success. Others were in dire need to go to a lavatory and had to beg the guards to take them. Reluctantly, they were accompanied one by one for no more than a couple of minutes each.

Around 5pm, after we had been sitting on this hard floor for almost four hours, a guard gave each prisoner one piece of bread and a slice of cheese. A stream of curses, growing progressively louder, broke the silence. Someone was coming – someone none too sweet-tempered and big. The noise of his army boots on the concrete floor of the corridor seemed like an elephant! The thumping stopped as the cursing hit full volume. The owner of the boots and voice was in the hall with us, and it was obvious that we were the object of his cursing.

'Watch out, it's Haji Davoud!' whispered a prisoner.

'Hypocrites, atheists, socialists and communists', his deep voice boomed around the hall, 'You are in the Golden Fortress. Here we break your bones in quarantine! If you do not repent we will break your souls and your spirit to doomsday! In the unlikely event that you survive this, we put you in front of the firing squad! Only total surrender, full conversion to Islam and becoming a Tavab can possibly save your souls. Welcome to the Golden Fortress!' This was to be no convalescence after my ordeal at Evin and the Komiteh. 'Who wants to become a Tavab and save his soul? Stand up if you wish to spare yourselves!'

Five or so who had been Tavabs at Evin stood up. They were told to walk over to the far side of the hall. 'So, you refuse Islam's mercy – you prefer to go to Hell, do you? Well, we will be sending you there soon enough!' Haji Davoud bellowed at those of us who remained.

'Take these infidels and hypocrites off to quarantine – they are inhuman, just animals, donkeys even!' The guards pulled us to our feet and prodded us sharply with their gun barrels into groups of five or so. As the heavy footsteps of Haji Davoud left the hall, he shouted over his shoulder 'I'll see you in quarantine!'

Chapter 8

Quarantine

We marched through the maze of grey corridors and I could hear prisoners in each block – they were calling out, talking between themselves or moaning from their injuries. At the end of this journey we found ourselves in the block called quarantine. Sounds like we are in for some special treatment here, I thought. We will probably be kept here together until our resistance is broken before we are integrated into the normal prison blocks.

The Golden Fortress had four sections and the political prisoners were kept in the first three. The regular police ran the fourth section for everyone else. Each section had four large blocks, and four small blocks called mujaradi – solitary. Each block had 16 small cells, measuring around 1.5 by 2.5 metres. These were designed to hold two to four prisoners. There were also eight large cells that were about 3 by 5 metres and were supposed to hold about twice as many. In practice, up to 40 prisoners were squeezed into the larger cells and 15 to 20 in the small cells.

Hardline prisoners were permanently locked down in block 1. Each section would hold between 2-2,500 prisoners, excluding solitary cells which were built to hold 20 prisoners. Some 11,340 political prisoners were held in the main three blocks with 750 prisoners kept in section four.

Quarantine was a special block with 16 identical cells, each measuring 2.5 metres by 1.5 metres and about 3.5 metres high. Three bunk beds were stacked against one wall for inmates who were either newly arrived from other prisons or judged to be 'intransigents' – men and women who the Tavabs decided showed signs of resistance to the Islamic regime. In reality, it wasn't possible to be a troublemaker. The Tavabs ensured that communication and association between prisoners was almost non-existent. The Tavabs presented false evidence when they took a dislike to a prisoner..

In the third block of section three was the quarantine area for women prisoners, irrespective of their age, who were in any way suspected by officials or Tavabs of being intransigents.

Blindfolded as I was, my first impression of my new 'home' was the salty, sour stench of human sweat that hit me when the cell door opened. It was unbearably humid, like a steam bath. I was pushed over the threshold, the door clanging shut behind me. I removed my blindfold. Thirty-five people, crushed together in a tiny space, stared at me expectantly. At my back was an iron barred sliding door, through which the other four new arrivals and I had just been pushed. On the left side of the cell were three bunks. The top two had wooden bases, the bottom one nothing, so that it provided a frame within which seven people could sit, knees cramped against their chests. Seven people sat on each of the two bunks above; backs to the wall, with the cell so narrow that the soles of their feet pressed against the opposite wall. Seven others sat on the floor opposite, facing the seven below the bunks. Six of us sat with our backs to the iron barred door and six opposite. Some hung off the bunks racked against the wall. People were stacked up like baked bean tins in a supermarket, crammed in like slaves on a prison ship. You could stand up and, picking your way between the others' legs, walk from one end to the other to relieve the cramps in your legs, and try and release some of the stress through this micro-stroll.

One of the 35 watchers rose and welcomed us to quarantine on behalf of the cell commune. He introduced himself as Farid and while we talked, he went to fetch us some food, stored in old plastic bread wrappers hanging from the corners of the bed frames. 'You must be starving', he said, 'New arrivals from Evin always are.' We ate stale bread and dried dates from this cell larder. Still, it tasted like kebabs to us and we were locked away from Haji Davoud and the guards.

Farid asked everyone else to introduce themselves to us. When this small ceremony was over, Farid laid down the cell ground rules. 'We have organised the cell as a commune. Everything here is common property – except your toothbrush and spectacles. What money we have goes into a common fund, as does the money sent from our families each month. All individual expenses are paid out of the common fund – that includes stuff like your toothbrush and so on. When anyone leaves the cell, we give them an emergency stipend from the fund, so they have cash to tide them over for a while. But if any of you would like to go it alone, then you can do so at your discretion and still count on our help and co-operation.'

We five expressed our willingness to join in the communal arrangements, handed in the cash in our pockets and were allocated spaces which changed daily so that no one was stuck in the worst corner. Farid supervised this. I was the oldest and, as a result of Komiteh, 209 and elsewhere, I was the most frail. Farid suggested I should get a top bunk place close to the corner. Everyone agreed and I got the cell equivalent of the penthouse suite.

The others shifted position every two hours, those sitting on the floor against the narrower walls moving up to the bunks, giving them two hours of relatively comfortable sleep. We would also take it in turns to walk up and down the centre of the cell – although there was never any room for more than one person at a time to do this.

Each prisoner was given one aluminium spoon, one dirty plastic plate, and one plastic cup – black with ground-in grime, though it had once been red. Two hours after our arrival, I heard the rumble of trolley castors trundling down the corridor. The undefinable lentil mush and bread was pushed into the cell and the cell monitor called after the guard to remind him that the food we had was barely enough for 35, and our cell population had just risen by five. The guard shouted back, 'We'd rather kill you than feed you' and carried on his way.

It was very difficult for our monitor to divide such scant fare among us. The broth was so watery it was possible to count the lentils floating in it. Its only seasoning was the prison cook's special – bromide. We also had a bucket of yellowish water, looking like it had been drawn off a rusty oil drum. This served as tea. Every 24 hours, each prisoner would be given three cups of this, along with four sugar cubes. Shortly after the meal, a guard came to escort us to the bathroom to wash up.

Once every day, the cell door would be opened for about 10 minutes to allow us to hurriedly wash our shirts and dishes, or revive ourselves by cooling down in the corridors, or douse ourselves in cold water. Two people would be delegated to wash up the dishes in one bowl, and the rest of us would use the three or four other bowls to wash ourselves. This gave each of us about one to one-and-a-half minutes to wash and go to the lavatory. If we overran, we would be beaten by the guards.

Every 15 days we would be allotted 15 minutes to shower, with as many as ten of us cramming under one of the three shower heads. We crossed the corridor and were able to hear voices from other cells. Quarantine living had its own peculiarities. The physical and mental pressures of having to survive, 40 to a box, were horrendous. We had the all-pervasive prison broadcast system: Koranic catechisms all day and all night. After a week I was sure that I would never get out of it alive. At least there were no Tavabs to note our every action and we all looked after one another. I have never experienced comradeship like it, even from prisoners who were not left wing.

But the pressure was unbearable. Some were crushed by it and their collapse was a devastating blow to those who had come so close to them in quarantine. Habib was a Mojahed supporter of about 16 who had been in the cell for about five months when we arrived. His mental condition was sound but incessant squatting had given him chronic piles and incontinence. He had to sit with his hand between his legs to keep his rectal passage inside him. Every minute was torture for him. Others had infected bladders, could not hold their water or, like me, pissed blood when they did. The guards were deaf to our appeals for more time at the lavatory, and beat everyone when we protested. We kept a bucket in the cell.

In the cell opposite us, there was a young man who would scream, cry and curse at the guards, Khomeini, Islam and the Koran. The guards retaliated by tying him to an iron bed frame and giving him up to a hundred lashes from his neck to his ankles. We could all hear the crack of the whip and his screams. But it didn't stop him. He was too far gone. There were others like him and their sounds became familiar but always horrifying to hear. One evening after we had eaten and the whole of quarantine was engaged in subdued discussion, the calm was shattered by a scream of hysterical laughter. There was no joy in it: it was insane and terrifying. It started a chain reaction. The deranged young man in the cell opposite joined in this hellish wail. From the far corner of the corridor, another voice howled out in solidarity with his comrades in madness. Everyone else was shocked into silence. You could feel the block inmates hold their collective breath, awaiting the outcome of this manic eruption. The inmates of one cell began to drum on their door. Soon we all joined in, hammering out an angry beat with spoons, plates, cups and fists. The whole block was beating out a rhythm of hate against the prison system that had sent those who had started this crazy demonstration over the edge.

The guards had left their usual vantage points along the corridor to attend prayer. Twenty of them returned and charged in with clubs, fists and boots. In the centre of this pack was Haji Davoud. They hauled the screamers out of the block, beating them as they went. Then the rest of us were ordered out of our cells, forming two lines along the corridor, blindfolded, faces to the wall. The guards systematically attacked us from behind. Haji Davoud's wolves went from one side to the other until they were too exhausted to continue. Then they ordered our human wreckage back to the cells. 'The next time you riot, it will be the firing squad!' Haji Davoud shouted.

One week later, the three screaming prisoners who had been taken out were brought back. They looked extremely frail. They had been put in solitary for a week, and repeatedly beaten. They had broken jaws, gashes on their heads, and were black and blue. Two had slashed their wrists, including the young man from the cell opposite ours.

CHAPTER 9

THE PRISON REGIME IN THE GOLDEN FORTRESS

Between June 1981 and the end of 1982, some of those who had been arrested in street battles – particularly in the Mojahedin militia and left groups who had taken up arms, were given a stark choice – go to the firing squad to be shot or go to the firing squad to do the shooting.

Those of us who remained in our cells while the massacres went on around us were revolted at living with those who had chosen to kill our comrades. When they returned from the firing squad, you could see and smell the blood on their clothes, and the horror of death on their faces. But even this became commonplace and they began justifying what they were doing. Gradually, they came to see their actions in these slaughterhouses as a defence of the Islamic regime. They became proud to be Tavabs.

This phenomenon, of Tavabiat, embryonic in Evin, was transformed into a mass force in the Golden Fortress. In Evin, the Tavabs comprised less than one per cent of the total prison population. In the Golden Fortress, this disease had reached epidemic proportions. More than ten per cent were hard core Tavabs, and another ten per cent were passively. The regime hoped to erode the morale, political identity and discipline of its jailed opponents through the physical assaults of the Tavabs and the demoralisation which we felt because of their very existence. Then there were the Tudeh and Fedayeen Majority, who still supported the Khomeini regime. Prisoners from those organisations formed another divisive force. And finally political prisoners who had overthrown the Shah were deliberately mixed with prisoners from that era.

I was dropped between these opposing forces when I was moved out of quarantine into the regular cells in section 3's block 1 in the autumn of 1982. On my arrival I was surrounded by a group of Tavabs. After some questioning, they decided into which cell I should go. Between one and three Tavabs were put with each group of prisoners. Each was expected to make a daily report on the cell.

The central block corridor was about three metres wide, with cells either side. The large cells were at the far end of the corridor. The further down the corridor you were, the more anti-regime you were seen to be. The prisoners from cell 17 onwards were intransigents. Cells 6 to 10 held the prisoners who leaned towards the Tavabs but would not actively collaborate. Cells 10 to 16 held those whose sympathies lay with the intransigents. These were the 'passives'.

The most vicious Tavabs congregated in cells 1 to 3. The first cell was called the control room and housed the chief Tavab. He allocated cells rather than the prison authorities. He was the link between the block and the officials, handpicked by them on the basis of atrocities he had carried out for the regime in previous prisons. His underlings lived in the cells around the control room. There was a division of labour between them: one gathered information from the prisoners, another took charge of food distribution and a third would take prisoners to interrogation. They ran a gangster-like operation.

While we were held in 24-hour confinement, the Tavabs would sit on top of the bunk beds. There they could observe everything we did or said. In the small cells we had three lots of three high bunks – in the larger cells up to 15 beds, so the Tavabs would be watching in three different positions. On one occasion they were able to implicate a group of seven intransigents with trying to write a manuscript on political developments in the government. All seven were shot.

Any indication of fellow feeling for another prisoner could endanger you. It was seen as 'communal activity' or propagating 'communist spirituality'. Anyone convicted would be sent either to quarantine or to 'doomsday'.

About 30 prisoners were kept in my cell. At meal times individual plastic plates would be given out by the Tavabs to ensure that we all ate on our own. You could not even help the injured to eat. To help another prisoner to eat his food would be seen as fomenting 'spiritual resistance'. In this 'Islamic University', organised by Imam Khomeini and managed by Haji Davoud, any human relationship would be seen as a great crime against the Islamic regime.

I was being held in a closed cell – I was under lockdown, under constant Tavab observation. Even in the blocks of the Golden Fortress where some free movement was allowed, prisoners were constantly followed. Tavabs followed conversations between inmates, made notes of what was said and then passed them to the control room. Usually, prisoners would be taken away for questioning as a result.

However, if the subject of discussion was considered to be especially serious, such as criticism of the regime or political opposition, the Tavabs would beat the prisoner and often make him stand blindfolded through the night. I was beaten and

punched by the Tavabs many times. On occasion I was made to
stand for ten hours.

The Golden Fortress was governed by a scrap iron dealer with
a yard in South Tehran. The south of the city was the epicentre
of the black market, drug dealing and prostitution, and this man
was one of the organisers of an Islamic Committee in the area.
In this way he came into contact with the office of the Islamic
Revolutionary Prosecutor, and so wormed his way into being
the sole representative of Khomeini in the Golden Fortress.

He was an obese man. It was said he could eat a whole sheep
in one sitting. He did the rounds of the prison blocks himself,
flanked by guards, intermittently stopping to cuff an
unfortunate prisoner or send another flying by buffeting him
with his stomach. He was bald, with a large black beard almost
entirely covering a bloated face in which were embedded a pair
of piggy little eyes. His nose was a bulbous monument to heavy
drinking. Flat-footed, broad-shouldered and immense, he
waddled rather than walked with a heavy step that shook even
the concrete prison floors. He was also sentimental. The mere
mention of Khomeini would have him dabbing his eyes in
remembrance of his benefactor. The lives of more than 10,000
men and women were placed in his hands.

As a result of his elevation from scrapyard to slaughter house,
he began to consider himself a theorist. In his own eyes he
became a great authority on every subject from imperialism to
the atom and would inflict a lecture on these matters at any
provocation. He believed he was an expert on political prisons
and their inmates. Yet this devout servant of the Imam was also a
dirty old man. He forced one group of women involved in
prison resistance to confess in public alleged sexual activities in
safe houses. This performance was filmed. The women were so
broken by the brutality of quarantine and doomsday that they
acquiesced to this show trial in the hope that it would get them

out. As much as they tried to plead the sincerity of their repentance, the Tavab section of the crowd would shout 'Death to the hypocrites and communists! Down with Israel, America and the Soviet Union! Long live Khomeini, Imam of the epoch!' Following the orchestrated barracking, a pronouncement would be made: 'You have not passed this test of sincerity. You will stay here until you rot.'

These show trials took place many times, usually in the early afternoon, and would go on till eight or nine at night. The Tavabs would direct the prisoners from each block down to the main corridor and order them to sit. Thousands of prisoners provided an audience for hours at an end, crammed in, squatting on the floor, with the privileged Tavabs in the front row seats. It was not simply those on the platform who were undergoing psychological torture. The audience was a seething mass of the injured, diseased and infected.

This was not the only public duty of the prisoner. Each was required to pray five times a day. Imagine, six to seven hundred prisoners in a block, all forced to leave their cells to pray in the corridors. We would be assembled into groups of six, sometimes more than a hundred rows of us. The front were always reserved for the Tavabs. One of them would lead the prayer session. Nobody could avoid attending prayer sessions. All but the Tavabs despised them and would try to conduct their own prayer afterwards with their own appointed Imam. Some prisoners suggested that prayers should be conducted individually, not en masse led by Tavabs, arguing that God would accept individual prayer. But the ritual was part of the brainwashing prison system.

Groups of prison guards or Hezbollahi (hand-picked thugs, trained in the martial arts and conditioned to attack without provocation) were tasked to attack prisoners following Tavab reports. Sometimes a cell would be singled out, sometimes even the entire block. They would come with wooden clubs and whips made from steel cabling. These raids would also occur if the regime had suffered a setback in the war, had been humiliated by Saddam Hussein, when an assassination attempt had been made on the regime and on holy days.

The Islamic guards would be assembled in the corridor. They would be singing or shouting 'God is great!', 'Khomeini is Imam!', 'Down with hypocrites, down with communists!' Then they would launch their attack. Anything in their way would be broken up. Prisoners would be taken away with them on Tavab intelligence. Three or four guards would attack a single prisoner.

Those not selected would be sent out into the prison yard. The guards would then launch a search and destroy operation, ransacking cells, searching through belongings for any material that constituted opposition to the regime or subversive material. They would attempt to locate an owner to interrogate. Sometimes everyone in the cell would be taken for questioning. Whatever the outcome of these raids, the guards would leave a complete mess behind them. All of our belongings would be thrown across the floor, many items would be ripped up or broken. It would take us hours to clear up and restore normality, or at least what we understood as normal life. Despite covert attempts by prisoners to help those injured by the guards, the Tavabs would be on the lookout to report any signs of co-operation. Indeed, they would often take part in the raids. A report would be made by the Tavabs on the effectiveness and findings of the raid, directly precipitating torture and even the death of many prisoners.

Everyone in the Golden Fortress had a unique tale to tell. Each revealed the upheaval that had shaken our whole country – particularly its poorer sections, the landless peasants, the workers and the youth. One story was that of Mohsen, who left the land and came to the tin shanty towns on the edge of Tehran. At 14, he became active in the upheaval against the Shah and went on to be an organiser in his shanty town, distributing leaflets and papers. He was a well-known activist of the left.

In 1981 he was picked up by the local Islamic committee and brought to Evin. He went through all the stages of interrogation, was sentenced to five years by an Islamic court and sent to the Golden Fortress. His conduct in the prison was good: he stood by his comrades and so he was sent to cells where the intransigents were kept. He came across another boy, Mohammed, from a similar background in his neighbourhood, but who had become a Tavab. Both were around 16 or 17 at the time. Mohsen told me that he was talking to the Tavab to convince him to at least become neutral. As a result of these discussions, both of them moved to a passive cell.

Mohsen was picked up from the block and sent to the prison central office. All of us associated with him became worried. Maybe he had been singled out because of his links with other prisoners. Three days later he returned, exhausted and beaten about the face. He told us that he had been made to stand for three days and nights and that he had been beaten with a stick.

Mohsen had been singled out, he said, because Mohammed had claimed that Mohsen had made a sexual advance towards him. Mohsen went back to the intransigents, Mohammed back to the Tavabs.

In truth, it was the Tavabs who were guilty of uninvited sexual advances. A physical attack on a prisoner could turn into a sexual assault, especially for women prisoners. Young people would often be put under the care of Tavabs, to protect them from 'corruption' by the intransigents. These youths – often only children – would be vulnerable to sexual abuse by the Tavabs and had no way out.

CHAPTER 10

DOOMSDAY

In the still of an autumn night in 1983, the quiet was shattered as about 50 guards attacked the cell blocks, concentrating on the intransigents' cells. They targeted anyone who looked un-Islamic or unrepentant in any way – which they took to mean anyone with glasses or a moustache.

It was a regular raid. They marched down the corridor, two or three of them staying by the doorway of each cell. As the 'wild bunch' reached the last cell, they turned and began their most savage attack, pulling prisoners from their sleep and dragging them into the corridor. They were beaten until they could no longer stand. The contents of the cell were turned upside down again. Then they would move to the next cell and repeat the process. All the while the Tavabs looked on and sometimes joined in the beatings.

The governor always made sure that he was at the heart of these raids. Here he was in his element. He loved this carnage. Running around, in and out of the cells, he would be drenched in his own sweat, panting heavily as he heaved his bulbous frame from one cell to the next. Anyone unfortunate enough to catch his eye received a beating.

That night I saw him slapping and chopping at Mohammed Abrandi, a prisoner in his 70s we called *Amou* – uncle. Amou was an oil worker who had criticised the Tavabs in the block. Then, with one wild movement of his arm, the governor lost his balance and his colossal bulk came crashing down. He landed heavily on his right arm, which promptly broke and he screamed in agony. It took five of the guards to haul the howling governor to his feet. As they left, they shouted 'God is great, long live Khomeini! Down with communism!'

Far from being a cause for amusement for us, we knew that Haji's misfortune would spur on the other guards. The blameless Amou was quickly surrounded by guards. As he looked up at them encircling him, they started beating him on all sides with fists, feet, clubs and lengths of cable. He was pushed from one guard to the next, in a savage game of pass the parcel until he lost consciousness. Then the guards meted out the same treatment to others in the cell.

Amou had been singled out for rough treatment. When he arrived in the block, the guards put him low down the danger list, in cell 5 close to the control room. They thought he was just an old, sick and illiterate worker. One day Amou offered some of his food to a young cellmate who he thought looked as though he needed it more than he did. The Tavab overseer in their cell, who was only about 16, grabbed the food from the young man and threw it into the plastic bag in the room that served as a rubbish bin and shouted to Amou that he would report this 'communist behaviour'. Amou had been simmering with anger ever since he had been put in that cell. The Tavabs incensed him. Now this anger exploded.

Amou would have been naturally tall, over two metres, with long, gangling arms and legs and big hands and feet. Now, though, he was bent almost double. But he drew himself up to his full height and slapped the Tavab across the face, a stinging blow that knocked the brat to the floor. This won Amou a beating by five other Tavabs and an immediate move to cell 24 – promotion to intransigents and elevation to hero status in the eyes of the prisoners.

The night of the mass beating in our block, between one and five prisoners in each intransigent cell were punched, kicked and stamped unconscious by the guards, and then dragged out of the block by the Tavabs. This happened throughout the prison that night and those that followed. This was the start of what was called 'doomsday' and included attacks on the women's blocks. Those prisoners taken away were moved to another complex in the prison. They were put in front of a wall, given pencil and paper, and asked specific questions about their attitude to the Islamic regime, the war with Iraq, Israel, the US and the Soviet Union. They were asked questions about the different prisons that they had been at, and how they had acted in them. Pressure was put on them to identify other prisoners who had shown opposition of any form within the prisons. They were asked similar questions about others in their cells. The last question was, would they become a Tavab? If the answer was 'Yes', they were expected to prove it, by giving all the information withheld so far – details about their political activity before their arrest, about their family and friends, and information gathered within the prison. In particular they were pressed for information about the activities and identities of the intransigents within their cell and block.

Those who managed to pass this test, some giving evidence they knew to be out of date, could get back into the regular blocks. Some found themselves back at Evin's 209 with lengthier sentences and beginning a new round of interrogation and torture. Those who refused to co-operate, or had nothing further to tell, made up the doomsday block. This regime, which had developed in an ad-hoc manner, involved the prisoner in solitary: blindfolded, standing facing the wall, forced to listen to a constant barrage of sermons, speeches and Koran readings broadcast around the clock. These were interspersed with replays of interviews with oppositional leaders who had capitulated to the Islamic regime. Khomeini was heard crying in front of adolescents about to be sent to the front in the war against Iraq, 'I wish I was a Pasdar. You are God's chosen. Dead or alive, you will go to heaven. I am the loser, because I have not been chosen to share your glory'.

There would be live broadcasts from the trenches the night before an attack as the young Pasdars psyched themselves up to go over the top. They were used as human mine detectors, one detected mine equalling one boy blown to bits.

At its inception, doomsday inmates were forced to stand for days on end, deprived of sleep, and kicked back onto their feet when they collapsed from exhaustion. They had three breaks a day to eat and to go to the lavatory. Further punishment was equally arbitrarily imposed. The prisoner would be forced to sit cross-legged on the floor, blindfolded and facing the wall, presumably because the Tavabs had grown tired of kicking them to their feet. This lasted for a couple of days. The last stage was the separation of prisoners from each other with plywood partitions.

Doomsday's laws evolved from day to day as the governor, the guards and Tavabs patrolled doomsday. No one knew what was forbidden and what was not. The residents of doomsday would discover a rule when he or she had broken it and earned a beating – this rule, though, might have changed entirely by the next morning. Moving your hands got you beaten. Stretching your legs got you beaten. So did turning your head, or adjusting your blindfold. Whatever you do, do nothing was the message.

The guards seemed equally at sea. What appeared to be a carefully thought-out strategy to disorientate, confuse and distress the prisoners in fact was the opposite – random, ill-conceived and inconsistent... but hell, nevertheless. At 11pm, all doomsday's prisoners were ordered to lie down. At 6am they were ordered to sit back in position; facing the wall, legs crossed. Bodhiramma, the Buddhist saint, squatted for years facing a cave wall. That was his choice: the prisoners in doomsday had no such luxury. Days rolled into weeks, and so into months. Some inmates capitulated. They would cry out, 'Bring in the papers. I'll write anything you want'. They were filmed and used in the performances that the governor staged, where they confessed to things they had never done. Often, they would sit on the stage, sobbing or laughing uncontrollably. Others crumbled physically and mentally through trying to hold out. Of those who returned, some had lost their voices. Some could no longer concentrate and lost their memory. Many developed twitches. Suicide was not uncommon.

One man who spent ten months in doomsday would wander back and forth in a straight line, talking to himself, totally oblivious to his surroundings. During his time in doomsday, he had learnt to trust no one, to associate with no one, indeed to forget himself. Four years after his experience in doomsday, he too killed himself. Years after others were released, some still chose to end their lives as a result of what had happened to them. It was from the scattered testimonies of these human husks that we discovered what was happening in the governor's latest creation.

CHAPTER 11

THE RED PRIEST

M ojtaba was born in a village called Khomein in central
Iran sometime in the late 1940s, not far from where
Khomeini himself came from. Mojtabah's father was the village
shopkeeper. This was a stable and respectable background,
where the remnants of Iran's feudal past still clung on tightly.
Religion and the patriarchal family dominated. As a young man,
with the encouragement of his proud parents, Mojtabah entered
a small seminary in the locality from which he graduated to
Iran's religious capital, Qom. Here he was given financial
support and a roof over his head in order to continue his
religious studies, under the guidance of some of Khomeini's
closest associates.

He was a pupil of Gilani, who would become the most
senior judge of the Islamic revolutionary courts, responsible for
the execution of tens of thousands. After the establishment of
the Islamic regime, Khomeini handpicked Gilani as one of the
founding members of the Council of Keepers – a religious
body that oversaw all legislative matters dealt with by the

Majlis. Without their explicit approval, no law could be enacted. At the time of writing, he was still the most prominent member of this body.

As opposition to the Shah gained strength in the late 1970s, Mojtabah, along with many of his young contemporaries in the clergy, organised a group to distribute Islamic propaganda material, including reprints of Khomeini's speeches and writings from exile in Najaf, the religious city in Iraq. They would circulate pamphlets among the pilgrims who flocked to the holy city of Qom. This political activity led him to visit Tehran regularly, opening him up to secular contacts. He wanted to get into the student milieu, to widen both his knowledge and his political activities. Once he was picked up by the Shah's secret police and received a beating within the holy Fatima al-Masumeh shrine itself! He was so sore after this that he could not journey anywhere for several weeks to spread his message of freedom.

By 1977 Mojtabah had established a foothold in the most vibrant areas of opposition— among students, in the universities in Tehran – the centre of political opposition to the Shah's regime – and in the seminaries of Qom – the centre of religious opposition. He sought out prominent student activists and tried to convince them to make a stand of religious opposition. He had some success in this, but as the movement deepened and expanded, so did his own reading and experience. The rising power and confidence of the workers' movement, and its political expression in the Marxist left, set new questions that neither the Koran nor Khomeini could answer in the opinion of this inquisitive and socially conscious priest.

Each summer, the seminaries in Qom would close for three or four months. The religious leaders there would assign him to travel to remote villages to preach to the peasants. In addition to daily prayer sessions, there would be weekly sermons during which Mojtabah would subtly criticise the rule of the Shah and present the teachings of Islam and Khomeini as the only salvation.

In February 1979, Khomeini made his famous journey by Air France jet from Paris, arriving at Tehran airport to be greeted by eight million people. Emerging from the luxury of his 'Ayatollah Class' cabin, he and his entourage were driven towards the city centre, where millions thronged the streets hoping for a glimpse of him. So dense were the crowds that he had to be taken by helicopter the last few kilometres to Tehran's newest and largest graveyard.

Amid the headstones, Khomeini denounced the Shah for creating the most thriving industry in Iran. The bitter irony that history so often repeats was later to see this same graveyard extended a hundred fold, stretching out into the desert. Khomeini himself is buried there, in a golden mausoleum for the faithful to visit.

Mojtabah was present at Khomeini's version of the Sermon on the Mount and even helped organise it. He was one of the trusted bodyguards that day. But Mojtabah heard nothing from the man they regarded as their saviour about freedom and democracy – which he had come to see as the necessary outcome of the approaching revolution. He came away instead from this massive gathering among the graves with massive and grave doubts.

It didn't take Mojtabah long to realise that Khomeini's agenda was very different from that of the masses. Within the first year of the Islamic regime, he began to look for alternatives. It wouldn't be found among the minarets of Qom, but through the left organisations represented among the students he worked alongside in Tehran University.

Here, he was drawn towards the revolutionary left, and soon became the organiser of one of the bookstalls there. He came to believe that the Islamic seizure of power was a counter-revolution and advocated its overthrow. Where he had previously distributed Khomeini's works among the pilgrims at Qom and the students in Tehran's universities, Mojtaba now circulated Marx's writings around the campuses in the capital. Where he had previously handed out religious material decrying the despotic regime of the Shah, he now distributed pamphlets calling for the overthrow of the Ayatollahs' state apparatus.

Mojtabah's enthusiastic apostasy was bound to bring him to the attention of the Hezbollah. When the universities were closed under the pretext of carrying forward the 'Islamic cultural revolution', many students and professors were weeded out. Mojtabah was one among thousands thrown out of the lecture halls and into the prisons. Like so many of us, he was tortured and interrogated in Evin's block 209, and then rushed through a mock trial. His judge was none other than his former mentor, the senior judge Ayatollah Gilani, now the head of the Islamic judicial system.

Gilani combined this day job with a little early evening moonlighting. He hosted a popular show on TV: indeed, he was the regime's equivalent of Oprah. He discussed at length – literally – how far it was permissible for the penis to penetrate the vagina before it became sinful during Ramadan. So many inches were still consistent with fasting. A good, all-sheets-to-the-wind fuck would have been deemed gluttonous and profane. Popular viewing as this was, it caused a real problem for families in getting the kids away from the tube.

Had one been able to dine out in prison, Mojtabah would have dined out for years on his account of the exchange between him and his old tutor he gave to trusted comrades in the Golden Fortress.

'What is your name, my son?' asked Gilani, who knew the answer very well.

'Mojtabah, Haji Aghah'.

'Why have you turned your back on Islam, God and Imam Khomeini?'

'Ah, through bad associates and bad advice at the University', sighed Mojtabah ruefully.

'Do you know that what you have done is blasphemy – a crime which merits immediate beheading?'

'No, I haven't blasphemed. I was only politically active.'

'Why did you lose interest in being active on behalf of God and Islam? What made you become active in politics against God?'

God obviously didn't dabble in politics. Be honest, when did you last see a deity with a placard?

'It was a mistake,' said Mojtabah, playing the misguided political naïf – if his inquisitors had detected any sign that Mojtabah was convinced in these beliefs they would have taken pleasure in hanging a renegade former mullah that very night.

'God will be watching you in prison!' Gilani shouted across the court room. 'Any ungodly behaviour will bring you instant death!'

This 'trial' took about three minutes. A short trial and a long sentence – ten years, and all the time his neck would be under the axe's blade. The news of Mojtabah's arrest brought shock and outrage in his home village and the first person to disown him was his father – less out of devotion to God than a desire to maintain his status among his customers in the village. In contrast, his mother, although amazed and distraught not only by his activities but also his plight, was more understanding. For many years, she would be the only person from the village to visit him in different prisons.

With the death sentence hovering over his head, Mojtabah was understandably more cautious and restrained than many other prisoners. He would be careful to whom he spoke, and about what.

There's a lot more that could be said about Mojtabah. Like many others, he deserves his own book. This cannot be it, and it is unlikely to be written, at least not yet. Mojtabah survived his prison term with honour and, like all those that did, has to watch his back while the Islamic regime survives. So I shall say no more.

CHAPTER 12

THE VIP
LOUNGE

Nineteen eighty-five was a year of change for prisoners at the Golden Fortress. Many political prisoners were sent to other jails throughout the country. Iran was experiencing a crimewave, brought about by deteriorating social conditions and the Fortress was earmarked to hold the non-political prisoners.

International protest and pressure from prisoners' families over conditions in the Golden Fortress made it necessary for the regime to shuffle the pack. This eventually led to the replacement of Haji Davoud and his cronies with a new broom, Haji Meysam, who had been the governor of the large prison in the south at Shiraz. He was associated with Khomeini's heir apparent at the time, Ayatollah Montazeri. This grouping was calling for a regime of Islamic indoctrination within the prisons. Things, hopefully, would be easier, at least for a while.

At the changing of the guard, while the jailer's key ring passed from Haji Davoud to Haji Meysam, there was something of a hiatus within the prisons. Formal religious education in classrooms replaced the constant radio barrage, and we were given the right to organise our own classes, and have textbooks sent in to us – on approved subjects, of course.

I was transferred to another block in the Golden Fortress, Mujaradi block 4 in section 3, which allowed greater freedom of movement but, paradoxically, I was less inclined to use it. The reason for this was the prisoners we now had to associate with. These were the supporters of the Shah, and included some luminaries of the old regime: four-star generals, heads of Savak, government ministers and the Shah's ambassador to France. Members of the royal court were held here, even the Shah's dancing master.

A second group, closely associated with the first, were leading members of the Islamic regime's army who had taken part in a failed coup d'état. Most of them were army officers from the Shah's time who had stayed on after the Khomeini takeover. Some had distinguished themselves in the suppression of the Kurdish uprising of 1980-8. They boasted loudly of having 'put down the communists'. These two groups made up about 60 per cent of the block.

Those of us in the forefront of the fight against both the Shah and Khomeini – the socialists, communists and Mojahedin – comprised about 15 per cent. There were members of Rahe Kargar, the Fedayeen Minority and Mojahedin and the Tudeh. Then there were supporters of the National Front, a liberal tendency among a thin layer of intellectuals, merchants and employers. One, Amir Entezam, was a former deputy prime minister and main spokesman of the Islamic government after the overthrow of the Shah. Other ousted politicians included supporters of the Islamic regime's first president, Bani-Sadr, who hadn't been quite quick enough in getting out of the country when their leader fell out of favour with Khomeini after the seizure of the US embassy in Tehran.

Lastly, there was a mixed bag of South Tehran hoodlums and

other big city gangsters, mullahs with qualms about the regime, or who had been caught with their fingers in the till. Then there were another couple of mullahs, caught with their fingers in other people's underwear.

Mixing up more than a hundred incompatibles in this block was essentially an exercise in mischief-making by Haji Davoud. There was no common ground across these main political divides. The left would co-operate with the Mojahedin, but never the royalists, mullahs or gangsters, and vice versa. Unsurprisingly, left wing political prisoners were unwilling even to sort out a toilet rota with those who had tortured them under the Shah in this same prison or slaughtered their way through Kurdistan.

The royalists for their part did not want to associate with non-believers, and some would report on us to Haji Davoud. They were 'ready made' Tavabs in this respect. The royalists blamed the left for the downfall of the Shah and consequently the rise of Khomeini. Citing the Tudeh and Fedayeen Majority's defence of the Islamic regime, they would tell us, 'You communists gave full support to Khomeini. You are responsible for this!'

We left wing prisoners lived communally, each supporting the other. The new conditions meant we could talk more freely together, associate in the yard – even play football and volleyball with tightly packed rags. Later, the prison officials even condescended to sell us a plastic ball.

Money brought by our families every 20 days was pooled, and used to provide food and the like from the prison shop, bought for us with the money by a guard. Special needs were catered for out of the money, too. We would of course extend this to comrades who received no visits and no money. If a comrade fell ill, others would always take care of him. Decisions were arrived at democratically by the prisoners' weekly cell meeting – although we were careful to make sure that no one outside knew about this, as it would have brought trouble down on our heads. Eating, too, was communal. The food supplied by the prison, along with the supplementary food we had bought, was spread out on a plastic sheet on the floor, around which we would sit. Each prisoner could then help himself. This had been the practice of left and Mojahedin prisoners, even under the Shah.

Our approach was in stark contrast to that of the royalists and the others. What each of them could get, he made damned sure he kept for himself. Five cells on the opposite side of the corridor to ours were occupied by royalists and army would-have-been coup leaders. All were long-term prisoners: from ten years to life. The cell whose bars faced ours housed eight of them: generals and one air force colonel; a famous flying ace. Most had grown beards, and were doing their level best to act the part of the obedient moslem. They probably had the most over-used prayer mats in the prison. They had actually been worn to threads! Any time a prison official visited, they complained of our presence in their block. They protested that they had served the Islamic regime before, were penitent for their misdeeds, and wanted to do so again. The presence of communists in the block tarred them by association: we lowered the tone of the neighbourhood.

Each of them had access to much more money than the whole group of left prisoners put together. Any one of them would spend more on one meal than the 14 people in our cell would spend all week. We would watch from our cell, as the eight men opposite got out eight separate plastic trays and dug in to eight separate meals, not one with a thought of sharing with another. Each ate with his back to the others and to the cell door, so that no one could see what delicacies he had procured.

Most of the royalists and army grandees were filthy rich. Many would pay the equivalent of thousands of pounds into the private coffers of Haji Davoud to make one short call to their families in Europe or America. Even if they couldn't buy themselves out of prison, they wanted to make sure that the weight of their wallets would lighten the weight of their work. They would hire the hoodlums or other impoverished non-political prisoners to do their dirty jobs, like a valet. They would even get them to do their own personal washing. Left wing prisoners would not – and to the best of my knowledge never did – lower themselves to this. We were no one's servants. Even in prison, the royalists maintained their class distinctions.

The royalists not only hated the left, they also deeply distrusted each other. Haji Davoud was therefore able to use some of them not only to inform against the left, but to sneak on each other. Occasionally this would get out of hand, as we saw in one farce played out before us in the four-star generals' cell opposite.

A member of this royalist cell was brought before Haji Davoud after a report that one of his 'comrades' had made against him. The prisoner – a general – explained that the informant had a grudge against him, and that the report Haji had received was rooted in personal animosity and not in fact. To prove his sincerity and love for the Islamic regime and Khomeini, the general proceeded to grass on brother officers in his cell. They had bad-mouthed the regime, cursed Khomeini and so on. Haji Davoud called in each of these prisoners, one by one, to put the accusations to them. Each one responded exactly the same way – denying the charges and squealing on his fellows, until each one of the eight was implicated several times over.

Haji Davoud loved this. A scrap dealer from the wrong side of the tracks had made fools of the leading lights of the Shah's officer corps. As a finale to the farce he called them all into his office, and demanded that each one repeat their charges in front of the others. They must all have gone bright purple with embarrassment and fury! Haji then berated them: how could he believe anything anyone had told him? It was obvious that there was not one among them who had an ounce of personal integrity or honesty! After the scrap dealer had finished carpeting the generals, he sent them back to their cell with their tails between their legs.

We found out about this tribute to the discipline and integrity of the Shah's generals as they arrived back in the block. They were pushing and shoving each other, tearing at each others throats and shouting, 'How could you say that my prayers were not sincere?', 'You liar! I've never criticised Imam Khomeini!', 'I did not denounce the Islamic revolution!'. We were treated to their recriminations for a whole week after. So much for the top brass' esprit de corps.

There were one or two establishment figures who stood out from the pack and could be respected. One was a four-star general named Jahanbani. His brother had held the same rank and had been shot by the regime. Jahanbani was sentenced to life. Although he had no thought of resisting the regime, he refused to engage in the backstabbing and sycophancy. Another was Amir Entezam, the first deputy prime minister of the Islamic regime. Not only was he honest in his dealings with others, but he was vocal in his criticisms of the prison conditions to officials and would argue, chapter and verse, why these went against Islamic law. He is still in prison.

The regime had trouble maintaining its discipline over some inmates. One colourful character was a mullah of about 30 who was jailed for his subsidiary profession – rent boy. He plied his trade inside as well as out, among the hoodlums and one or two willing royalists. This was another way that class structures reproduced themselves in the prison. Sex of this sort was possible for the royalists since they bought all their foodstuffs from the prison shop. We were dosed up to the eyeballs on the standard, bromide-enriched prison diet. No one else even thought of sex any more. It was also felt that such associations could implicate political prisoners in a situation that carried a heavy penalty. There were enough dangers without adding to them. The regime constantly moved the gay mullah around in an attempt to find somewhere 'safe, and preserve the 'morality' of the jail.

Another mullah we shared the block with, more mindful of Islamic propriety, was Ahmad Moftizadeh, a Kurdish leader of a large Sunni sect. He had collaborated with the regime's repression of the Kurds during the crushing of the Sanandaj uprising in 1980. On finding his way to the inner sanctum of the regime barred, he had attempted to secure an independent base by voicing criticisms of it. This had earned him a jail sentence. With him were four followers who acted as personal servants. Everywhere he was to be found, they were in attendance. They would wash his hands and feet, obey his every command. He would lead them in prayer, the others kneeling behind him. Because of his status as religious leader, Moftizadeh got preferential treatment. When his wife visited, he did not have to speak through a screen for a painfully brief five minutes, as we did. Every so often, he and his wife would be escorted to a house on the other side of the prison, where they would be allowed to spend the weekend, alone and undisturbed.

This oil and water mix of prisoners resulted in a lot of mutual distrust and hostility – hostility that often teetered on the brink of open and wide-scale confrontation. The royalists looked for any pretext to get us expelled from the block. We knew they were conspiring against us; some of us had been put into solitary as a result. I remember one occasion when a full-scale riot was about to erupt in the block. All the prisoners were expecting it and had prepared. Rocks, iron bars, handmade knives and anything else that could conceivably be used as a weapon were concealed about the cells. This was not something that we looked forward to. Violence would result in heavy punishment by the prison authorities, and anyway the left was heavily outnumbered in the block. Fortunately the situation was defused through negotiations between representatives of the different factions.

In our cell there were three Rahe Kargar members, two from the Fedayeen Minority, two Tudeh sympathisers, two Mojahedin, and five from smaller left organisations. I got on well with a member of Rahe Kargar called Heydar Zaghi, the son of a poor tea vendor in Tehran's bazaar. He had been the head of the organisation in the industrial city of Kazvin, where he had been working to establish a solid foothold in the factories. While driving from Tehran to Kazvin his car was pulled over by the Islamic guards. A bundle of the Rahe Kargar newspaper was found in the boot, but he claimed that he was just transporting them. Heydar was sentenced to three years at his trial.

At the end of his sentence, he had been asked if he was prepared to denounce Rahe Kargar in a televised show trial. He had refused and was sent back to his cell. Release dates don't mean a lot in Iran. The following year, new information came to light which indicated the prominent role he had played. He was taken to 209 for a new round of interrogation, re-tried and given a further ten-year sentence.

Heydar was an energetic debater in the cell. Although he lifted the morale of the cell with his love of discussion and conversation, he also had a deeply melancholy aspect – or maybe just pragmatic. 'They'll never let me out of here alive', he would occasionally ruminate, head in hands. Unfortunately, he was right. As his sentence drew to a close in 1988, he was executed.

Also among my cellmates was Mohammed Abrandi – Amou. Amou was a veteran of more than half a century of struggles in the southern oilfields. Arrested as a Minority supporter, he became very close to Rahe Kargar in the course of prison discussions. Amou was a popular, respected and sociable man. Even the royalists enjoyed his company. They sought to enlist his sympathies and so use him to liaise with the left prisoners. Amou was often a guest in their cells, where they would ply him with good coffee, imported chocolate, cigarettes and sandwiches. This old worker was treated as a dignitary among the dignitaries. Of an evening he would often be found in the cell shared by the ambassador to France, the Shah's dancing master and a four-star general.

In the tense environment of the block, such courtship was not appreciated by the left, and Amou was often criticised by his comrades – myself included. But in the prisons, fine coffee and good cigarettes and celebrity company are powerful arguments, outweighing our verbal ones. Anyway, the old oil worker, whose body was bent, scarred and calloused after a lifetime keeping the indolents supplied with rum truffles, was no doubt amused by finding himself in the bizarre position of being served them by those who had fed them to the Shah.

Amou's hobnobbing aside, this block was more treacherous and threatening than most. Fortunately, it was transitory and we were soon moved on again.

CHAPTER 13

THE END OF
THE ROPE

Firooz Alvandi was a medical student at Tehran University. Around the campus in the late 1970s, roadside pedlars would see a well-dressed, good-looking young man hurtling back and forth on a Honda 250cc motorbike. He would race out of the University entrance to the bike and, wearing a shiny red fibreglass crash helmet, fly off down the road. Sometimes they would see a young woman riding on the back.

Firooz came from a well-off family in north Tehran. He was also extremely clever; one of the lucky 100 who passed the medical school's entrance exam out of the 400,000 who sat it. Looks, money and intelligence made him a centre of attraction for female students. When the revolution happened, he was in his fourth year at college.

Firooz wasn't worried about tomorrow. His family was secure and affluent and he would soon qualify and be able to make his own fortune. Ambition for greater money and status directed him to dentistry, the fast track to success in Iran's medical profession.

He must have felt satisfied and lucky then; he had few unfulfilled desires. But he observed conditions around him, and wondered at the situation of those less fortunate. Probably every young man wonders about such things, but the turbulent conditions of the time drove him towards practical solutions that may otherwise have remained the musings of another student on the way to the good life. He became involved in some of the activities against the Shah's regime organised by opposition groups at the University, although this part of his life ran counter to his upbringing.

Firooz's family was Bah'ai and they were strong supporters of the Shah. Bah'ais teach non-interference in political matters and this was impressed on their children. Political activity of any kind was frowned on, and that against the Shah was totally taboo. But this was probably not the only rule Firooz broke without his family's knowledge.

Before the revolution, Firooz had no political affiliation. Like a million other young people, there were a thousand things more important than activism. But the spirit of the times swept away this apathy. Firooz along with millions of others was drawn into resistance to the Shah's regime. But for the extraordinary revolutionary conditions of the late 1970s, Firooz would now in all probability be an affluent dentist in north Tehran, and no doubt something of a ladies' man; haggling over the price of land or a Caspian villa, phone in one hand, pen and prescription pad in the other, with a queue of patients in reception.

The closure of Tehran University by the Shah in late 1978, and the occupation of its administration building demanding it be reopened, helped push Firooz towards activism. He would take part in the daily demonstrations through the streets surrounding the University in support of the occupation. With those of us inside the university on 24-hour red alert, Firooz's Honda became part of the supply train that brought food to those occupying the University. He quickly became one of a small group of illicit suppliers, passing goods through the barricaded streets surrounding the campus under cover of darkness. It was inevitable that our paths would cross. We would frequently exchange words of solidarity or a conspiratorial grin as he passed over his cardboard boxes of food.

He was one of our major sources of information, as we couldn't trust what we saw on the television and weren't at liberty to go wandering round the streets to find out for ourselves. Since this information was of an inevitably political nature, I found myself more and more able to engage in political conversation with him. This would sharpen both our perceptions: me as an old hand of the left who was fed desperately needed information on what was going on outside our barricades, and him about the wider nature of our fight. As the days progressed I witnessed a naive young student become an invaluable and keen-minded activist.

One night when Firooz was smuggling meat, vegetables and rice through the back door, he witnessed a poorly dressed, middle-aged woman, delivering two boxes of pastries. With great emotion, she handed over the boxes to a professor at the service entrance. With the boxes came a message: 'As a representative of the hundreds of working mothers who have lost their loved ones in the fight for freedom and democracy in Iran, I want you to know that we support your campaign to reopen the University. With the overthrow of the Shah's regime, we'll see the light of freedom, democracy and social justice'.

She was the mother of one of those who had taken up the gun to fight the regime. It wasn't just the intellectuals who opposed the Shah: masses of working people like this woman and her son were the very cutting edge of the struggle.

What she said deeply affected Firooz. As she left, he followed and engaged her in conversation. She told him that her son had been captured in Kurdistan and executed. Now she lived in the shanty town behind the University, and took in washing to survive. Firooz went back to her cardboard hut and spent the rest of the night listening to her stories. She told him how her family had been uprooted from their village in Kurdistan by the landlords, and about how they were forced to come to Tehran in search of a livelihood.

That night had a decisive effect on Firooz. He wanted to become like her son: to fight for, and make real, those same ideals. But he had to come to terms with his past and present. to make a clean break from the affluent college playboy if he wanted to live up to what the woman's son had died fighting for. Firooz continued to visit the woman, learning from her, as he became ever more involved in radical student politics, and the struggle against the Shah.

His activity intensified until the Shah was overthrown. But decline came hard upon this highpoint, and the consolidation of theocracy placed new questions before Firooz. He could not stand aloof and become like his parents. And now he was in no position to ingratiate himself with the new regime.

Firooz fought back. He became an active supporter of the newly formed Rahe Kargar, and could now be seen running its stall in front of the University. From now on he planted both feet firmly in the revolutionary camp. There was no going back. He threw his energy into selling books and distributing pamphlets. Bundles of literature, piled head high, replaced the girls on the back of Firooz's Honda.

This work totally absorbed Firooz. It cut him off from his parents and made his home life difficult and lonely. As the first shots were exchanged with Iraq, the family sold up and fled to the 'paradise' of America. With his parents gone, the essentially conservative Bah'ai community severed their strained ties with Firooz. At the same time, the Hezbollah took over the University. All that was left for Firooz to focus his energies on was the fight to overthrow the Khomeini regime – but in a way that was placing him in an increasingly isolated and vulnerable position.

Firooz was blacklisted as a known subversive and was arrested in front of the University one day in 1981. His Honda was confiscated, the books on the back burned. The Hezbollah raided his home and took whatever they wanted. Firooz was taken to Evin for selling books and pamphlets. His 'crimes' were manifold: a socialist, communist, militant atheist – and a Bah'ai! Enough to earn him a ten-year sentence after a five-minute, Islamic kangaroo court hearing.

He kept his mouth shut right through interrogation and torture in Evin, not giving one name away. He was then transferred to the Golden Fortress, spending two months in quarantine. It was there that I met Firooz again, in December 1984. We were roommates, of a kind. I moved in to the bunk below his. The happy noisy and vigorous young man of pre-revolutionary days had become introverted, and would not communicate with anyone. We would study the faces of others in prison. Each prisoner becomes an expert at 'reading' those around him; able to tell the degree of pain inside from the expression outside. Marks of unsettled and unsettling questions in Firooz's mind were deeply imprinted on his face.

His day would begin at one in the afternoon, when I would wake him for his lunch. He would eat little and silently. After he had finished lunch, he would pick himself up and walk hurriedly to the prison yard, looking only ahead, smoking as he went. Here he was finishing a project he had started a month before my arrival in the block. He had collected five or more empty 50kg rice sacks, made from plastic twine. He would unravel them into long single strands and then wind them together into a rope. He had created a rope of more than 50 metres long.

One day in the spring of 1985 I went out after him to see what he was doing. He had tied one end to the far corner of the yard and was standing in the opposite corner, twisting the threads into rope with a rubbing motion between his palms, hands held above his head. He was completing the final touches.

Firooz's project was a nuisance. He had diagonally bisected the yard with his rope, preventing the 600 other prisoners from exercising by running round the perimeter, unless they were prepared to limbo dance under Firooz's rope twice each circuit. I asked him what he was up to.

'Making a rope', he said, continuing with his winding, not even looking at me as he talked.

'I can see that. Why?'

'To hang my clothes on.'

'What's wrong with the common rope that we all use?'

'I don't want to use it. I've decided to make my own.'

'But why are you making it so long? You don't have that many clothes! One shirt, one pair of trousers and underpants won't stretch to 50 metres.'

'Well, if my clothes won't fill it, at least it fills my time.'

I was still perplexed, but Firooz hadn't much patience with conversation. I left him to it.

After the exercise period had finished, Firooz coiled up the rope and returned to the block. He tied one end to the bars at the far end of the corridor, sat at the other, and continued as before. He gave the impression that he was committed to finish this work as soon as he could, almost as if he was working on a commission. There were no guards in the corridors – often no guards would come along for 24 hours at a time.

Firooz had come under a great deal of pressure from Haji Davoud and the Tavabs in the past. When Haji Davoud visited the block, Firooz was always singled out for the first beating, often at Haji's own hands. Firooz would be mocked for being both a Bah'ai and a communist. Many prisoners reckoned that Firooz's rope project was his way of cutting himself off from the other political prisoners and so reducing the pressure from the authorities. It was not unusual for prisoners to occupy time by making themselves a rope. It was the prison equivalent of knitting. But other prisoners made ropes of 10 or 15 metres, not 50.

After supper, Firooz went back to bed, putting the finishing touches on a painting he had started almost three months ago. He continued this through the night, even though he only had moonlight to work by. Between midnight and one, he would rise, take a pack of cigarettes and walk to the small toilet area, where he would pace backwards and forwards, smoking, until around 3 or 4am. Initially, this led to a beating from the Tavabs, but when they saw that he had isolated himself from the other prisoners and immersed himself in his rope project, they left him alone.

Firooz lay on his bed, lit by the moon through a small window, finishing his painting. It was of three tulips. There are two types of tulips native to Iran. One stands straight, head upwards. The head of the other bends down and grows in the mountainous areas, on the slopes of Kurdistan. We call them weeping tulips. Firooz's three tulips were all weeping. He had sketched them in black pen and painted the petals a deep burgundy. The people working in the kitchens could always supply materials of any sort for payment. That's how Firooz got his pen and paints, and the rice sacks to turn into rope.

By 30 April, Firooz had finished both his tulips and his rope. That night he sat on his bed and showed his tulips to everyone. Some cellmates, unhappy with him for cutting himself off from us, said nothing. Others openly admired his fine work.

It was my day as elected cell monitor. I had made the tea and was handing it around the others. Firooz sat on the bed, rope coiled beside him and the painting propped up against the wall by the bed. Unusually, he was openly discussing politics: American foreign policy towards Iran. I offered him a rather strong tea; again unusual, as this was regarded as showing favour.

Normally we made the tea weak to stretch out our resources. A cellmate questioned my generosity.

'I know my customers,' I joked, 'This one only takes his tea strong.' But really it was to encourage Firooz because this was the most positive he had been for a long, long time.

The Tavabs called lights out and we all went to bed. As usual, Firooz lay a while then went to the toilet with a pack of cigarettes. Prisoners whose bladder infections and injuries forced them to go to relieve themselves frequently saw Firooz pacing back and forth and smoking in these confined and reeking toilets.

When I rose at 5am the following morning, I went to collect his share of breakfast, so that he could eat it at lunch when he eventually woke. He was not in his bunk, but nothing registered with me about it. As we sat over our common breakfast, I asked if anyone had seen Firooz around. No one knew were he was. Someone suggested that he might have been moved from the block because of illness. I asked at the control room. They said that no one had been moved. We became more concerned, and went from one cell to the next in search of him. Some comrades then went to the showers, and I went to the toilet to look.

I couldn't see him pacing up and down, so I checked each of the six cubicles, shouting out his name. As soon as I pushed the fourth door I saw him. He was hanging from his rope, quite dead. His eyes bulged from his face. But he smiled.

Firooz had hanged himself in what we call the Palestinian way. He had looped the rope over the water pipes and then through his legs, noose about his neck, in such a way as when he lifted his feet off the ground, the rope snapped taut and killed him instantly.

We informed the control room. Officials turned up, took a photo of Firooz as I had found him, and then instructed four of us to remove him. We took his body outside the block. Shock and grief spread through the entire block. Shock both because of Firooz's suicide and because we had been unable to prevent the death of a comrade who had so strongly and courageously withstood the barbarity of the regime. But we could not show any of this openly, under the noses of the Tavabs.

Later I talked to a comrade in the block who knew Firooz and whom I trusted. I had a long discussion with him about what had happened to Firooz. He had snapped under the pressure meted out to intransigents within the prison. He had been constantly attacked by the Tavabs and guards in their visits to the blocks. He had it worse than other political prisoners, as he was a Bah'ai as well as a communist. He had been beaten to get information from him. They'd failed, and he was sent straight back to the 209 torture chamber at Evin after two years in the Golden Fortress.

In 209 the interrogators had demanded information on his links outside prison to Rahe Kargar, and what information he had about prison activists. As a trusted activist, Firooz knew a lot that could have put the lives of others in danger. He had been offered the chance of release, and to continue his medical studies, if he became a stooge. But they would not let him leave the country to join his parents; he was a hostage, as his family had fled Iran and taken their money with them.

He was told that he could get out quickly if he signed over his family's house where his grandmother lived. She used to visit him and had been his only contact with the outside world over the four years of his imprisonment. She could only visit once every six or seven months, as she was old, frail and afraid of the guards. Then they threatened to put him in front of the firing squad if the Tavabs found out he had been involved in any prison resistance.

Neither the stick nor the carrot influenced our comrade. We knew this because none of the contacts he had built up through the years in prison came under attack. On his way back to the Golden Fortress, Firooz decided that one way to lessen the pressure would be to find out who had informed on him. To do so, he decided to withdraw from his prison activity and to limit his contacts. In this way, he would limit the total number of reports made on him. Firooz did eventually locate the man who had been whispering against him: one Esfahani, a Rahe Kargar Tavab in the Golden Fortress who had known him well from the period before his arrest.

But Firooz's policy of silence had unfortunate repercussions. Everybody knew that he had been taken to Evin and put under pressure. Some leftist prisoners considered his withdrawal a sell-out. They refused to talk to him at all and told others to do the same. This came as a devastating blow to Firooz. He had no other world than that of prison comradeship. Now pressure from the prison authorities was combined with that of his former colleagues.

By the time I joined him in the block, this was his state of mind. Most prisoners had wrongly lost faith in him. They were on my back to watch what I said with him, but I took every opportunity I could to get him to open up, and often tried to draw him into political conversation. He seemed to respond and wanted to be fed information on developments after his imprisonment, especially on what was happening in Rahe Kargar. In prison he had heard that it had been disbanded – untrue – and was keen to find out was happening.

Grief wasn't an adequate response to the tragedy of Firooz's death. It demanded an answer from us as to why it had happened, and what responsibility we bore for it. Each shade of prison opinion interpreted it differently to start with, as heated debate spread from block to block. The leftist prisoners argued that Firooz's suicide was the result of him simply breaking down under pressure; his way out. But this was not a convincing argument. If Firooz really had given up, he would have revealed the names of hundreds of people both in prison and still free. Firooz didn't give enough information for even one arrest – ever.

Firooz paid for his role within the prison. He had become a flag of resistance. Haji Davoud wanted to destroy the morale of those around him, those who looked up to him, by breaking him. He was targeted in the same way that an army would focus its attack on the standard bearer of its enemy on the battlefield. The tragedy was that his own side opened up their ranks around him to let the assault take place. When he needed the moral support of those he had given support to, he found their backs turned.

Firooz weighed all this up with a stunned calm. His work on the painting of the tulips and the rope were no deranged retreat into an internal life of his own. Maybe at the beginning such diversions had been to keep Haji Davoud and the Tavabs off his back. But the symbolism of the tulips and the brutal functionalism of the rope became so clear and so strong after Firooz's death that it was clear to even those prisoners blinded by more than the prison hoods that he had set his feet on the road to this end at least three months before. He even had the date chosen at the beginning.

We managed to obtain a Persian dictionary. This explained the symbolism of Firooz's three weeping tulips. Weeping tulips live through the spring and die at about this time. In fact, you could predict their death almost to the day: the day Firooz died.

Firooz was telling us this was the night of his Last Supper – if we had been able to understand. He was saying his goodbyes and showing us that he was going out fighting. He had given in to no one, and would die before he did.

All this was analysed intensely within the block. We eventually reached the conclusion that each and every one of us in prison could only defend ourselves by defending our common security. We could not afford to let anyone be isolated, as this endangered not only that individual, but created a fissure in our ranks, endangering us all.

It took Firooz's death to make us appreciate exactly what Haji

Davoud was trying to do. We had to make sure that the lesson was not forgotten. Our self-criticism was passed to the other blocks and through visiting relatives to the wider movement.

CHAPTER 14

HOLY GANGSTERS

Haji Yusef was my father's closest friend. Although my father was a carpenter by trade, he drifted and started drinking and taking opium. That was how he fell in league with gangsters like Haji who could supply him with what he wanted. Haji was also a cut-throat who had once attacked and killed an innocent man with his dagger. As a result, he had been jailed for several years under the Shah. He bought his way out and emerged a strong supporter of his regime. He participated in the CIA and MI6 organised coup d'état in 1953 against prime minister Mossadegh, who had dared to nationalise the oil industry in Iran against the interests of BP. Haji Yusef had been a leader of a gang that had organised the prostitutes and hoodlums to attack Mossadegh's house, ransacking everything in it; slashing up the Persian carpets too big to steal in one piece, and even taking out the window frames to sell. The main gang leader, to whom Haji Yusef owed his allegiance, was 'Brainless Shaban'. As a result of the Shah's return Shaban christened himself Shaban Taj Bakhsh – the Kingmaker. 'Brainless' stuck, though.

Such ransacking raids continue to play a large role in fundamentalist 'politics'. The irony was that such 'confiscations' were not just conducted against such 'unbelievers' as Mossadegh, or people like myself after the 1979 revolution. Ayatollah Montazeri, Khomeini's heir apparent who fell foul of his mentor, suffered the same indignities at the hands of these carrion. After one such raid on his home in October 1994, Montazeri penned an open letter to his students turned persecutors. 'Firstly, if those who attacked my house had official authorisation, they did not need to organise such armed force so as to cordon off the whole neighbourhood, cut telephone lines or use electric drills to gain entry. Secondly, the official court generally would not be interested in my personal belongings, including vacuum cleaners, tape recorders, wall-clocks, car spares, electric shavers, precious gold coins and so forth. Thirdly, the officials of the court should only confiscate belongings in the presence of the accused, who should be given an agreed list of all items removed. These people have even confiscated some of the housekeepers' belongings and they broke into every room and every cupboard in the house. While ransacking the place, they even fought amongst each other over some of these items.'

Considering that Montazeri, who remains one of the most outstanding theoreticians of the Velayate Faghih (theocracy) and who claims among millions of followers some 120 deputies in the Majles, is today subjected to this treatment, imagine the kind of savagery directed at an unbeliever such as me in 1982 or Mossadegh a quarter of a century earlier. It's how Haji Yusef and his ilk made their money, stripping the homes of sanctioned victims like locusts. Their handlers also took their cut. Haji Lajiverdi, in particular, has amassed vast wealth through the violent seizure of property. These confiscations created a whole layer of people who enriched themselves in this manner, unsurprisingly becoming the most protective of the regime which sanctioned their theft.

At the time of the ransacking of Mossadegh's house in 1953, Haji Yusef was at his physical peak: built like a wrestler, at least six-and-a-half feet and weighing 300lbs. I used to see him around, especially in the public baths, from when I was about eight. His appearance both frightened and fascinated me. Not only was he gargantuan, but heavily tattooed from the neck down. On his expansive chest was a big picture of the Shah. Two crowns were tattooed on his shoulders. Queen Fouzi, the Shah's first wife and the sister of King Faroukh of Egypt, was tattooed on his back.

When the Shah divorced Fouzi and married Soraya, Haji Yusef had Soraya tattooed on his right shoulder. When Soraya was in turn divorced and the Shah married Farah, she went on the left shoulder.

After the 1953 coup Haji Yusef was used by the Shah's regime as a stick against the left, the student movement and workers. In return, the regime turned a blind eye to his drug trafficking. In our neighbourhood he had enough power to run a centre for selling opium and other hard drugs. Each day, a hundred addicts would queue at his headquarters to get their fix. Most addicts were hoodlums, thieves and lumpen elements of the area who supported their habit by working for Haji Yusef.

On the side, Haji Yusef was also the head of an Islamic association in the area. Each Monday night, 50 to 150 workers, destitutes and street kids would gather for various Islamic rituals; to sing hymns and to beat themselves to the point of fainting and to recite the Koran in Arabic – even though almost all of them could not even read and write in their native Persian. At the head of this association stood a handful of rich bazaaris, or merchants, and landlords and some emerging capitalists. These organisations, known as 'Basiges', were everywhere and they all had a Haji Yusef-type gang leader as a frontman.

For a long time after the 1953 coup only the police, Savak, army and gang leaders like Haji Yusef and 'Brainless' supported the Shah's regime. But during the revolutionary upheaval that led to his overthrow, these gang leaders abandoned the Shah and flocked to Khomeini. Haji Yusef became the head of a large Islamic committee as a reward. It was responsible for the arrest, torture and execution of hundreds of people. Most of the other members of this committee were his criminal sidekicks.

Five days after Khomeini seized power, Haji Yusef approached me to join his new committee, on the strength of my record of work against the Shah. I could see where such committees would lead and refused diplomatically – 'Too many other responsibilities. Sorry!'

Declassed destitutes, uprooted from the land in their millions and unable to integrate into the urban workforce, provided the support for these Islamic committees and other arms of the regime. They were at the sharp end of the class divide, making shacks out of cannibalised oil barrels, the contents of which had kept the Shah and his friends in their marble palaces.

This strata became a catalyst for both the revolution against the Shah and at the same time the Islamic counter-revolution. They took part in the revolution against the Shah's despotism, and were as active in helping Khomeini establish his theocracy. They were Khomeini's storm troopers in his attacks on the short-lived democratic institutions that flourished in the spring of freedom after the February 1979 revolution. Their Islamic committees provided our guards and interrogators in the prisons. The lower ranks of repressive state organs were staffed by these destitutes, the higher echelons by a rag-bag of clergy, gang leaders, bazaaris and hoodlums.

How does a passionate monarchist end up as a cog in the machine of the Islamic Republic? After the Shah's so-called White Revolution – a programme of land reform imposed on the Shah by the Kennedy administration in the early 1960s – it became clear that any effective land reform would open up a conflict between the monarchist state and the religious hierarchy. This was because the hierarchy owned about 15 per cent of arable land in Iran before the reform. It was the second biggest landowner after the Pahlavi dynasty itself. The reform meant that the hierarchy was in danger of losing the land on which it relied for income. Any encroachment on their source of rents would not go unopposed. Khomeini's opposition to land reform put him at the head of a mass opposition movement, even though he was an unknown, relatively young cleric.

This movement broadened its base through appeals to anti-Western and anti-imperialist sentiment. Attacks on the Pepsi-Cola plant were instigated and plants owned by Bah'ais were wrecked. This was where Haji Yusef came in again. He mobilised an attack on Pepsi in 1963, smashing, ransacking and torching it, as he had done to Dr Mossadegh's house 10 years before. He had a talent for this kind of work.

In the play-off between the Shah and the religious hierarchy, he threw in his hand with the latter. Any attack on the old feudal structure threatened the parasitic existence which Haji Yusef eked out in its cracks. So he switched his allegiance, breaking from those mullahs who still gave their support to the Shah and going along with Khomeini.

The regime, on the other hand, hoped that the likes of Haji Yusef would return to the fold. It was unwilling to crack down on the Islamic societies for fear of alienating them further and giving them greater confidence to express their own interests, hostile to those of the regime. Furthermore, the Shah was aware that he might have to rely on them as a bulwark against an independent working class movement.

After Khomeini seized power, Haji Yusef became active in organising Islamic committees, growing his beard longer to fit the part. On the face of it, he was more respectable than in his youth. Former members of Savak, royalist army officers and others from the old regime who had come to grief under

Khomeini would come to kiss Haji Yusef's hand in the hope that he would 'see them right'. His 13-year-old son was also killed at the front while acting as one of Khomeini's human minesweepers. He had moved up from street rat to venerable old man.

But Haji had a problem. In the weekly Islamic obsequies, he could not remove his shirt to beat his breast, as required of an Islamic organiser. After all, he carried the entire Iranian royal family around on his torso! This cursed insignia would not let him rest, even after death. He tried to atone for the graven images on his body by praying hard, forehead pressed into a prayer stone from Mecca, in the hope that the marks of his devotions could be seen from afar.

To avoid posthumous embarrassment, Haji Yusef demanded in his will that his wife would not take his body to the mortuary to be washed publicly seven times, as Islamic ritual decreed. No one but his wife should wash his sacred body. But because he was so big, his wife couldn't even lift his leg when he died in 1981, let alone wash him from head to toe seven times. So he had to be taken to the mortuary, followed by a crowd of thousands, including many respected mullahs and Islamic officials.

He was laid out on a slab, and in went his wife along with a confidant to assist in the ritual scrub down. I wanted to see those fascinating tattoos on the giant that I recalled from childhood. My family being close to his, I tried to get in. But his wife was adamant, 'It is against Haji's will to be seen by anyone while being washed and wrapped.' And so he went to meet his maker, with his embarrassment hidden by the shroud brought back from his pilgrimage to Mecca.

Haji Karim was of the same ilk: a man with a considerable criminal record for theft as a youngster. He had been a member of a gang that robbed people on the roads. I was only around ten years old then and very scared of him. For many years he peddled opium and other hard drugs to the youth in our area.

After the revolution he became a member of the Islamic committee in our neighbourhood and a trustee of the local mosque, which became the centre for the distribution of necessities using ration coupons. This committee, run by thieves, came to control all distribution in the neighbourhood from bank credits to sugar to televisions. They organised the population in the war effort, in particular recruiting young people to the front.

Shortly before my arrest I went to my father's shop in the neighbourhood. There was a crowd of people sitting around the shop, some obviously Revolutionary Guard members, with khaki uniforms and Kalashnikovs. I knew many of the faces; among them Haji Yusef and Haji Karim. I said 'Hello', and sat close to the door. The nature of the company – and the Revolutionary Guards' guns in particular – made me think that when I left, it would be a good idea to leave quickly.

As I sat down, my father turned to me and said, 'Three days ago, Haji Yusef lost his dearest 13-year-old son at the front against Saddam and the Great Satan.' I was shocked at the news, and extended my condolences to Haji Yusef. But he refused to accept any sympathy. 'You should congratulate me for having brought up a son who could become a martyr for Islam and Khomeini at 13!'

I did not know how to react. My father said that the Martyrs' Foundation had sent a check for 200,000 Touman (about $28,500 at the official exchange rate of the time) to Haji Yusef. He also said that Haji Karim's 14-year-old had just met a similar end and that they would be organising a funeral ceremony later in the week.

I asked whether the Martyrs' Foundation had also sent money to Haji Karim, who turned to me and said, 'Thanks be to God, the Islamic revolution is merciful, and I have received the same amount of money. The Foundation will also pay most of the expenses for the funeral and wake.'

'Congratulations on your achievements,' I said, trying to sound not too sarcastic.

My father asked, 'How about you? Aren't you going to go to the front?'

'No thank you!' I snapped, 'I guess I'm just not "holy" enough for martyrdom. Looks like you won't be lucky enough to get a cheque out of my corpse!'

Before I could move, my father leapt up to slap me round the face. Others intervened to restrain him. For a moment we stood glaring at one another in silence. Then I turned on my heel and left. I never went back.

It was five years before I saw my father again, through a soundproofed prison screen.

CHAPTER 15

THE RISE AND FALL
OF THE TAVABS

From the early days of the Islamic regime, the prison
authorities used the Tavabs – 'Repentants' – in a systematic
way. The fact that the Tavabs played such a role demands
examination.

It is possible to draw a comparison between the Tavabs and
those prisoners called 'capos' in Nazi prison camps. They were
all inmates who acted as stooges and thugs for the prison guards.
Indeed, that was our name for them. The difference was that the
Tavabs where much more ideological, being compelled to
become devout Muslims to prove their loyalty to the prison
authorities. According to prison officials, Tavabs were those who
had acted against the will of authority and committed a capital
offence. If the person sentenced was to repent, and this
repentance was accepted and verified by the religious
authorities, the interrogators and torturers of the Islamic courts,
then their life might be spared.

Firstly, it needs to be borne in mind that almost all of those in jail were not active members of an organisation, had not tried to use force to overthrow the government, but were often picked up for reading a taboo newspaper or having a left-wing leaflet on them. Most of them were between 15 and 20 years of age. These ordinary, young and generally naive people were put through the Islamic torture mill. It was often this, rather than the pamphlet they might have been reading, that politicised them.

Politicisation, though, did take place under conditions of the defeat of the 1979 revolution, the rise of the Islamic regime, and the consequent dispersion, confusion and crisis of the left. Consequently there was a vacuum on the left. The coup attempt by the Mojahedin leadership in 1981, which led to the ejection of Bani-Sadr from the presidency and the massacres of opposition forces, all contributed to the collapse of resistance among wide swathes of previously active young people. Within the jails, the wave of executions plunged many into cynicism and despair.

The prison system focused on depriving the individual of his or her identity. Massive force was marshalled to cut the prisoner off from any associations, and to break his physical resilience. Once this had been achieved, the prisoner was their prey. Estranged from his comrades, he would be deprived of the links and ideas by which he had previously identified himself: freedom, democracy, social justice. Heart and mind had been emptied out by the prison system. The ground had been laid for total submission. The prisoner would be in a cultural and social vacuum, which the regime would then attempt to fill with its alienating and degrading values.

Before being accepted as a Tavab, each individual subject to this had to provide all the information he had, covering his relationship to political trends, inside and outside of prison, and all information regarding his family and close associates. Some young Tavabs got their whole families arrested as a result.

Unrestrained terror was used against any individual or group

142

of prisoners who gave any sign of resistance. The prison population was divided between religious and non-religious, Islamic and non-Islamic, Tavab and intransigents.

Prison officials used every opportunity to deepen the divisions between the left and religious organisations, and within the left itself. Former leading activists from such organisations as the Mojahedin, Peykar, Tudeh and Fedayeen Majority were used with devastating effect by officials after they recanted. These broken but still capable prisoners produced a publication, *The Tavabin*, and were put in front of the cameras to 'confess their sins'. Kianoori, the leader of the Tudeh Party, and Ehsan Tabari, its leading theorist, are the two best-known cases. Some leaders of the Mojahedin uprising played a prominent role in these show-trial charades. The Mojahedin was probably the most vulnerable to this ideological assault because of its religious perspective. In addition, the Mojahedin possessed more teenage members than any other group.

Other Tavabs went so far as to assist in the arrest and execution of their erstwhile comrades, some even becoming full-time interrogators in Evin's 209 and I had the misfortune to be one of their subjects on a number of occasions.

Hussein Rohani, from Peykar's leadership, Ataolahi from the Fedayeen Minority, and Hussein Riyahi of the guerrilla group the Communist League, all took the stand in televised show trials. Their first proved to be quite an occasion.

Haji Lajiverdi organised a show trial in Evin. Many imprisoned leaders, of Peykar in particular, were lined up before the assembled thousands brought unwillingly from their cells to witness another spectacle. By Haji Lajiverdi were the Peykar leaders Hossein Rohani, Jigarehi, his wife Manijeh Hodayi, along with chief Tavabs from other organisations. This was in 1982, about two months after the Peykar leaders' arrest. One of their number, Peykar's general secretary Ali Reza Sepasieh

Ashtiani, had already died under torture as a result of his courageous resistance. Haji Lajiverdi introduced them, and said that they were assembled today 'to share their experiences'.

First up to the microphone was Rohani. He told how he had been active for over 20 years, passing from the leadership of the Mojahedin to Peykar. He spoke in a calm and level tone. After summarising his political development, he went on to condemn it: 'I have abandoned Marxism and embraced Islam.'

Manijeh Hodayi asked to speak. Instead of damning her political past, as expected, she turned her derision on Rohani: 'Mister Rohani didn't know what he was talking about when he was a Muslim in the Mojahedin. He didn't when he was a Marxist in the Peykar. Listening to him now, as a "born again" Muslim, it's obvious he still doesn't…'

Lajiverdi, the Tavabs and the guards stood in shocked silence as she continued her attack. The thousands of prisoners, squatting cross-legged before the stage, were lifted by this unexpected display of courage. We could only watch as armed guards and club-wielding Tavabs strode up and down our ranks, looking for anyone that might appear in the slightest bit satisfied at this unexpected outcome. That had to be the only advantage of the women's veils: they couldn't see you smile.

Eventually, the guards regained their composure and the microphone was taken from her. Rohani pleaded with Haji Lajiverdi for time to answer. But his response wasn't what Haji Lajiverdi might have hoped for: 'I was extremely impressed with what Manijeh said. It took real guts. I can't stand here and support the Islamic regime after this woman has put herself on the line defending her convictions. I retract that support, and reaffirm my commitment to Peykar.'

Haji Lajiverdi watched open-mouthed as all his careful preparation crumbled before him and 12,000 inmates. There had rarely, if ever, been such a collective lift to prison morale. He strode to the podium, snatching back the microphone.

'Look at yourselves', he sneered at those on the stage, 'You have such weak personalities that a woman's whimpering can change your minds within a minute.' Then he turned to face the crowd. 'These are the leaders that you have invested your faith in. You must be really naïve to be fooled by the likes of Rohani and Hodayi'.

Rohani asked for the microphone again and, surprisingly was given it. Now, he rejected Peykar and gave his support, once again, to the Islamic regime. It was apparent that he was totally confused; a shell of the man that had been arrested only two months before. These show trials were intended to shake the ideological foundations of the opposition, and tear them up from the roots. It was an attempt to flaunt the bankruptcy of any alternative to the Islamic regime.

Lajiverdi looms large in any account of Iran's jails and demands an account of his progression to the de facto role of Lord High Executioner. He first came to note in 1969. He and six others were charged with throwing a Molotov cocktail through the window of the El-Al airways offices in Tehran: as they saw it, defending Islamic values against the 'Zionist menace'. Up until his arrest as a part-time terrorist, Lajiverdi had been a small shopkeeper, selling pocket handkerchiefs in the bazaar. This little group of petrol bomb hurlers drew most of their support from people just like him.

Lajiverdi really personifies those who became the core of the Islamic regime. These were the men of the lower middle classes – small shopkeepers and bazaaris – squeezed by the development of capitalism in Iran. As they watched the traditional economy disintegrate, they felt the ground crumble from underneath them. They could neither prevent its forward march, nor understand why it was happening. For such people, the Shah's attempt to enrich his dynasty by dragging Iran kicking and screaming into the latter half of the 20th century posed a palpable threat to their culture and livelihood. They bitterly resented this process.

They loathed even more the working class movement which was emerging as a result of the industrialisation. It had a secular and democratic agenda which they felt was a threat. The greatest sacrilege of all, it challenged their last bastion of authority – their domination of women in the home. Around them they drew the ever increasing mass of landless ex-peasants, who had trekked from the countryside to surround the cities with their shanty towns built from corrugated iron, oil-drums and cardboard; an army of millions, vainly looking for work and a leader to champion their cause.

Lajiverdi and his six co-conspirators were tried *in camera* under penal code 310, one which was specifically directed at underground communist groups, which must really have offended Haji Lajiverdi's good Muslim sensibilities, and given heavy jail sentences.

In the course of his incarceration, he became known for continually agitating for a separation between Muslim and non-Muslim political prisoners – a division that Savak lapped up. He and his ilk wouldn't shake hands with a non-religious prisoner, or eat food touched by one, deeming it befouled. They used to hang up their own washing line in the small prison yards, refusing to let any left prisoners have use of it. In the confined space of the yard, this often meant that there was no room for any other line, a situation which inevitably led to fights between political prisoners.

The group was characterised by propounding this line, becoming known as the 'Clean-Untouchables', referring to the Islamic/non-Islamic division. Even at this time, this group's hostility to the left far outstripped that shown to the Shah's regime. As a result, of course, the majority of the prison population boycotted Lajiverdi, increasing his isolation and is bitterness against the left.

Many of Lajiverdi's cell-mates and co-thinkers in block 2 at Evin immediately before the revolution were to take prominent positions with the consolidation of the Islamic regime. Rajai, who became the Islamic regime's first prime minister and second president, met a bloody end from a Mojehedin bomb. Haji Katchoui, the first post-revolution governor of Evin prison, was blown up by one of his own guards in the jail. Abbas Shaybani, is now a four-term Majles deputy.

Háji Lajiverdi's enthusiasm for the Tavabs during my time in prison seems ironic, since he himself was a 'repentant' under the Shah's prison regime. In 1978, when the Shah was on his last legs, Savak's chief interrogator Rasouli asked each cell in turn 'Who has repented their crime?' Lajiverdi was one of the people who raised his hand, and was given his freedom as a reward for his capitulation. Rajai was another.

Lajiverdi slunk out of Evin's gates under a cloud, having been identified by those inside and outside the prison for submitting to the regime. He nurtured this shame, turning it against those he blamed as being responsible for it: the left prisoners who had stuck by their guns, only freed by the hundreds of thousands who smashed through Evin's gates in a giant human wave in the revolution, only a few months later. Nevertheless, Lajiverdi and his entourage did well out of the revolution. They went on to become the heads of the Islamic regime's prisons, with absolute authority over all those within.

Lajiverdi, who was assassinated by the Mujahedin in the early 1990's, was a very little man – and not only in stature. His mean-mindedness towards those with more courage than himself was to take a terrible toll when he came to have direct authority over them. He did not respect another for his or her independence, but only felt secure with someone when he could completely dominate them. He didn't have the intellectual or physical strength to impose this through his own qualities. He was nothing without the whole weight of the prison regime. This man was the epitome of a spiteful, inadequate non-entity, given power over life and death.

Lajiverdi was short and cross-eyed, his face wearing a permanent sour look. Although I had stood within feet of him a couple of times, I had never used the opportunity to take a close, hard look at him. With such a man in such a position, you avoid any possibility of eye contact. To have your eyes meet with Lajiverdi's when you were under his control often meant being summarily shot. The man's very presence radiated a sickness born of his callous slaughter of tens of thousands of defenceless prisoners.

We called him the Eichmann of Iran. It is difficult to say which of these two butchers suffers most in the comparison. To be sure, Eichmann murdered far more people. But Eichmann had the opportunity. One can only be grateful – if that is the word – that Iran since 1979 is a smaller concentration camp than Europe under the Nazis.

The Tavabs organised and controlled the prison blocks, which covered every facet of prison life, from allocating food rations and cleaning to conducting prayers and looking after cells. Some Tavabs worked as torturers' assistants. This was particularly the case in quarantine and doomsday, where they were given a free hand to break prisoners. Tavabs would also act as goons in the raids on the cells.

One way this worked was through what we called the Ku Klux Klan – Tavabs wearing Klan-like hoods to conceal their identities. They were brought into cells and the prisoners were ordered to take off their blindfolds so that the 'Klan' could identify those with any links to opposition groups. These visits spread fear among the prisoners: those picked out by the Klan would be sent to the torture blocks for the most intensive interrogation. Some of those picked out either died under torture, or in front of the firing squad.

The leader of one such gang of thugs was an ex-Mojahedin

militia leader called Behzad Nezami. Before his arrest, he was responsible for the assassination of 17 people identified as collaborators with the regime. Faced with the choice of the bullet or repentance, Nezami chose the latter – with a vengeance. He organised his old militia group as a sort of Tavab flying squad. Haji Davoud gave it free run around the Golden Fortress. At any place within it, at any time, Nezami and his heavies could burst in. They were the Tavab's trouble-shooters, being called in wherever any disturbance was feared.

The beatings they meted out were ferocious. As their confidence grew, so did their brutality. Nezami's squad began to drag boys of 13 or 14 from the cells to be gang-raped. On one occasion, a comrade of mine, Gholam, then 15, confronted these thugs. This young man told them that they would have no one from this cell. Nezami responded with a heavy blow to the neck. The effect to the carotid nerves in the neck was such that his head still twitches to this day. He lay prone in his cell for months after the assault. And, sadly, another young boy was taken from the cell.

Using the Tavabs, Haji Davoud was able to infiltrate a group of intransigents in the Golden Fortress. Seven intransigents were working on a document containing an analysis of the regime; but the document never got out, and neither did they. All were shot. All the prisoners with whom they had contact were sent to doomsday, resulting in more Tavabs.

After this episode the Tavabs became a far more important element in prison. Any friendly gesture from one prisoner to another, even the offer of a puff on a cigarette, would be taken as upholding collective resistance, the organisation of a 'cigarette commune' and the propagation of communist attitudes. The same was true if one prisoner assisted an injured fellow. Everything was noted and reported.

In a cell, where up to 40 men might be held, any contact between them was held to be a threat and was severely punished.

During the short exercise periods along the block corridor, you would be shadowed by a Tavab. Any words exchanged between prisoners that could be construed as political would be reported and punished. If two prisoners were seen talking, they were separated and quizzed about their conversation. If the two stories did not tally, then both men were in trouble. We got into the habit of constructing alibis before we spoke to each other, to counter the constant surveillance.

Tavabism went through many different phases through the first ten years of its existence. The contradictions in its development manifested itself in different ways. In the beginning, as far as the Islamic regime was concerned, a Tavab was a prisoner who had recanted, rejecting anything not Islamic and fully embracing Islam. It is interesting to note that many Tavabs not only abandoned their old norms of behaviour, but failed to adopt those presented to them by the Islamic regime. They became not so much immoral as amoral. Theft and the sexual abuse of teenagers in the prison was rife among the Tavabs. The forced adoption of a morality that they could not accept led them to abandon any morality. As time went by, these tendencies became clearer. What was happening to the Tavabs, was in stark contrast to the respectful and comradely stance of other prisoners.

Tavabs had to deal with the divorce between their behaviour in prison and outside after their release. Tavabs most active in the torture and murder of other prisoners sometimes expiated their guilt in the most spectacular way after leaving jail. For instance, they would wire themselves with explosives and then go to Friday prayer meetings where some would sit near representatives of the regime. When they detonated their bomb, killing themselves instantly, they would exact their revenge. Others would don the uniform of a Mojahedin militia man, to take up arms against the regime.

These cases show that the regime's policy of enforcing their ideas was often self-defeating. Those who repented in prison would recant their repentance once outside. Tavabs were an inherently unstable force.

The presence of Tavabs in the blocks increased the friction, often drawing the prison authorities into unwanted confrontation with prisoners. Each time a crisis developed between the Tavabs and other prisoners, the authorities would be forced to intervene. The Tavabs became the tail wagging the dog. By the mid-1980s, the regime wanted to adapt its prison policies in response to pressure from prisoners' relatives and human rights groups. But Tavabism had built up a momentum of its own, and presented a barrier to the change the regime wanted. By this time many of the Tavabs were coming over to the opposition and saying what they had done to other prisoners. As such they became a bigger threat to the regime than they did to the prisoners. This put the regime in a dilemma about how to deal with the Tavabs, who were no longer under control and no longer collaborating with the regime. The crisis of the Tavabs led to intense bickering within the regime: some of the prisoners' families lobbying for change were influential with strong ties to the clergy and the politically significant bazaaris. Iran's human rights record was also turning it into a pariah state, condemned repeatedly by the UN General Assembly. As Iran tried to renew trade links with the outside world after the war with Iraq, this was all bad news.

It was the supporters of Ayatollah Montazeri, Khomeini's heir apparent, who undertook the dissolution of Tavabiat, a move that caused profound ideological and practical dislocations for the regime. The usefulness of the Tavabs had come to an end, and a very bloody end at that. Having used the Tavabs who had come from the leadership of the various opposition groups, the regime turned on them. Between 1983 and 1985, the main Tavabs were sent to the firing squad, in a 'cleansing operation' administered by 'the Eichmann of Evin'. While a number of them, such as Kianoori, the leader of the Tudeh Party, were kept alive longer (in this case, so as not to create too many waves with the Soviet Union), the vast majority of the Tavab leaders were killed at this time.

The crisis of Tavabiat engulfed those who had been its prime movers and patrons. The crisis went so deep it even scorched the holy robe of Haji Davoud. He had misused his authority to the point of selling favours to the imprisoned heads of the Shah's regime, pocketing between half a million to a million Touman in the process – almost $100,000. Such activities did not stop at the prison walls. At one point, nearly $30 million of iron girders that Haji Davoud had acquired for prison construction were unearthed on the black market, the proceeds having gone into his personal account. This is a clear, and not untypical, example of the moral fabric of our 'religious guardians' in the prisons, the stalwarts of Tavabiat.

A number of tensions grew between members of the Islamic regime, the judiciary, the Majles and prominent members of the clergy – in particular Rafsanjani, the Speaker of the Majles and the president. These two, in particular, held out for continuing the harsh repression within the prisons. Every so often, we would see emissaries from the authorities inspecting the prison. These people had been handpicked by Khomeini himself and so they would be sent into prisons with definite objectives in mind.

On one occasion, of the three emissaries who visited, one was a representative of the head of the regime's judiciary. Nothing stays still, and life does not develop in a linear fashion. The regime wanted an immutable prison guard to uphold its immutable laws, but what it created had its own dynamic, going through continuous changes of both a quantitative and a qualitative kind. Eventually, it became its own antithesis. The Tavabs became a major stumbling block to the Islamic jailers, forcing the regime to cut itself free from what it had created.

As these tensions within the regime were played out, in

particular between Khomeini and Montazeri, we also noticed that an open debate was being conducted in the official newspapers by Montazeri as to who was and who was not an Islamic Tavab. In essence, the regime had to justify doing away with the Tavab system. The remedy proposed by Montazeri for Tavabs was *ershad*, the ideological indoctrination of the prison population as opposed to the physical elimination of prisoners, which was proving impossible to carry out. As these debates ensued, Khomeini changed the personnel heading the prison authorities – a sign that Montazeri was winning the argument. We only heard about all of this through visits from our families – the prison regime ensured that it was kept from us. So the prison visitors became known to us as 'Montazeri's Brigade'. This was headed by a young clerk called Ansari, a man who had been active in the occupation of the American embassy in the early 1980s and who was later elected to the Majles. Through his role in the prisons he became known as a reformer.

The first sign of real change was the removal of Haji Davoud as head of the Golden Fortress. We noticed that he had not been seen for a whole week – then we met his successor, sent from a provincial prison in Shiraz. But our ears, eyes and whole bodies remained on the alert for signs of Haji Davoud. Then a number of prisoners were taken from the Golden Fortress to Evin to be freed at the completion of their sentences – and as they passed through the office for discharging prisoners, the person in charge was none other than Haji Davoud himself! Imagine, the man who had made life so unbearable within the Golden Fortress was now reduced to a mere clerk, rubber-stamping release papers. Though representing a now inappropriate method of prison management, the likes of Haji Davoud were still retained by the regime to keep order when directions from above changed abruptly.

The new broom at the Golden Fortress introduced changes which affected the structure of the organisation and the control of the prison blocks. Although there was still a Tavab in charge of my block, the control room was marginalised. Now they no longer had the authority to beat anyone. In each block, a number of prisoners were asked whether they would be renouncing their past activities in opposition to the regime. They were told that if they were ready to record appropriate interviews on video they would be pardoned and released. Strangely enough, except for the Tavabs who were doing everything possible to leave prison, no more than 25 to 30 per cent of the prisoners agreed. Even more strangely, the Tavabs were most likely to be turned down for release after their videotaped confessions. Because they had become part of the opposition, the regime was wary of releasing them in case they stirred up trouble in the country at large. In fact, many of the Tavabs were shot in the 'massacre' which took place all over the country.

But the Tavabs were absolutely devastated at not being released in the numbers they expected after their video interview. This led to widespread demoralisation within their ranks. It was the final blow that ended the Tavab reign. The regime no longer required them so they were now being shunned by both sides – by the other prisoners and now by the regime – their Islamic masters! Their only way out was to renounce Tavabism and to join the ranks of the intransigents.

The process began with some leading Tavabs calling for a general meeting of prisoners within a block. Each Tavab would confess to all the atrocities that he had committed. Every now and then, when a Tavab was confessing some atrocities, a fellow prisoner would raise his hand and recount episodes that had been omitted by the Tavab, usually an incident in which he had been at the receiving end. This was our day of jubilation as we saw the former allies of the regime recanting their 'repentance'. One of the most hated forms of prison life had evaporated in front of our eyes and we saw that we had won an important moral victory over the regime. Our solidarity had been vindicated, despite everything, and we rejoiced.

CHAPTER 16

GETTING BETTER
ALL THE TIME

The Montazeri reforms opened up the potential for freer movement within the prisons. Cell doors began to open, allowing us to associate. Without the Tavabs constantly looking over our shoulders, these opportunities were seized upon whenever they presented themselves.

From being locked within our cells 24 hours a day, we began to be allowed free movement around the block and in the exercise yard throughout the hours of daylight – considerably more freedom of association than is permitted, say, in British jails. This didn't apply to prisoners identified as ringleaders of prison resistance, who were still under 24 hour lock-up in solitary cells. There was no abrupt shift to a more liberal prison regime. The authorities wanted to maintain control and ensure that there was no danger of it running away from them. In some prisons, the transition occurred relatively quickly. But in the Golden Fortress the officials only gave away every concession grudgingly. For instance, when we attempted to elect block representatives to liaise with the prison authorities, they refused to countenance such a move – one which had already been put into action in other prisons, such as Gohardasht and Evin.

Our attempts to organise communal exercise in our block met the same stony response. In the early days of this handover period, the new governor visited the block. Unlike his predecessor, he arrived without club-wielding retinue and visited each cell in turn. He introduced himself as Haji Meysam, sat on the floor and invited his inmates' comments on how to make this place more liveable – leaving the main gate open would have been nice.

As he passed down from the Tavabs towards the intransigents, his stops at each cell became longer. When he reached our cell at the very end, he spent nearly two hours squatting on the floor. Men from other cells, including Tavabs, gathered around the room to listen to the discussion, often chipping in. Those who couldn't get in stood in the corridors, some standing on tiptoes to see over their comrades' shoulders. The head Tavab of the block sat close to the governor, but did not have much to say. The whole tenor of the discussion was not pleasant for him.

The governor offered us group exercise. Haji Davoud had banned this, fearing that it would reinforce the prisoners' solidarity. But this proposal was conditional on us accepting a Tavab as its organiser. One cellmate, Saíd, insisted that the main problem before had been the Tavabs, and as long as our activities were conditional upon their supervision there could be no real improvement. We would not take part in any cosmetic exercise of this sort. But the governor insisted that this was the bottom line. 'We'll give you three names, and you choose one, but there must be a Tavab present.' This was not good enough. Saíd replied that as long as we had Tavab watchdogs, we would boycott all the events that they were supervising. The whole cell murmured its agreement.

We argued each other to a standstill. Our demands were not

met there and then, but a couple of weeks later word came down that we could organise our own exercise sessions. Our determination had paid off. Our demands were conceded in such a way that Haji did not lose face by giving in at the meeting. I am certain that this was no isolated incident. He must have got the same message wherever he had gone in the prison – get the Tavabs off our back or no deal. And we won.

We were also offered a ping-pong table – if we clubbed together 2,000 Toumen to pay for it. Were we being bribed? some wondered. The Mojahedin and some small left groups argued that this was a shallow public relations scam by the regime to conceal its atrocities. Of course it was, but then so was our weekly kebab and we weren't going to turn that down.

Within a week of this cell discussion, prison food markedly improved – although we still had 'prison seasoning' – bromide with everything. Minced meat kebabs with rice were added to the prison diet, along with two or three rice-based meals. Guaranteed three days' rice and meat meals per week, we ate better food than we had in years.

Education was brought up at this meeting. Some young prisoners had been arrested at 14 or 15 and had now spent around five years inside. There were thousands of young men and women like this in the prison system. Haji Meysam allowed us to carry on education among ourselves, with the aim of getting prisoners through exams, which were externally organised. It gave us the right to organise classes, something which would never have been allowed under Haji Davoud. He accepted the right of prisoners to receive educational material, textbooks and the like, from their families – after they had passed under the watchful eye of the Hezbollah.

We were now able to organise a form of block library. Each cell would 'lease' all its available books to the whole block. The entire stock was listed. If you saw a title you wanted, you just put your name down for it and hoped it was not too popular.

The central prison library was partially opened to us for the first time, making non-Koranic texts available through the official channels. No one was going to let us get hold of Che Guevara's *Guerrilla Warfare*, but approved anti-Soviet or anti-Marxist texts were made available to us – ironically enough, including the Persian translation of Tony Cliff's *State Capitalism in Russia* and Charles Bettelheim's *Class Struggles in the USSR*.

Haji Meysam's little public relations exercise short-circuited the whole Tavab system. They got the message that they were no longer in charge; the Islamic Republic no longer required their services. This would have also been impressed on them privately, but the regime wanted to make it public, so that we knew they no longer held the reins.

These changes made possible a freer relationship between inmates, which in turn developed a deeper and more profound political discourse between the different trends within the prisons. We still had to watch for informers, and would not open up to anyone we did not trust, but debates could now extend further than a hurried, furtive whisper.

We relaxed. We even permitted ourselves some festivities at times, grouping together in cells to celebrate key dates. I remember one Persian New Year vividly, celebrated on the first day of spring 1987. The week before we had done a full week of spring cleaning in the blocks: scrubbing down the walls, washing the floors, cleaning out the toilets, all of us working with an almost child-like enthusiasm and frisson of expectancy.

When we had convinced ourselves that the grey concrete walls sparkled, representatives of each cell met to plan out the night's celebrations. Different cells had responsibility for providing different dishes for a communal meal. Kurdish, Persian, Baluchi, even Turkish and Arabic dishes were prepared in as authentic a manner as conditions allowed. Decorations were prepared from paper, and we sought to brighten the grim uniformity of the block with anything of colour that we could lay hands on.

A month in advance an Armenian comrade began to build a guitar from scratch, to help the musical entertainment on the night go with a swing. Musical instruments were banned, as the religious authorities felt that such things would 'degenerate men's souls'.

The strings were made out of plastic threads picked from rice sacks. All of us ripped off wood from packing cases to build the body and neck. In its raw state, it was unusable: unshaped and too thick. It was sanded by making it wet and rubbing along the grain on the abrasive concrete floor until it became more flexible. The pieces were then left in the sun, each one laid at an angle calculated to warp it to just the right shape. These pieces were then painstakingly bound together with plastic twine so that the join was airtight. No craftsman ever produced in more difficult conditions with so few resources. With two days to go, the guitar was ready and hidden away.

All political groupings pitched in to make the party a success, although such co-operation was at times uneasy. In our cell, a couple of Peykar and Minority people were adamant that they did not want anyone from Tudeh or the Majority visiting their cell even to convey New Year greetings. 'But if we visit their cells, they'll naturally want to return the compliment,' others objected. To preserve peace in the cell, we conceded to the selective inhospitality.

We did our best to replicate the festivities outside, but such vital trappings as bonfires were out of the question. Entertainments were planned, as was block security, to ward against the discovery of our solemnities by the guards.

Yet while our New Year may have been covert, it was the same outside. Khomeini condemned New Year festivities as pagan, warning, 'We cannot celebrate until the war with Saddam has been won.' Small children became subversives as they built secret bonfires, scattering as the armoured cars – attracted by their blaze –bulldozed them under their wheels. So, this New

Year, we had clear common cause with the people of Iran outside our prisons. We all celebrated in the same arduous position, feeling the same warm glow of satisfaction of having done it anyway.

The centrepiece of the celebration was to be a cake, which our cell had volunteered for. Baking was out of the question, so we had to find other means. The base for it was bread, dried over our primus stoves, which we had bought from a shop in the jail that was run by the guards rather than by the prison itself (you could get anything for the right price) and pounded into a powder. We then mixed it with a little water to make a dough, and flavoured it with coffee and jams. The mix was augmented by figs, dates and raisins. We then moulded the mixture with our hands into a cake about three feet in diameter. It was placed on a plate made of pieces of cardboard stuck together in layers to allow us to move it. The cake was then left to dry and set. Like digging an escape tunnel in Stalag 17, this was a big job that demanded teamwork. Lookouts were posted. At any sight of a guard, the cake was shoved under a bunk, and blankets were hung down to conceal it.

The final touches were icing sugar decorations: in white on a dark brown cake. We wrote 'The New Year will bring happiness and victory to the workers' above the cake's centrepiece, a five-pointed white icing star, on either side of which was an icing hammer and sickle. The Armenian guitarist organised a vocal group around him, with rehearsals taking place *sotto voce* at night.

All day on New Year's Eve, religious programmes were broadcast over the PA system and Khomeini's New Year message was shown. He dabbed at tearful eyes, telling the boys going to the front, 'I wish I was a Pasdar, so that I too could be a martyr.'

From 5pm on, each cell was itching to serve its delicacies and carefully honed artistic talents. We prepared a communal eating area in the main corridor, with large plastic sheets as a makeshift tablecloth, again bought from the guards. Along the lengthy of the corridor, around 600 prisoners emerged, waving and smiling at each other. Men milled around, sampling food from along the tablecloth, mingling and talking. Our banquet lasted from 8pm to 10pm. When people had eaten their fill, the entertainment began, and our cake was carried out, shoulder high, by four men.

Our Armenian guitarist and his band took centre stage. Songs in Turkish, Kurdish, Armenian and Persian followed one another, reflecting all the different cultural elements that make up Iran. Individual performers then came up – poets, singers and comedians. I got up to sing, but my tuneless voice brought howls of derision. I gave up, my cracked notes collapsing into laughter.

Over the PA we heard the 20-cannon salute that announced midnight and the New Year. We all embraced those around us, wishing good luck to their families and freedom to themselves. Words of encouragement were exchanged between comrades. For two hours, 600 men threaded through their fellows, wishing each a happy new year.

As we got happier, we got louder. It was inevitable that we would attract attention to ourselves, as noise of the revelry seeped from the block. Few, unfortunately, seemed aware of this at the time. Those who appealed for quiet were ignored as killjoys. Then the main door burst open and large numbers of guards tore into the crowd, beating the men around them and kicking the food to the floor. We were all ordered and pushed towards our cells. We watched from behind cell bars as the New Year decorations were torn apart. The guards began to systematically search the block, looking for revolutionary poems, homemade wine or anything else remotely incriminating – which was most of what we had for the party.

As the guards reached the end of the corridor, where our cell was, they gathered in horror around the still uncut cake, with its star and hammers and sickles. 'Who is responsible for this?'

demanded a guard. 'Fucking godless communists,' he cursed, 'Haven't you learned your lessons yet?' Those of us in the nearby cells were set upon. One of my cellmates, Massoud, watching others falling under hails of blows, shouted out 'It was me!'

'Pick the cake up,' ordered a guard. He struggled to pick it up, with a guard supporting it on the other side, so heavy was it. Both marched down the corridor with it and out of the block. Massoud was held in solitary the following week and we made a point in toasting him in his absence. He gained much respect from the whole of the block for his brave and selfless action, which saved many others from a severe beating.

Although the night's celebrations had been abruptly terminated, the whole week was spent in a continuous circuit of visits of prisoners from one cell to another. These visits turned into mini-parties, with songs and food offered round those present. If I enjoyed any time in prison, this was it.

All this was a prelude to the phased withdrawal of the Golden Fortress from the political prison network. During the next five months, all politicos were moved to other jails, and the Golden Fortress was given over entirely to criminals. The politicals were divided into three groups. Those from the provinces were returned to jails from where they came, so that their families could visit them easily. The other division was made in the interests of prison security, we thought. On what seemed like arbitrary criteria, one group was sent to Evin, the other to the prison of Gohardasht.

CHAPTER 17

GOHARDASHT

Gohardasht was a prison built in the dying days of the Shah's regime. He never got to play with his new toy, as he was overthrown before it was completed. Then the press was given a tour of this new Bastille of the Iranian revolution (Evin prison had always been considered the first Bastille). It was a warren of thousands of solitary cells and interrogation units. The new regime declared initially that it would be turned into a university, but no lecture theatres were ever built. All that changed was the name: Gohardasht Learning Centre.

Within three years, the regime had filled the jail with thousands of prisoners, whom it hoped would never emerge. Many spent four years and more in total solitary confinement. There was a name for those sent to Gohardasht: the forgotten ones. Swallowed up by the sprawling jail, never to be heard from again. Haji Davoud would send those prisoners he could not control in the Golden Fortress to this place.

Many lost control of their limbs, which would jerk spasmodically as they walked, talked, sat or lay. Others became mentally disorientated – mad. I shared cells in Gohardasht with some of these forgotten men.

The governor was Haji Mortazavi, a cleric and an Islamic judge in southern Iran, responsible for sending thousands to the gallows. He had also served as an officer in Hamadan prison between 1982 and 1983, at a time of large-scale massacres. Now he became part of the prison reform process.

When the prison regime was 'liberalised', just before I was moved to Gohardasht, many of the walls of the solitary cells were knocked together. Small coffins for the living dead were made into larger ones where the forgotten could mingle. Blocks of 32 former solitary cells were knocked into five communal cells and now housed between ten and 30 men rather than one or two. Six solitary cells were retained. The prison also kept a number of the solitary cells in the other blocks.

The Tavabs had never gained the upper hand here. The revised prison population was made up of old inmates at Gohardasht, and prisoners from Evin and the Golden Fortress. None were prepared to see the Tavabs take control. Resistance was often physical, especially by those from solitary.

Our block held about 200 inmates, most of whom were left-wing prisoners. Of these, about 40 were Mojahedin supporters. Each cell elected its own representative. He communicated the wishes of his cellmates to other cell representatives and argued and voted in line with his cell mandate in block decisions. He was the cell 'MP' – or, rather, delegate to the block soviet. All cell and block representatives were democratically elected and recallable by inmates. By this arrangement, each of the different political groupings would be assured of representation at decision-making meetings of the block.

This did not come about overnight. It took weeks, sometimes months, of debate and experiment. For instance, when it came to organising a block library, a small minority of leftists in some blocks refused to co-operate with the Tudeh and Fedayeen

Majority, at a time when they had abandoned support for the regime and were taking a full part in prison organisation and resistance. Yet their critics argued that these people could still expose our security. At the end of the day, the library was organised without the co-operation of the opposition.

Block 1, my own, was divided along political lines. The Mojahedin, Tudeh, Rahe Kargar and so on would all organise their funds separately. Some individuals, haunted by memories of Haji Davoud's persecution, chose to organise their affairs in complete isolation. Occasionally two of these hermits would get together. Likewise, they abstained from any attempt at prison resistance.

The Mojahedin had a 'welcome one and all' policy, incorporating everyone within the communal structures, even former Tavabs, some of whom had switched allegiance once more and taken on responsibilities in the communes. Tudeh and the Majority also adopted the same line but the left was wary of this apparent 'forgive and forget' approach, and much less ready to reincorporate its former Tavabs.

Our block was well organised, but in other blocks communal co-operation was even higher. Block 4 not only made every attempt to produce a representative and democratic structure, but organised a block commune that cut across political divides. A block fund was set up. All the money that came through family visits would go into this and be distributed according to need. Clothes would be handed out in the same manner. It even became possible to reverse the cashflow and send money from the jail to families who were in dire need.

This commune was administered by an elected committee of three. Cleaning rosters, food allocation, activities and so on were also handled by elected representatives. Embryonic open resistance was taking shape because of this emerging form of organisation. Where there is unity there is strength. The unified approach to things as straightforward as organising the library, sport or negotiating with the authorities, involved more than 90 per cent of all inmates and gave us the strength and confidence to compete for control.

Block 18, which held persecuted Bah'ais, was organised along similar lines. Religious traditions were adapted to prison needs. The commune was more paternalistic, where the elected officials were the religious elders. I spent about two months here. They organised classes in English, Mathematics and the like, constantly trying to uplift one another. One or two were still snooping on the rest. One of these Bah'ai prisoners was the nephew of Hojabrah Yazdahni, a prominent businessman who had made himself millions of dollars under the Shah's protection. The nephew was universally despised for acting as a stooge inside block 18.

In this new environment, where distrust between fellow inmates was waning, discussion intensified as members of different political groupings dissected and analysed. From the contacts I made with some Mojahedin leaders in the different blocks, I found they had asked their members and supporters not to engage in political discussion with the left. The excuse for this was to maintain security but the reality was different.

Many Mojahedin prisoners were young, with little political experience, and were therefore seen as vulnerable to serious political challenge. Their leaders were strongly protective of the rank and file and would do their utmost to prevent any discussion between them and the left. I did not try to shove Marxism down their throats, but to answer questions they might have. As almost all of them were from working class back-grounds, they were in theory our natural constituency, but there was little to be gained in prising them away from the Mojahedin. This would often weaken their resistance to the regime's propaganda, playing, as it did, on a shared Islamic outlook.

The most hotly debated subject was the Iran-Iraq war. There were three perspectives. One was that the Islamic regime was bound to continue the war until one government or the other was destroyed. This was how the Mojahedin and some left groups saw things. The second argued that if Khomeini accepted the UN Security Council's peace resolution, No. 595, the result would be the abandonment of expansionist aims in the Gulf, Afghanistan and the like. This was the route to accommodation with the West: live and let live with the 'Great Satan'. This was a view I shared. Lastly, some believed that the regime could accept the peace resolution without any noticeable change or policy shift. This was the perspective of Tudeh and the Fedayeen Majority.

We held structured debates with written contributions on such matters as the prospects for revolution, its international character and our allies and enemies. Another written contribution that circulated was on the importance of the working class in the revolution, and the task of organisation under present conditions. Inmates also took part in the debate over the nature and structure of the Islamic regime; to what degree it was revolutionary or counter-revolutionary.

We were able to organise links with other blocks through which we were able to circulate discussion papers. 'Discussion paper' is perhaps a rather grandiose term for what did the rounds. We were not suddenly provided with writing and printing materials. The papers that circulated were small, narrow strips, filled with tiny, tightly cramped writing, and could easily be concealed and smuggled from cell to cell, block to block. They were folded into pellets and wrapped in plastic. Couriers would swallow them and wait. In one end out the other. Debate flowed with the rhythm of bodily functions. Responses to the original papers were encouraged, and there was a healthy exchange of little paper pellets, concluding in an overview of the entire debate.

I used to act as postman, passing the document pellets from our block to a comrade in another. The paper was folded up to the size of the last thumb joint, and usually wrapped in my blindfold, which was in turn stuffed in my trouser pocket. We always kept our blindfolds close to hand even when we were not compelled to wear them, as a visit from a guard or official would mean we had to wear them again.

Deliveries took place on Wednesdays when it had darkened sufficiently to make it hard for the guards to see what we were up to. Sometimes packages would be exchanged both ways. The guy I had to get the paper to didn't use the same exercise yard as our block, although his block overlooked our yard. So, instead of simply switching the paper from palm to palm as we met, we had to fashion some way of getting it from the ground to the second-floor window of the block's toilet. The toilet was used so that, in case we were seen, no particular cell could be identified for punishment.

The paper was not heavy enough to throw that distance. The wind could take it straight to a guard's feet. Even if I could have thrown it with any accuracy, the bars on the cell windows were too close together for the recipient to put his finger through. Instead, he would dangle a thread out of the window to the ground. I would sidle along to it and tie the small package to the end, while a number of comrades kept watch around me. Up in the second-floor toilets, lookouts from that block were posted to give warning should the delivery be seen by the guards. Then the paper would be hauled up, I would walk off nonchalantly and my lookouts would disperse. The simple exchange of such a small piece of paper would take at least six men from each block.

One particular day, I walked over to the wall and indicated that I had a message to pass up. This was done by making loud conversation to a lookout walking with me, which allowed whoever waited above to hear certain coded phrases. A voice from the toilet window similarly indicated that we should circuit the yard a couple of times while he prepared to lower the thread. Even though we couldn't see each other, we recognised each other's voices. We had known one another for over ten years.

So off I sauntered, making light conversation with the lookout at my shoulder. All the while, our eyes scanned the yard and overlooking buildings, searching for any sign of guards. On our return, the lookout stood in front of me, obscuring sight of my hands, as I fumbled with package and thread, to tie it up as soon as possible. The message then began its speedy ascent and we walked off without looking back.

The next circuit, two of us in the yard held our loud conversation below the toilet window, trying to discern if the other block had received the message OK. I looked up. Two guards were looking daggers at us from the roof of the block opposite. They knew something wasn't right. Within seconds they were in the yard, and I was hauled off to an interrogation room on the second floor. I was kicked and punched, as I knew I would be as soon as I had seen them. Between blows, they demanded to know what I was doing.

'Nothing, just talking to the guy with me.'

To say anything else would have meant much more trouble for all of us. It was much wiser just to take the beating now, and have done with it, however bad it might prove to be. The guards threw me in solitary for a couple of days. Then I was back on the block as usual. But you can believe I was a lot more careful in my role of postman after that.

The Islamic regime attempted to cleanse the prisons of 'subversive' literature, some of which had been circulating in the jails for more than 20 years. Often books would be copied out by hand, in the fashion of a medieval monk. It was this sort of material with which the regime wanted to fuel its bonfires.

Khomeini followed Torquemada in his paranoid censorship. Anything that was considered 'un-Islamic' was confiscated –

even language textbooks were seized. Prison culture adapted to defend its stores of knowledge. We transcribed books onto small sheets of paper, and hid them in unimaginable places, from burying them in the prison yard to rolling them up and stuffing them inside the iron bed frames. If a prisoner was being moved, he would tell a trusted comrade where his illicit treasures were stashed – handing on the title of keeper of the scrolls.

When the period of liberalisation opened up, buried treasures were dug up and bed frames emptied as these secret libraries came into the light of day. Teams of 20 inmates would copy and recopy key texts: books on Iranian history, literary critique and so on. The works of Marx and Lenin became available in the cramped hand that was the trademark of the prison scribe.

Once produced, these new editions would find their way around the prison in the same way as our discussion papers. An itemised central store would be kept in a particular cell on each block: our central library. This was on open display, which meant that anyone could share it. 'Open display' literature was usually educational, or the sort of political stuff the regime could handle. Sensitive material remained carefully hidden. There was an ever-present danger of a raid and confiscation of all the material we had spent so much time and effort assembling.

Family visits were now permitted every fortnight instead of each month. Brothers and sisters under 30 were now allowed to visit. If we had small children, they would be allowed on our side of the security screen for a five-minute period, so that we had some physical contact.

My eight-year-old son – who, like all the other prisoners' children, was terrified by the visit ordeal – was allowed around the screen. While I held him in my arms, I put a cotton cap on his head, woven for me by an Iraqi comrade in the jail. Any exchange was forbidden but fortunately the guards missed the gift, assuming he'd come in with it as he left. The hat itself was symbolic: on the top was a big red star, blending in with the rest of the colourful pattern. So at the end of the visit, off went my young son with a badge of prison resistance emblazoned on his cap, mocking the guards whose weapons he walked under. Now in his thirties, he still has the cap.

On another occasion, I hastily wrote the frequency and time of clandestine radio broadcasts from our organisation, Rahe Kargar, which were taking place on the border with Iraq and Iran, on the inside of his arm. He was already street-wise, and made sure that it could not be seen. When he was searched by the guards at the end of the visit, he jumped around, waving his arms and singing, playing the hyperactive little boy. The guards couldn't get a grip on him to frisk him properly. I watched through the screen in silent trepidation as they tried to search him. If they found the numbers on his forearm, I was in serious trouble. In the end, they despaired of keeping him still, and one guard propelled him on his way with a frustrated slap on the back. Of course, this was risky stuff. But in prison, if you don't take risks, you're dead anyway.

For the first time we were permitted to write to our families on a special form with a maximum of five bland lines. Anything more than this would go straight in the censor's bin. We could pen these notes once a month. At New Year, Noruz, our five-line cards wishing our families 'better times in the coming year' were censored, as the authorities were suspicious that the correspondent was encouraging his family to resist. Many prisoners were questioned about the 'subversive' nature of their new year's greeting.

Yet the prison thaw encouraged a real community. We had our own library, sports club (of sorts) and social welfare network. Groups engaged in debate more freely. We built up a solid reservoir of strength to deal with issues about the mental and physical wellbeing of prisoners. The possibility of resistance became real.

One of the first tests of this new-found strength was when the left wing prisoners asked to be given meals regularly and punctually during the Islamic fasting month of Ramadan. At this time, we would get only two meals a day: one between 2am and 3am, and the other of bread, cheese and tea at about 6pm. There was nothing to eat between, other than what we had saved from these scant meals.

While I was in prison, Ramadan fell during the height of summer, so it was not hygienic to store food in hot, sweaty cells. In its new 'liberal' guise the regime did not enforce fasting, but neither did it give us regular food so that we would not have to comply! We could have food sent in, but the prison cooks were definitely working to rule during Ramadan. If food was sent in, it would not keep, and many prisoners contracted diarrhoea and food poisoning through rash attempts to supplement their diet.

Low rations and rotting meat provided the spark for a revolt. As discontent spread from block to block, only the Mojahedin stepped back from confrontation. As good Muslims, they did not want to demand additional servings during Ramadan, but felt bound to fast – or at least to maintain the pretence. The hard-line Islamists within their ranks were adamant about this and fasted with religious zeal. The liberals flouted the regulations but the majority in the centre upheld the principle of Ramadan, while ignoring it in practice. Still, they refused to combine with the left wing in demanding the full regular portion of food.

Discontent erupted during the first ten days of Ramadan in 1987. There was resistance in almost every block. In some, inmates from left groups would gather at the doors and demand to see the prison authorities. In block 1, 20 to 30 inmates maintained a continuous presence at the door. We did not want to go out on a limb or be left behind so we kept a careful eye on what was happening elsewhere in the prison.

In our block, about 120 men took part in this resistance, with the Mojahedin and the hermits looking on. After a long debate, it was decided to boycott the early morning prison rations. We handed back the vats of food untouched, except for those who were not taking part in the boycott.

This tactic was adopted by other blocks and other prisons, as word was spread via our families and prisoners. As a result food supplies went back to normal throughout Ramadan. The mullahs had given up on our souls, and been forced to pay a little more attention to our stomachs.

Our victory was all the more remarkable when you consider that throughout the country restaurants were closed outside restricted hours at this time, and anyone seen eating in the street could be arrested. Our fight upset the sensibilities of none other than Haji Mortazavi, who came to our block at the height of this affair. 'How can you infidels demand warm food?' he asked. 'Our Islamic soldiers are fasting on the front line against imperialism, even while they fight, while you want injured veterans to play the chef for you. It is impossible!' Impossible it may have been, but we got it.

Group exercise was another flashpoint. On this issue, the regime had the Mojahedin in its sights. They took exercise in the yard, about 30 from our block grouping at a time, going through light exercise or sometimes with one among them giving instruction in karate or the like, which would often attract members of other groups.

Then a directive was issued banning group exercise. The left joined the Mojahedin in resisting this. More than 70 prisoners took part in a jogging group, round and round the exercise yard. We did this each day from 9 to 9.30am. A couple of older prisoners, who had been jailed under the Shah, acted as pacesetters, to make sure the younger, more energetic prisoners did not leave the pack behind. One was a Tudeh Party central committee member, and the other was from Rahe Kargar. They were at the front, and no one was to pass them. The rest followed along behind – sometimes as many as 100, sending clouds of dust from our heels as we pounded round and round.

If the regime could stop us organising sport, we knew it could stop us doing everything under the sun. It was necessary to stick together and repulse this attack with all our might. The old and frail joined in – me included – and it gave confidence to the younger comrades to see those weak with injuries and illness in the line alongside them. There had not been such a united struggle from the blocks up until this point.

Unprepared for a head-on confrontation, the authorities looked on and the head guard threatened us with a 24-hour lock-up if we persisted. We were not deterred and the run continued every day. But the threat was real. One day there was no run round the yard – we could not get out of our cells. We talked it through. What would be the consequences should we carry on? Would it get those who did not run with us – the quitters – locked up with us as a result?

Discussion continued for several weeks, and most of us agreed to continue the runs as soon as we were allowed back in the yard. We heard that other blocks had got the same treatment; locked up en masse, or runners picked off, beaten and held in darkened solitary or the steam room. The steam room was a small room where 40 or 50 prisoners were crammed in so tight they couldn't breath properly. Steam was pumped in and the men would sweat like hell, dropping like flies from the humidity after one or two hours. When all were totally exhausted, the guards would burst in with fists, clubs and cables. But clubs and steam were not enough to make us concede the fight and so it went on.

We were told that if word of our fight got out, the offenders would be put in solitary. Whole blocks defied this order by ensuring that each and every one passed the message on during visits, making it impossible for the authorities to deal with all the offenders. Word spread and resistance consolidated. Throughout

Gohardasht, 'to be or not to be' in the solidarity jog became the main question, overshadowing political differences inside and contradictory developments outside.

When guards came to the cell, we would encircle them, insisting on our right to exercise, arguing that it was necessary for our health. We also pointed out that if we did not run together, then we would get in each others' way as 200 prisoners milled around in the confined space of the yard. It would be chaos.

One day we were visited by the head of prison security and riot squad, Haji Davoud Lashgari. We clustered round, badgering him. He screamed back, 'I'll open the gate but I'll break the neck of anyone that runs together!'

The gate opened at 8am the next morning. Men went to the yard to hang their clothes, stretch their legs, chat and mill around. At 9am sharp the solidarity jog was back pounding around the yard. The guards on the roof immediately reported this disturbance. We completed the run – tired, breathless but happy. To run or not was a political question, rather than simply a dispute over recreational amenities, and would determine the next phase of our struggle within the prison system. We carried on for two more days under the eyes of the rooftop guards.

Day three was sunny, and we filed into the bright and warm yard on the stroke of 9am. Five minutes from the end, when we were sweating and panting our way through the last four or five laps, a small gate leading to the main corridor opened on one side of the yard. Out stormed Haji Davoud Lashgari, leading 30 members of the riot squad, smack into the front of the column of joggers. Each one down the line was bundled through the gate. The remaining members of the riot squad pinned down those further away, ensuring no one got away.

As each man was pushed through the gate, he was flanked by two lines of guards, in the narrow landing and up the staircase – the only way out. One by one, we were forced to run a continuous gauntlet of baying, vicious guards, up three landings. It was the most horrendous beating I have ever been through, from Komiteh, Evin and the Golden Fortress. It felt like the worst of all of them rolled into one.

Some of us didn't make it to the second floor, and had to be dragged, semi-conscious there. We were now on another block, blindfolded, and forced to stand facing the wall on either side of the corridor. The guards lined up behind us. Anyone that fell had all hell beaten out of him until he got back on his feet. We were then beaten mercilessly for an hour. Anyone who cried out got beaten worse.

I shouted, 'How can you treat people like this for just running?' I could hear them really laying into our elderly pacesetter and shouted for them to leave him alone. I heard Haji Davoud Lashgari just behind me: 'You dare to question our brothers? I'll teach you a lesson you'll never forget, you bastard!' He began to chop at me from all sides. One hand struck my floating ribs on the right side and I blacked out.

I came to in an infirmary bed. Two guards stood over me, alongside them two Mojahedin prisoners from my block, looking at me anxiously. I could feel an oxygen mask over my mouth, and that my left arm was attached to a drip. Night had fallen. All around us was dark.

I found my tongue and yelled with as much strength as I could muster – it was probably more of a croak – 'Why don't you leave us alone? What sort of Islamic justice is this? Why don't you shoot me, so I can end this day-to-day torture?'

It seemed that I had been taken back to the cells by my fellow joggers. But when my cell mates could not revive me, they hammered on the door until the chief guard came and decided I should be taken to the infirmary. The two comrades from the Mojahedin had volunteered to carry me.

When I was fully conscious, I was jacked full of pain-killers, and the two Mojahedin were told to haul me back to the cells.

My return was greeted by prisoners from across the political spectrum. The Mojahedin had spread the word of how I had challenged the guards in the infirmary, and this seemed to have gone down well. Two of my cellmates looked after me. For two nights, groups of prisoners came to see me, to wish me well and check on my recovery. It was a much appreciated sign of solidarity.

Those painful days and nights passed quickly. We had to make a decision about how to counter this latest attack. We decided to refuse to leave our cells, all but a handful of prisoners who went into the yard to exercise alone. Others went to play football: solitary figures kicking a ball with half a guilty eye on those watching them from inside. We also told our families about the horrendous beating.

The prison was divided over our next step. Some argued that group exercise was not our problem but the Mojahedin's, and that we should not put our necks on the line for them. Most felt that how we exercised affected all of us.

In the meantime, struggles broke out elsewhere. Some feared the return of doomsday and quarantine. News came that a left prisoner who had been in solitary for a long period because of his resistance had managed to prise apart the thick steel slats that covered his cell window, like heavyweight Venetian blinds, to squeeze through and hurl himself from the third-story window to die on hitting the yard below.

In another block, occupied mainly by the Mojahedin, one mentally disturbed prisoner had found a quiet moment in the bathroom and hanged himself from the door frame. In block 3, which faced ours, one Mojahedin prisoner had managed to save enough petrol from his commune's heating and cooking ration – the amount of food we received from the jail was never enough, so food was bought from the guards' shop whenever we could afford it – and had set himself alight. We heard the horrified cries of his comrades as they ran to put out the flames… too late.

These were not isolated incidents but charted a drift back to despair by many who had suffered so much. In our own block was Hassan Sedighi. He was an experienced prison militant who had come through the torture rooms of Savak never even giving his name. As a former Mojahad he joined the nucleus of Rahe Kargar in its formation in prison and spent almost half of his life, 14 years, in the prisons of the Shah and Khomeini. He killed himself late one night in the shower. There he could swallow cleaning fluid without disturbance. He then returned to his cell as if he'd just paid a visit to the toilet like any other night. I was unable to sleep because of pains from my injuries and saw him sitting in front of his cell with a book on his lap.

I sat down to talk to him, asking him about his book. 'I'm not interested in it, really,' he answered, 'It's just there's nothing else to do'.

His face was dark, and he looked unwell. 'Are you sick?' I asked.

'There's nothing wrong with me', he said.

When I got up the next morning I was told that he was extremely ill, that he could not even breathe properly. We tried to get the guard to take him to the infirmary but this was refused. We persisted in this all day: within hours he was vomiting blood. Eventually he was carried to the infirmary. By the time he got there he was unconscious. The doctors tried to force him to vomit but were unable to help him.

Upon hearing of Hassan's death, several friends and comrades met to discuss what could be done as a mark of respect. The concept of some sort of ceremony took shape. Not only to commemorate Hassan but also as a show of defiance to the authorities for allowing him to die and as an opportunity for prisoners to gather in solidarity.

This was our proposal: a short speech about Hassan's political struggle and his opposition to the authorities within the prison system, followed by some songs and poems. And then perhaps messages from individuals and organisations. We would hold the ceremony in the prison block's prayer room which could hold up to 200 people at around 3pm – at this time most guards would be asleep after a hefty afternoon meal and so security would be at its laxest.

Some comrades were asked to contact the other political groups, cell by cell, to explain the need for such an occasion and to win support for it. I was to obtain support from the Mojahedin and Tudeh prisoners. In all I had to speak to 18 cells – eight Mojahedin, five Tudeh and five Majority members.

I first approached the cell representative, asking for an opportunity to put forward a proposal. They would then give me a time to return to put my proposal, as each cell would have its own agenda for discussion each evening. I would then talk briefly about our comrade Hassan and our plans to commemorate his death. I was then asked to leave the cell while the prisoners discussed the proposal. The discussion was thorough and intense. They would debate the proposal, hearing arguments both for and against. Each cell would then vote on the proposal and then tell me the outcome.

At the end of this week-long period of consultation, out of 22 cells, 20 had voted in favour of our proposal. In each of these 20 cells, the great majority of prisoners were in favour. One cell, that of the passives, was not approached as their non-participation was anticipated. The last cell, made up of Minority and some other leftists including Maoists, voted against the proposal. Ironically, Hassan was from this very cell. We were given a brief summary of the debates from each cell by the cell representative, but we were especially interested in the arguments in this last cell. They felt participation in such a large scale event would allow the prison authorities to identify prisoners who were prepared to take part in acts of resistance and defiance. Prisoners would thus be at a personal risk of identification and punishment – this they considered too dangerous.

This argument was put forward in other cells, but was mostly defeated by the Mojahedin who argued, incorrectly as it happened, that such a ceremony or commemoration would have religious overtones and would not annoy the authorities or unduly attract their attention. This issue continued to be a topic of debate throughout the block even after cells had made their decision.

The ceremony was held, as planned, in the block prayer room. Of 200 prisoners within the block, 170 attended as requested. The ceremony was held promptly at 3pm on a sunny afternoon, exactly two weeks after Hassan's death. His family had already collected his body and, under orders from the prison authorities, arranged for a discreet burial with no ceremony. Some of our families had been made aware of Hassan's death so the prison authorities knew that they had to be careful or there would be an international ruckus about his death inside the prison. With this in mind, we knew that we could push our luck a little bit further than usual with the authorities with our daring commemoration.

The prayer room was a large square room with a stone floor which rarely fulfilled its intended purpose of Islamic prayer. On this occasion, the room would again not be used for prayer. Everybody filed into the room and sat on the floor in one large circle. The ceremony started with a call for a minute's silence for Hassan. In order to avoid being seen from outside, we remained seated.

I had prepared a short statement on Hassan's life and death entitled 'A Prisoner of Two Regimes'. I described Hassan's life, of which 14 years had been spent in the prisons of the two regimes – seven under the Shah, seven more during the Islamic regime.

Hassan had been captured while a member of the Mojahedin by Savak just as he had entered the University of Tehran as an engineering student and been put through the most vile torture. He was said to have been the most resistant captive that Savak had ever known. His refusal to even identify himself for a long period had brought upon him the most savage torture methods.

This bravery had become widely recognised among opposition groups inside the prison. During the revolutionary upheaval he was released from prison by thousands of people who stormed through the walls of Evin and other prisons to free the Shah's political prisoners.

Hassan then joined the nucleus of Rahe Kargar upon its formation. He was given responsibility for organising among students at the university. Shortly after the Islamic 'cultural revolution' he was again arrested. He was brought to Evin for a second time, after again suffering a period of severe torture. To his amazement, he found that some of his interrogators and torturers had been his fellow prisoners under the Shah! He was given 'special' treatment as he was not only an opponent of the regime but had also turned his back on Islam on leaving the Mojahedin. He had become at once an unbeliever and an apostate. He was, in fact, lucky not to have been shot while in Evin.

We had assembled to commemorate Hassan's murder by the prison regime and to remind ourselves that Hassan took his life as the prison authorities had given him nothing to live for. He had become a martyr because the Islamic regime would not respond for a full 24 hours to treat him to save his life. For this reason, we held the Islamic regime responsible for his murder in Gohardasht.

I read this tribute in a loud, clear and emotional manner. The meeting was taut with restrained emotion. Some comrades began to weep. There then followed a revolutionary poetry recital by Karim, a young Mojehad who had been jailed when aged just 15. During a six-year period of torture and interrogation he had become a Tavab (under Haji Davoud's

Golden Fortress prison regime) but since the period of increased resistance and the demise of the Tavab system, he had once again become an active member of the Mojahedin.

Upon hearing of the proposal for the ceremony, he had asked me to allow him to recite poetry. I consulted with others before answering him. Some were concerned about his past Tavab activities, but the commemoration organising committee was prepared to accept my recommendation to allow him to recite his poetry. It was possible that more Mojahedin would be attracted as a result. In security terms, he would be jeopardising his own rather than ours.

Karim chose three political poems, well-known by most prisoners. One was written by Said Sultanpour, who had also been a prisoner of both regimes – he had been arrested at his wedding ceremony by Islamic guards and was executed almost immediately after reaching Evin for a second time. The poems were recited with great conviction and emotion and many people remarked later how moved they were. Karim was to be executed in 1988–89, despite his prior activities as a Tavab.

A third section had been planned in which messages from organisations and individuals could be read out. But although one Rahe Kargar comrade read out his personal message to Hassan, understandably no other message was delivered. To have done so would have identified individuals with specific organisations – something that no one was prepared to do. Thus the ceremony ended with one comrade standing up and thanking everyone for attending. People were then asked to leave the room discreetly so as not to attract undue attention.

The whole ceremony, its organisation and the period of consultation brought about a new mood of unity and co-operation in the level of resistance offered to the prison authorities. Hassan's death had acted as a spur for us to organise ourselves better to oppose the regime's oppression of all prisoners.

The prison authorities increased the pressure from then on. There were mixed reactions from the prisoners. Some would look back to the Golden Fortress – the Tavabs, quarantine and doomsday – and retreated back into themselves, fearing a return to such conditions. Others felt it was even more important to show the utmost resistance, to make it hard for the officials to reassert their total authority over us.

Even with this division, the mood in favour of fighting back was strong. The flash point occurred in the spring of 1987. The officials cut our paraffin ration in the wake of a suicide and the same week prison guards confiscated all our paraffin cooking stoves. This was a significant attack on our living standards. Prison food was not enough to live on, so we had to supplement our diet with food from the prison shop. But if we could not cook it, we could not eat it.

Even those who wanted to finish their sentences with the minimum of fuss reacted angrily to this. There was no point keeping your head down if it meant starving to death. This brought together prisoners in a way the exercise issue, which could be seen as a Mojahedin-only problem, had not. The provocative action of the officials united prisoners in all blocks, without exception. Each block, according to its capabilities, organised its own way of resisting. The officials tried to defuse the anger by telling us that they would pay for the stoves, but under no circumstances would they return them.

In the discussions about the way to proceed, a number of proposals were submitted from our cell. A block-wide hunger strike was proposed by the left. The right countered with a wait-and-see attitude. Some of us suggested that on the visiting days, we refused food and explained the situation to our families, to involve those outside. This was eventually accepted by the cell, and forwarded to the block.

Other cells proposed that we should boycott the prison shop, apart from washing and cleaning materials. It was also proposed that we should refuse to use the exercise yard. We decided to leave the shop boycott and use of the exercise yard to the discretion of each cell, as many prisoners needed to use either or both for health reasons. The proposal from our cell was adopted by the block, with the addition that the first ten prisoners called for a visit would not go, and the next ten would go to explain why this was the case. We hoped that this would lead families to put pressure on the officials immediately – which is what happened. So this struggle between the prisoners and their jailers broadened out to include our families, who acted as the backbone for our resistance.

During the first week of our co-ordinated fightback, we crowded round the big iron door to the block, hammering on it and demanding to see the officials. Every trend and organisation was keen to be represented in this campaign, which continued day after day, in the hope of wearing down the authorities.

We have met Amou – Mohammed Abrandi – already in the Golden Fortress. An old worker, weathered from the sun of the oilfields and bent from a lifetime's labour and living in shacks constructed out of oil barrels. He'd never been to school, but taught himself to read in Persian and Arabic so fluently that he could write poetry in both.

When he was young, he was a giant of a man – wide-shouldered and long-limbed, with a reputation as no mean fighter. He had taken part with other oil workers in strikes in southern Iran after WWII, and remembered bitterly the capitulation of Tudeh at this time. Amou brought his experience to bear in the development of the movement that overthrew the Shah. The oil workers played a crucial role in this opposition movement. Their strikes and protests cut off the regime's life blood.

With the consolidation of the Islamic government, Amou joined the Fedayeen, the largest left group in Iran. When the organisation split, he sided with the Minority, which refused to support the regime. He was still active among the oil workers, despite his advanced years. His troubles began when *Time* magazine photographed him addressing a meeting of striking oil workers and printed it in full colour on their front cover. The Islamic regime took this as irrefutable evidence that he was inciting workers.

When the regime cracked down on the left, the Minority encouraged the development of armed cells in factories and towns and Amou was associated with one such group. Within a year, in 1983, he had been captured. He was tortured in 209 and, in unimaginable pain, he gave information which led to the capture of the woman who was the secretary of his cell. She was shot.

Amou was sentenced to seven years and sent to the Golden Fortress. Many captured with him from the Minority refused to speak to him and asked others to ostracise him as well. Ironically, according to what Amou told me, this boycott was organised by a member of the Minority who agreed to be part of a firing squad in Evin. When Amou, further down the same line, had been asked, he excused himself as being 'too old and too frail for that kind of stuff'. This person, Amou said, was trying to cover his own tracks by maligning the old man but because Amou had shown weakness under torture, few would listen to his story. He was blanked and became lonely and isolated. He lived as an intransigent throughout, refusing to associate with the Tavabs. But he met a blank wall of hostility from many fellow prisoners.

When I arrived at the Golden Fortress, he told me the circumstances in which he had given information in an effort to win my sympathy. 'I'm a typical working class activist,' he told me. 'There was no way I could be effective in the Minority's armed cells, disconnected from the workplace. We were just waiting to be captured there – fish out of water, flapping about on the beach. In effect, I got burned out. I only really began to read Marxist works after the overthrow of the Shah. I got arrested too soon – I was only just beginning to get to grips with the essentials of Marxism. I needed to learn this. I was a good speaker, a good activist – the form was good but I lacked the content that Marxism could give me. I really felt the lack of this talking to workers during our oil strikes.' He would fall into despondency, which accentuated his hunched appearance and sigh, 'I don't think we will live to see the daylight of revolution and socialism in Iran.'

I was constantly warned not to associate with him. But I felt I understood his strengths and weaknesses, and knew I was safe with him. In fact, I tried my best to integrate him back into the main body of left prisoners, with some success. Amou's own (generally) buoyant and sociable disposition helped no small amount.

On prison high days and holidays – such as they were – he would throw his all into the proceedings to make things go with a swing. We celebrated May Day, International Women's Day, the anniversary of the Russian revolution and the like. As the guards had their calendars ringed in red on these days and were on the lookout for any untoward joviality, we celebrated covertly and a couple of days in advance. Such festivities amounted to getting spruced up as best as was possible – a wash and shave was all that could be done – and go round the cells bringing greetings. Statements were read quietly, and certain individuals on your block would be invited to discreet gatherings in a particular cell some time later.

Amou, our master autodidact, would do the rounds of the cells with me and a couple of younger comrades. One May Day he composed a poem, which he had set to a jazz-like rhythm. He schooled us as his 'scat' backing vocalists. He read out his composition, while our backing group lined up behind him to set the tempo. 'Dang dang-dang dang, Dang dang-dang dang.'

Over this, Amou went into what was a rap, albeit performed by a septuagenarian Persian, about workers' unity and the road to socialism. Fluid, staccato Persian was interspersed with pidgin-English which made its appearance to cover key words and concepts which would have incurred the wrath of the guards had they overheard and understood.

The prison had discovered its own beat poet. Word went round the block and our performance became much in demand. The word went out to come to cell 24, one of the larger rooms in the block, on May Day after 8pm, when the presence of the guards was at a minimum. Each bunk bed became a tightly filled stall as the audience swelled in anticipation of the night's entertainment. Not quite Carnegie Hall, but it did much to lift morale, especially Amou's.

When the struggle hotted up in Gohardasht, Amou was at the forefront. He hammered on the door and harangued officials with the best of them during the protest over the confiscation of our stoves. On one such occasion, in the spring of 1988, he was snatched from the front of the crowd and dragged away. He was taken to the central office, where five guards set upon this old man. Fists, clubs and cables fell upon a body that bore all the scars of 70 years of injustice in Iran. Two hours later, he was thrown, half-dead, back into his block.

During the night, Amou burned up with fever and pain. His cellmates hammered on the door, demanding that he should be taken to the infirmary. The guards sneered, 'Let the old bastard die.' Amou did not recover. In the heart of that dark night, he closed his eyes, and never opened them again. The daylight he waited for is still below the horizon.

One night, at about 10pm, two officials came to our block. One of them was Haji Mahmoud, a young mullah from the religious city of Qom. He was one of the prison authority's troubleshooters and also a censor. They sat in the main corridor and asked about our grievances – although they knew already. Group after group told them, citing the particular needs of individuals who needed more food, exercise and the like.

Our demands were met with a rebuke: 'We no longer recognise your elected representatives. From now on, we will decide who we deal with on your block, or we will deal with no one.' So now we had another demand – to get our own representatives recognised.

The next day we drummed on the door with greater insistence. Between 80 and 100 angry prisoners queued, demanding to see the officials. The doors opened, Haji Mahmoud and a crony came forward and the mass of prisoners surged through. The two officials turned and ran, fleeing like frightened chickens. They had been humiliated.

Half an hour later, once we had been forced back inside, the block doors reopened, admitting 50 club-wielding guards. They went from cell to cell, starting where the disturbed and deranged were kept. Beating and breaking, they wreaked havoc in all 22 cells. Everything and everyone in the cell was smashed and thrown into the corridor. Not one possession was left intact, not one prisoner escaped a beating.

We were hauled to our feet and told to go to the prayer room. Those who couldn't walk were dragged. Those who could walk were ordered to take all their possessions, which were stacked in the centre of the room: a mountain of books, clothes, bedding, cutlery. The guards rummaged through each prisoner's sack, looking for anything that might be incriminating. Then we were instructed to return to our cells while the guards continued their search. Of course, we lost watches, money and other valuables. But our real worry was that they might unearth material that would allow them to send prisoners back to court for organising resistance. Books, letters, the fabric of our sacks, were picked through. Handwriting samples and books were taken out for further investigation.

Three large plastic cases of wine were also unearthed. We had been making wine in an Islamic prison! A poet, Kamal, was in charge of our illicit vat. We had fermented wine out of grapes, raisins and berries bought at the prison shop. Our moonshine was concealed under bedding and sacking in the corner of two or three cells – and in the prayer room!

Our sacrilege enraged the guards, who went from cell to cell trying to find out who the underground vintner was. Fortunately, not many people knew – the wine was a closely guarded secret. And with a knife at your neck, you learned to shake your head in denial. If you nodded, the movement of your head would push the knife point into the soft underside of your chin.

Beatings, threats and solitary did not yield any results, and Kamal's role remained hidden. He had another vulnerable point. He would write poetry on prison conditions and resistance, which he would ask me to translate into English, so that even if the guards found them they would not understand. But this exposed me: as the translations were in my hand, I could be shot.

We hoped other secrets would remain hidden. What they'd taken from the blocks in the form of messages on paper and in books was in carefully concealed code, which we hoped wouldn't be detected, let alone deciphered.

The next week was spent clambering over this mountain of possessions, trying to reclaim our shirts, bedding – even our bloody toothbrushes, buried somewhere deep within. Then came the slow process of putting our cells back in order. At the end of all this, there was stuff left unclaimed in the pile: possessions that had been at the bottom of prisoners' sacks so long, they'd forgotten they had them. So we 'nationalised' it. Anyone who needed anything from this residual pile could come along and take it.

But the authorities were able to piece together evidence of an organisational network among the Mojahedin in one or two blocks. A couple of prisoners were fingered and put into solitary. They caved in under tremendous pressure, and were paraded in front of the other prisoners in their block. They 'confessed', asked forgiveness and appealed for other prisoners to follow their example. This was the authorities' response to developing resistance. We heard on the grapevine that the fight was not confined to Gohardasht. In other jails in Iran, prisoners were rising up and asserting their rights.

At this time, each prisoner was interviewed by a panel. He or she would be asked, 'Are you a Muslim? Do you pray? Do you support the Islamic Republic? Are you ready to go to the front to fight Iraqi aggression? Do you still have any affinity with the political group you were working with to overthrow the Islamic Republic?'

All those who answered that they were Muslims and prayed, were put together in one block, whether Mojahedin or left. Those who said they were Muslim but did not pray, were put with us. Now all the blocks were arranged on religious lines.

Prisoners were also split up according to the length of sentence. Those serving more than ten years were isolated inside two blocks within Gohardasht. One block was reserved for intransigents, the other for passives.

Within a month of the interviews, the whole of Gohardasht was organised along these lines. This disrupted resistance and it was a number of months before we were able to get our bearings and once again build up our network of contacts.

CHAPTER 18

MASSACRE!

A new block was formed from Evin intransigents of men who had completed their sentences but whom the regime refused to free because they had not said the right things at their release interviews. They had refused to appear on televised interviews denouncing the opposition in Iran. Such prisoners were to be held indefinitely. Some had received two-year sentences but were still behind bars six years later. There were about 200 of them and their families campaigned for their release.

As tentative contacts were renewed, each block in turn began to test the regime's resolve. How would it react to a new round of prison resistance? In my block we established good contacts with those around us. But there was still a mood of suspicion over why we had been segregated in this new way.

The Iranian war effort was waning. Iraq was growing more confident and successful, and international pressure, focusing on UN Security Council Resolution 595 calling for the immediate

191

cessation of hostilities, was stepped up. The Iranian front line crumbled in parts of the north west and Iraqi forces broke through. Khomeini took the poisoned chalice of the forced peace.

For the first time prison television showed the advance of Mojahedin commandos from bases in Iraq. Then things changed: one Friday afternoon in late July 1988, a couple of days after this news item was screened, all televisions were removed, scheduled visits from our families due the next day were cancelled until further notice; exercise periods were withdrawn; access to the infirmary and all other medical treatment for the sick was stopped; and we were confined to our blocks. Our isolation was total: we were not even permitted to read the Islamic regime's official daily paper. Everyone in Gohardasht was in quarantine. Even the guards were not allowed to leave the prison compound.

Days passed. The daily radio news broadcast at 2pm was stopped. We were desperate for news. Inmates in blocks closest to the guards' quarters would try and overhear what was said on the guards' radio. At 2pm these blocks would go deadly silent. Those with the sharpest ears would lie on the floor, put their ears to the narrow gap between the heavy iron block door and the ground, and try to pick up the faint strains of the broadcast. What they gleaned would be relayed to other blocks by Morse code tapped out on the floor and ceilings. In this way we could compare notes on what each block had gathered, piecing together the fragments of half-heard news. Information gathering and dissemination became the particular remit of certain blocks.

We discussed the likely effects of the military defeat throughout the country – in particular, what its effect would be in the prisons. I argued that Khomeini would seek an accommodation with the West and reactionary regimes in the region to give the regime a breathing space. If the regime was forced to adopt such a policy it would have to reduce pressure in the prisons as part of the public relations exercise to ingratiate itself with the West. Other comrades were more hesitant and feared the worst. Unfortunately, their pessimism was to prove well founded…

We heard that the Mojahedin prisoners were buoyant, believing that their advancing forces would soon take Tehran and release them. Their leaders told them to pack up their things, and wait for the prison doors to swing open.

Then suddenly the prison was hit by an Iraqi Scud missile. It came screaming out of a quiet night. Part of the prison's west wing was destroyed and several prison guards were killed. The force of the blast left hardly a single window intact. Many of us were cut by the flying glass. Prisoners were picked up and thrown against the opposite wall of their cells by the impact. We didn't know what the hell was going on – it felt like the end of the world. Shock and panic exploded immediately after the impact. The insane howled, screamed and cried from their cells.

When we'd picked ourselves up and assessed what had happened, we took the view that Khomeini didn't have long left if the Iraqis were this close. It all contributed to the growing uncertainty in the jail. At a time when tension was high, the rocket blast acted as an additional force to push many prisoners over the edge.

Stress built up like steam in a piston. By the second month of quarantine, we were conscious of new developments in adjoining blocks. Normally at night we were aware of prisoners moving around in nearby blocks as their bodies broke the light from their cells as they walked. Then the frequency of this decreased, then stopped. Now no one obstructed the light opposite us. Then the lights went out permanently. Each of these blocks had held more than 200 Mojahedin. Now they were empty.

Information filtered through from other blocks that the same thing was happening in their line of sight. Either they had been moved to other prisons, or… we dared not think.

Some of us decided to buttonhole prison officials to find out what was going on. Of course, we knew the officials wouldn't tell us what was really happening, but we might be able to read between the lines in a face-to-face meeting. We needed to glean some idea of what was going on in their minds. What was in store for us?

Information was at a premium and had never been so scarce. It was necessary to have mass support if we were to take even one step forward. There was no chance of success for individual protest action. But some on our block were reluctant to take on the officials. Those on the right were opposed to any action in principle. On the left, others urged patience because of the unknown circumstances. We were groping forward, blind.

I went from cell to cell rallying support for our proposed course of action. We were in a total blockade. The withholding of medicines put many of our lives in danger. We had the right to know why this was happening, and how long we would be held in isolation. What new crime had we committed to merit such treatment?

After a week of extensive discussion most cells had convinced themselves that unified action was the right response. Eighty out of 120 people on our block agreed to this course of action. Next morning, we asked those who supported us to gather at the door of the block. The guard came in response to our drumming on the door, and we demanded to see a prison official. He left and we remained by the door. After standing there for about an hour, we started knocking on the door again. The guard returned, cursing us, and pulled me and three others through the door.

'Stay there!' he ordered us, 'I'll bring someone down to talk to you.'

We were blindfolded and each of us was stood in one corner of the corridor facing the wall. We stood there for two more hours before anyone came back. A low-ranking official with whom we were familiar came and told us to turn round and tell him what we had on our minds.

I said, 'I've been asked to tell you that many prisoners want to know why we are in quarantine. How long will it last?'

'The decision has been made at a level above prison management', he told us. 'We don't have to explain their reasons to you. And there is no way we can know when this emergency will end. By now you should have learned that in Islamic prison no one has the right to speak for anyone else.'

'Speaking only for myself, then,' I responded, 'I need medical attention. Without the medicine that my family brings me every month, my life is in jeopardy. Doesn't that give me the right to question why you are cutting off our essential supplies?'

'Dead or alive, you'll stay in this condition as long as you're told to! We're losing thousands of young Pasdars at the front – do you really think we give a toss if thousands of you drop dead in the meantime? You're lucky to be alive at all. Go! We don't want to hear you whining again.'

One of my fellow negotiators attempted to argue with him. The official ignored him, instead turning to the guard and telling him, 'Put each one of them in a solitary cell.' He turned on his heel and left.

We were bundled off and, once in solitary, tried to communicate with one another and with other inmates in cells around us, using morse code. Someone tapped through that many prisoners had been hanged. I was reluctant to accept this, believing that it could be a rumour planted by the authorities – a scare story to demoralise and intimidate us.

We were back in our block the next day. For reasons that became clear later, the authorities did not want to keep prisoners in that part of the jail because they were concerned about what we might hear.

I prepared a balance sheet of prison resistance and what it had achieved in our block. We managed to get it to the comrades from our organisation in the block below. In particular, I pointed out our success in organising a united opposition to the prison regime, although at least 60 per cent of our block were considered passives. This spurred on resistance in the block below, which took the form of a limited hunger strike. Their key demand was for information about what was going on.

Officials came to the block below a week after our protest. They had a list with the names of four prisoners, who were taken away. Two were members of Rahe Kargar – one named Hossein Hajimohsen, the other Ebrahim Najaran. The third was a Fedayeen Minority member, and the last was a Peykar supporter. They were put in solitary.

News was coming in from other sources throughout the prison that thousands of Mojahedin prisoners had been hanged, and that hundreds from the left had met the same fate. Patchy though this information was, it was all pointing to the same thing: a mass execution of political prisoners.

By covering and uncovering the iron blinds on the cell windows, we could send semaphore-style messages from block to block by night. In this way we received news about what was happening. Claims about the massacre spread in this way, but there was no way of confirming it, and we remained suspicious. Then more concrete evidence came in which dismayed us all. Three days after our four comrades were removed from the block below, we received this coded message, which was deciphered over three long nights.

'I was taken out of block 8 with 24 other comrades. We were taken down to the main lobby. There we were seated on the floor, facing the wall. One by one, we were taken to a room. We were told this was an amnesty tribunal. Each one that entered, came out a few minutes later and was led to the end of the corridor, where there was a big iron door leading to the large auditorium. When it was my turn, the guard grabbed my wrist and took me in. I was directed to a chair, and was told to take off my blindfold. The Tribunal was composed of four mullahs, the head of prison security and the prison liaison officer, also a mullah. I was ordered to introduce myself. On hearing my name, they asked me the following questions:

"'Are you a Muslim? Do you pray in prison? Why did you become a supporter of an ungodly organisation? Are you ready to condemn your past activity and the activities of all opposition organisations in a televised interview? What would be your response if you were asked to go to the front in the war against Iraq? Are you ready to co-operate with prison officials in identifying those inmates who oppose the Islamic government? Do you consider the Islamic regime an anti-imperialist government? If so, why?"

'This took three minutes for them to ask and me to answer. All the while they swore that I was a hardcore activist, just trying to cover my true nature. I was then cursed, kicked, pulled out of the room and directed towards the big iron door. Their parting shot was "Take him to the top floor".

'I joined a queue. More than 50 waited in line, blindfolded. An hour and more passed. Then a guard called out 25 names. All the while, I was trying to find out whether those around me had been given amnesty or were destined for the top floor. All I could tell was that the others in the queue had been asked the same questions as me, and we were all waiting as a consequence. Once more, a guard called out 25 more names, and the queue shuffled forward.

'Now I was at the front of the line, right up against the iron door. It was covered in a thick carpet to muffle the sounds of what was happening inside. The whole area was dimmed, lit up only when the door opened to let guards in and out. I noticed that these guards looked different from the normal ones. They wore no uniforms, were bare-footed, with sleeves and trouser legs rolled up. They had shaved heads and thick beards. As they passed, they shouted Islamic slogans. Suspicious of this change of routine, I wanted to see inside when the guards passed, but did not want to attract any attention.

'Eventually, the door opened enough for me to glimpse a pile of prison slippers, dumped like lorry-loads of potatoes. When the guard returned, I craned to look over his shoulder, as soon as his back was turned.

'I saw 30 to 40 bodies hung by the neck from blue plastic cords looped from a horizontal iron bar above the stage area. They had been executed. I recognised Hossein Hajimohsen and Ibrahim Najaran, both from Rahe Kargar. Now I knew what being "taken to the top floor" meant.

'Another hour passed. A guard came, and called out more names. Mine was first – but not quite. They got my first name wrong – Hossein, instead of Hassan. I stood and said: "Brother, my name is not Hossein, it is Hassan. There is a mistake, I should not be taken to the top floor. There is a Hossein, but with the same surname, in another block."

'He insisted I come with him. I tore off my blindfold and ran towards the tribunal door, chased by these new guards. I shouted as I ran, "I swear to God my name is not Hossein, I swear to god my name is not Hossein!" again and again.

'By the time the guards got hold of me, I was already in the room, pleading my case before the tribunal. One of the mullahs fished out another file from the stack on the desk. After poring over it quickly, he told the guards to take me back to my block.

'Judging by the mound of prison slippers I saw, they must have already killed thousands of our comrades.'

This story was substantiated by other sources. Disbelief crumbled. We now knew what had happened to those in the empty blocks and what was likely to happen to us too.

I have said that the Mojahedin were singled out first. It was a reality for them while it was still a rumour for us. When the survivors were moved from their now denuded and echoing blocks, I had a chance to talk to them.

They had seen their comrades based in Iraq advancing following the announcement of the ceasefire, and seizing ground from the Pasdaran. Some families had told them that the regime was crumbling. All this had created a feeling of elation in the Mojahedin blocks. Some packed their belongings, ready to take the walk through the prison gates into the clear, free air. So when news came of an amnesty tribunal, they thought that they were virtually home and dry, already feeling clean civilian clothes on their backs, and decent food in their bellies. They could smell victory – could see the regime crumbling and knew it could only be a short time before Rajavi, their leader, shoved Khomeini into the gutter.

Now, the Mojahedin leaders liked to keep their footsoldiers' spirits up with such stories, but this time it seemed to be confirmed by the Tribunal, which started holding sessions from the end of July 1988. The first batches of prisoners that came before the tribunals were told by the chief judge that its purpose was to give them amnesty. We're going home boys, we're going home, they thought.

Each man was asked, 'What have you been accused of? What organisation do you belong to?' Those that answered with the self-deriding '*Monafegh*' – the regime's term for the Mojahedin, meaning 'fake Mojahed' – were put in a forced labour block that they presumed to be a step nearer freedom. Those that stood straight, answering 'Mojahed', which means 'soldier of God', were sent to the top floor.

The Mojahedin felt they had good reason to be optimistic. Although they had answered, '*Monafegh*' many times before to such questions, some thought that they could now afford to hold their heads up. They were duped into putting their necks into the noose.

After almost three weeks and nearly a thousand secret executions, the remaining Mojahedin began to realise what was happening. Guards appeared on the block, calling out men in batches, often as many as a hundred – none of whom would be seen again. Like us, they looked anxiously from their cell windows to see empty blocks. In discussion, they agreed to answer '*Monafegh*' to the main question. But other questions followed: 'Are you prepared to do a TV interview and sign a petition, denouncing the Mojahedin organisation?' Those that said no joined the queue for the gallows.

Later the Tribunal upped the stakes further, as Mojahedin members tried to twist and turn out of the hangman's noose. Now the Tribunal asked, 'Are you ready to co-operate with prison officials and give us the information you have about other prisoners?' Those who agreed to do this were transferred to the blocks to be processed by the tribunal. Two of them were put in our block, but we were lucky enough to realise what was going on. The sudden introduction of two Mojahedin into a left-wing block was bound to ignite suspicion at this time of heightened fear and distrust.

Towards the end of the slaughter of the Mojahedin, the Tribunal became more choosy about what 'co-operation' entailed: total support for the regime, blanket condemnation of the Mojahedin and all other opposition groups, signed petitions and televised interviews were not enough. Neither was a vague promise to inform on fellow prisoners. The Tribunal now demanded the names of five Intransigents if the man in front of them was not to dangle from a length of cable.

The 'lucky' survivors from the Mojahedin blocks went to do forced labour. The other 80 per cent were hanged. It took the Tribunal a month to administer this 'amnesty' to about 1,500 men in Gohardasht. That's before they started on the left wing.

I had lived close to many Mojahedin during my years in jail. I was particularly concerned about those I knew. I asked about Habib, with whom I shared a cell in quarantine at the Golden Fortress. He had acute intestinal problems. Those who had been with him said he had been constantly warning, 'We're walking into the regime's net. We're being sliced through like a cucumber!' When he went before the Tribunal, far down the line of the Mojahedin inquisitions, they didn't bother to ask '*Monafegh* or Mojahed?' but straight away demanded information about prison resistance. He refused to answer and went to the top floor.

I asked about Karim, who had read a poem at the ceremony for Hasan Sedighri. Karim had been a Tavab years ago at Evin and the Golden Fortress. He had been tried early on, and answered 'Mojahed'. He was executed. Some Mojahedin comrades I asked about did survive, thankfully. But they were the lucky few.

Final confirmation that a massacre was taking place reached us from the ground floor of block 20, which faced onto a yard. From their window, they saw the coming and going of large refrigeration lorries, two or three at a time, day and night. Their curiosity heightened by the rumours, the men in the block posted a 24-hour watch. One day a lorry stopped within clear view. The back opened. It was loaded with large parcels. Guards jumped on top of the pile as similar parcels were passed up to add to the load. Each was wrapped in plastic sheeting, tied with twine at either end. From the unsteady way in which the guards found their footing on top of the load it was clear what was in the packages – bodies. There had been a constant movement of these meat-wagons to an unknown graveyard for at least two months.

These mass graves are still being unearthed in south Tehran. Bodies were dumped into shallow trenches by the thousand and hastily covered. Heavy rain washed away parts of the thin topsoil, exposing the corpses to scavenging dogs. After one storm, the destitute shanty-town dwellers in the area saw hundreds of dogs helping themselves at one partly-exposed mass grave. News spread fast, and Islamic Guards moved in quickly to pile earth over the exposed trench. But the place was known, and the families of thousands butchered in the massacre still gather at the site on Fridays to mourn those taken from them, often bringing food to hand out in the shanty town. Every year in September there is a big commemoration here, at which those who lost their lives for their beliefs are remembered and celebrated.

Tension increased to the edge of madness for many of us. The only ones not affected were those who had no sanity left to lose. Most of us thought about the barely conceivable situation obsessively, night and day. We would all have to go through these tribunals. How could we avoid putting our necks in the noose? How were we going to avoid this calamitous fate? Vigilance, and clinging to contact with other blocks like life itself – for that was what it meant – became the be-all and end-all of existence.

One morning we sat up to find the block below us was now empty. We knew where they had gone. Some very dear comrades had been taken away.

Long meetings were held about how to face the tribunal, what to say to it, how to survive it. We had relative freedom to associate within our own block at this time. The guards were mostly busy with their offensive, but we still had to watch out for anyone who might be listening and could pass on information about our discussions. We still had to watch for elements who might crack under severe pressure under these most extreme circumstances.

We agreed that it meant death to confess to being a communist or a socialist or, indeed, any oppositionist to the Islamic regime. But it was left to the individual as to whether he said if he prayed. At previous prison inquisitions, we had always managed to dodge this question. Each prisoner was asked to approach the question of 'co-operation' with the authorities carefully. The issue of whether or not one prayed was not the central concern; defending your integrity, your comrades and fellow prisoners was. I said it was better to accept death than to give any information that would lead to further arrests or the execution of other inmates. 'For me, the bottom line is, do you sacrifice your dignity and comrades, or your own life? If I was prepared to compromise, I would not have spent nearly ten years here'. In my own cell, this approach was agreed upon.

Certainly, this very same discussion echoed around every cell in the block, and in the cells of other blocks. As far as other prisoners were concerned, my position was that each prisoner had to decide for himself how he would conduct himself. The situation was of such an extraordinary nature that we could not possibly hold some sort of block vote to decide a general line that everyone had to follow: each prisoner was due to face an almost split-second decision-making procedure – each individual had to establish for themself how they were to survive and how they would protect their fellow prisoners.

And so my turn came.

The guards arrived at our block. We were all led from our cells and out of the block, blindfolded. From where we were located, on the second floor, we were taken down to ground level, in single file and in absolute silence. Each of us had our right hand upon the shoulder of the prisoner in front of us. We were taken to a long corridor where many prisoners were waiting, sat cross-legged on the floor in a queue. The queue led to the door to the 'inquisition chamber'. Here, prisoners were 'processed' one-by-one by this 'inquisition panel'. Such was the speed of each hearing that another prisoner would be called every two or three minutes.

It was a good two hours before I got to the head of the queue, but finally my turn arrived. I was taken into the room to face the inquisition. I was sat on a chair and was told to remove my blindfold. I saw six people. I recognised the faces of two well-known Islamic judges behind a desk. These two presided over Divisions 1 and 2, respectively, of the Islamic courts. They were responsible for dealing primarily with the left-wing organisations and other oppositionists and, as such, their department was responsible for executing thousands of prisoners between 1981 and 1988. Haji Mobasheri had dealt with me before, back in 1982 and 1983, and again in 1986.

The other two clerics of the inquisition panel were Haji Raisi, the head prosecutor, and Ayatollah Eshraghi, Khomeini's son-in-law, the biggest landlord in the holy city of Qum: a rich man indeed. Now this man, who had so mysteriously accumulated vast amounts of property after 1979, appeared before us as the chief judge of our morals, holding all our lives in his hand.

The tribunal had to establish during the interview whether the prisoner was a non-Muslim (or *Mortad*, one born a Muslim but who has since rejected Islam) and/or a communist, or if he was hostile in any way to the regime. They asked each prisoner the same questions, and had no individual case papers. This 'amnesty inquisition' had been set up at the behest of Khomeini, who had issued a fatwa to 'eradicate all the *Monafeghs*, Mortads and communists'.

They explained, 'The Imam has given us the task of distinguishing between those prisoners who continue to oppose our Islamic Republic, and those who do not. On this basis we will oversee the amnesty for suitable prisoners.' He had told other prisoners that the panel was there to 'look into any problems you might have.'

With this short explanation out of the way, it immediately became clear that we were the real problem. And so the standard questioning commenced.

'Are you a Muslim?' he asked.

'I was born into a Muslim family, but religious practice was never very strong in our house – my father was a constant drinker', I answered.

'But I want to know whether you are a Muslim now!'

'I consider myself as much a Muslim as my mother and father do'.

Second question. 'Did you pray before you came to prison? Do you pray here in prison?'

'No, I do not pray in prison. Neither did I pray outside of prison. In order to be true to myself and to others, I have not put up a show of praying just for the sake of appearances.'

Third question. The prosecutor, Haji Raisi, now took up the line of questioning. 'Which grouplet did you belong to?' He used the term 'grouplet' as a putdown, to belittle political opposition groups generally.

'All through my interrogation and three appearances in court, I have constantly stressed the fact that I have never been a member of any organisation'. This had always been my answer to this line of questioning throughout my detention. Not even now was I prepared to alter it.

Haji Raisi probed further. 'What is your analysis of the Islamic revolution and of the Islamic regime?'

'The Islamic regime is an untypical form of government, based on the authority of Imam Khomeini and the Shia clergy, which arose after the popular revolution of millions of people against the Shah's despotic regime,' was my answer, deliberately ambiguous, and similar to one of the left group's broader formulations dating back to 1981.

Fourth question. 'Are you ready to pray as soon as you get back to your block?'

'I have no aversion to praying, but I am unable to pray because I have a broken back. The infirmary has all the documentation on my condition.'

'Then you can sit on the floor and pray! And you can have 50 lashes for not praying in prison. And ten more for any prayer session that you miss from now on. Now get out! Next!'

And that was it. All over inside three minutes! Before I knew what was happening, I was whisked out of the room just as quickly as I had entered it. I had managed to manoeuvre sufficiently to spin out my allotted few minutes before the inquisition panel. But more importantly, as I had intended, I had given away nothing nor had I compromised or implicated anyone. In fact I had not even told an untruth. Those three minutes could have been the end of me, and I had managed to emerge with just a few lashes. But so many had not been so fortunate, so many had been lost before we had been able to formulate an 'escape plan' from the inquisition panel.

The guard walked over to me and tugged on my arm. 'Get up and put your blindfold back on.' I was led out of the inquisition chamber and off to the queue for the lashes. I could hear the screams of those who had been placed on the tables to be lashed. But on the other side of the corridor was a line of prisoners who awaited the gallows.

As I looked over to them, the voice of Haji Naserian called out. 'Oh, dearest Khomeini, in your fatwa you ask us to bleed these infidels to death!' This chilling invocation was directed at the line of prisoners awaiting the hanging chamber. Then another voice returned, 'Don't forget to make your will! Do not be too cowardly to make you own will!' Again, this was directed at the soon-to-be executed prisoners. Rhythmic death threats and morbid jeers, often in rhyming couplets, were accompanied by the screams of those stretched across tables having the soles of their feet lashed. These sounds echoed round the corridor like a chant from hell.

Our line moved quickly. The guards had set up a torture production line. At the head of the line of men, a row of tables awaited their next victims who were hauled across their length and held face down on the table by wrists and ankles, the lick of thick electrical cable cut across soles. If you jumped in pain and they missed with the next lash, you would receive a further three. And remember, we were the lucky ones.

At this time, news came from a comrade, Mohammed Ali Behkish, from block 20 where most of the Tudeh cadres were kept. This was at ground level and looked out onto the killing floor. Mohammed had overheard the two chief judges talking to one of the executioners.

'The executioner said, "Ten minutes is not enough",' said Mohammed. '"When we bring them down from the gallows after this time, some of them are still moving. Please give them more time." One of the judges answered, "We don't have that much time to spare. Ten minutes is enough." The executioner asked, "Why not just stick them in front of the firing squad? That will be much faster." The judge replied, "We don't have the facilities here. You'll get blood all over the streets from the removal lorries. Do you want everyone to know what we're doing here?"' Mohammed Ali Behkish was executed shortly after, as was his brother, Mahmoud Behkish.

The Tudeh and Majority members in block 20 badly misread their situation. Believing that the regime was only purging the Mojahedin and revolutionary left, and having given their support to the regime, they went before the inquisition stating they were communists who backed the Islamic Republic. As a result, almost all of block 20, including some Tudeh Central Committee members, went to the gallows. Only a handful of broken leaders, such as the general secretary Kianoori, and their main theorist Esan Tabari, were kept alive for show. Some said that they were spared because of the might of the Soviet Union. But there was no Soviet Union by then; it is clear that they kept their skins for other reasons: they were later to publish books that fully supported the Islamic regime.

Kianoori, who died in 1999, was the regime's pet 'communist' and churned out his 'confessions of a turncoat' for the Islamic regime. This included his 600-page memoirs, approved by Vevak, the Ministry of Information and Security, which had been printed and published by the regime (this in a country that jailed a newspaper editor for ten years in April 1994 for printing a cartoon of a footballer thought to resemble Khomeini!). Having the pseudo-communist Kianoori tucked under the mullahs' turban proved more useful to them than killing him. My own view is that the Islamic regime had no right to imprison him or anyone else, either now or in the past, for their political beliefs.

It was a measure of our success in interpreting and analysing the unfolding events of the inquisition panel that, from our block, only one comrade was executed. He defiantly told the inquisition panel that he was a communist and that he did not believe in God. The rest of us managed to slip through the net. But we were one of the last blocks to be processed; the losses overall had been very high. Overall I estimate that 1,500 of us were executed at Gohardasht.

After our lashings, those of us who had survived the tribunal were brought together in a new block. Here, at dawn each morning, around 4am, guards went from cell to cell, asking every prisoner in turn, 'Are you ready to pray now?' Those who were not, for whatever reason, were dragged to a lashing table erected in the corridor and flogged. It became clear that this was the norm throughout the prison. From the blocks above, below and on either side we could hear thick electrical cable cutting the air, followed by screams as it cut the soles of feet.

The morning after our inquisition panel, when the guards gave us their first sadistic 'morning call', two comrades from the Fedayeen Majority who had been passive throughout their prison term, and who had little political contact with prison resistance, refused to pray. This was a surprise to us as these men kept themselves to themselves, eating and associating separately. One of these men, Masoud Masoudi, had also been jailed during the Shah's reign. (His brother, Babak Masoudi – a leader of the more militant Fedayeen Minority and a founder of the Fedayeen back in the 1960s – had been executed by the Islamic regime in 1987.) Masoud told one of the guards that he considered it 'belittling to do something in which I have no faith.' Islamic guards and prison officials in general are not great free thinkers and both men were hauled off to the lashing table. We were all ordered out of our cells to act as an audience.

The more experienced of the two, Masoud, was strapped face down to the table, given ten lashes and asked, 'Will you pray now?' 'No,' he replied, defiantly. They gave him another ten and still his answer was, 'No.' A further ten lashes. After 30, 40 then 50, his feet were oozing blood; his face too, as he was being punched and kicked if he moved during the flogging.

Eventually, barely audibly, he croaked his assent when asked. He was dragged off the table and ordered to wait for his compatriot – not that he was capable of going anywhere.

The second man was strapped into place. He quietly took the first 30 lashes, and from then on screamed each time the cable struck his soles. He too nodded after the 50th.

These two comrades must have seen many others bruised, bloodied and broken throughout their internment. But this was the first time that they had learned for themselves what it felt like to be torn apart. They had never guessed that the simple act of refusing to pray would receive such brutal retaliation.

For those intransigents who could not imagine these passives doing this, their act of defiance came as something of a revelation. Any man could emerge as a fighter in the prison resistance, as these two had done – at the last minute, despite others' beliefs and even their own ideas about themselves.

They were not the only eleventh hour converts to intransigency. There were others, but to explain I must go back to sunnier days.

In the aftermath of the hectic and hustling days of the Shah's overthrow, when Khomeini had not yet sunk his claws firmly into the structures inherited from the Peacock Throne, two fighters from the still unified Fedayeen organisation were passing through the Niavaran area of Tehran, where the Shah's court had been. As they walked through the deserted palace in the early light of the morning, with their Kalashnikovs slung behind them, Jalil Shahbazi and Ali Zareh got a glimpse of how the other half lived.

Ali was a university student, Jalil a young worker. A Jeep belonging to the Islamic security forces pulled up beside them. This was a patrol to make sure the poor kept away from the court's palaces – at least until the mullahs had finished plundering them. Caught unprepared, these two armed Fedayeen were captured and thrown into Evin. At this time, there were no left-wing political prisoners in Evin, and Jalil and Ali found themselves keeping company with the Shah's top brass: army generals, who were responsible for civilian massacres which led to his overthrow, and with Savak's head torturers and the like.

For whatever reason, the theocracy's new prison officials decided to keep these two young men in prison. By default, then, they held the dubious honour of being the first leftist prisoners arrested by the regime – prisoners who were held onto until the last minute of the massacres and beyond.

Our paths crossed in the prison system a number of times, and I consider myself fortunate to have run across them, and talked to them.

While we were in the Golden Fortress, Jalil explained their prison history. 'Once in a while they pull us into interrogation, and ask about the Fedayeen and its development. When the split occurred, they wanted to know which side we had taken. As things developed within the Fedayeen and society, we lined up with the Majority. So we told them that we believed the regime was progressive and deserved support. During the first two years, we were treated fairly decently. In the first year, we were even given the opposition's publications.

'After the Mojahedin's coup attempt in September 1981, things went downhill. We were witnesses to the mass executions of innocent people in jail. Within the year, we were sent to the Golden Fortress. The Majority and Tudeh were seen as compliant, and kept separate from the other left trends. Ali and I were put in with this section.

'Later, Haji Davoud split us up, sending us to different blocks in an attempt to divide the prison resistance. Many prisoners shunned us because we were tainted with collaboration. Despite this, I was quite optimistic because the convergence of Tudeh and the Majority looked like resulting in a united party. The arrest of Tudeh's leadership, coupled with the regime's assault on the Majority, caught us by surprise. We were shocked by the confessions of Tudeh's leaders.

'Six months after this, I was taken to court for the fourth time. They could never find anything to charge me with as I had only taken up arms against the Shah and had consistently said I supported the Islamic government. The court, as before, could not come to a conclusion. We were neither freed nor charged. But this time, the judge ordered me to co-operate with the interrogators and divulge any information I had about other prisoners. Either that, or stay till I rot.

'So when I walked from the court, I knew I was going to be in prison uniform for a long, long time.'

During the 1989 massacre, pressure was put on Jalil to pray. He refused and was badly beaten. Before the next prayer session came around, he slashed his wrist with a jagged fragment of a glass jar. He was dead before anyone found him.

Ali was more fortunate, surviving his torture. He was released in 1990.

Each day at prayer, I would tuck myself away in the corner and watch the other prisoners going through the charade. Fractured vertebrae excused me from this – scrambling from feet to knees,

211

bowing and back again. Instead of touching my forehead to the ground, I was given a piece of 'Mecca mud' to lift to my forehead, when everyone else bowed down. It looked stupid.

From here I could see my comrades bowing up and down, cursing Khomeini, Islam and the regime under their breath in the most obscene terms to the rhythm of the muezzin's chant. Our Imam was of the most makeshift sort: an illiterate guard with a dirty matted beard, who smelled worse than we did and couldn't get the prayer right. He kept losing his place and mixing up the sequence of prayers. Even an amateur and reluctant worshipper like myself knew enough to spot his glaring mistakes.

We were forced to take part in this hollow pantomime five times a day. And each day we would witness comrades being lashed, or hear others scream from other blocks. This went on for months, well into 1990.

Political prisoners are scattered throughout Iran. Each province has its own representatives of the religious hierarchy and jails over which they have complete authority. And, of course, each jail holds its share of the disaffected. All can rival Evin and Gohardasht in their degradation. The level of struggle inside can be gauged by just how vile the prison conditions are and where one finds the most prisons. Kurdistan is well supplied, and not even the smallest district is complete without its own prison.

Just as each locality has its own jail, each had its own massacre in 1988-89. All local representatives of Khomeini were instructed to deal with their opposition. Often, even those oppositionists who had served their sentences and been released were re-arrested, re-tried and executed.

This was the reaction of a frightened regime defeated in war, trying to reassert its hold, made more desperate and brutal by the thought that things were slipping away from it. The war that Khomeini had called 'God's greatest blessing' became his curse.

The defeat at the hands of Iraq made it essential to step up the war against its own people if it was not to lose that too. 'The Front' became the gallows in Iran, not minefields in Iraq.

In Kurdistan, the massacre was carried out in the most blatant and barbaric ways. Public gallows were erected in town squares. The corpses of those executed were kept on display for days, sometimes weeks, to warn the population of the rewards for 'subversion'. If this was what went on in the streets, one can only guess at the slaughter dished out behind prison walls.

A sort of race developed between officials in the different regions as to who could deal with dissenters most speedily and callously. In places such as Hamedan, Rasht in the north, and Rezaieh in Azerbaijan, more than 90 per cent of political prisoners were executed.

Mass graves were discovered in Karaj, near Tehran, on 24 October 1988 – 725 bodies were unearthed. Others were found in Tehran, in Rudbar and Menjil, both in the Caspian region. It will never be known how many prisoners were murdered at this time, but the figure usually cited is between 8,000 and 10,000.

CHAPTER 19

CAT AND MOUSE

O ur sisters and brothers had queued for the gallows while
we had queued for the lash. In the aftermath of the
massacre we queued for interviews and interrogation.

Two or three times a week, blindfolded, each of us would
stand before a panel as they fired a stream of questions and
demands at us.

'Are you ready to condemn the opposition grouplets? Will
you sign a petition to this effect? Are you prepared to be
interviewed on television to do this publicly? Are you prepared
to co-operate with prison officials? Will you give information
on prison opposition? Are you prepared to go to a Jihad labour
block? Will you participate in a mass demonstration of prisoners
in front of the UN headquarters in Tehran, in support of the
Islamic Republic and against the so-called Human Rights
Commission inquiry into torture and massacres? If you are
released, are you prepared to co-operate with Vavak?'

These barrages were designed to wear us down, to force us to submit; they kept alive the climate of fear and suspicion in the wake of the massacres. I took time and care in answering these questions to avoid implicating myself, or giving the regime an iota of help.

'Brother, I have never been a member of any group, so I have never supported their programmes in the first place. Signing your petition would imply that I have had associations with them. I've always denied that this is so. The same is true for being interviewed. What can I say about these groups? I don't know much about them... Brother, while in prison I've kept myself to myself. I haven't mixed in prison politics, so I have no information to share with you... As to demonstrating, brother, as you can see' – I looked down at my body and shrugged expressively – 'I can hardly stand, let alone demonstrate at the UN... I can't co-operate with state security. I have no expertise or experience here. You're welcome to my expertise where I have it. I can teach for you if you want!'

This final – and only – offer to my interrogators provoked an upwardly extended middle finger from one of my interrogators. 'We're not letting you near a classroom again, you bastard!'

In the aftermath of these interrogations, the blocks were constantly reshuffled so there was little chance to build new links. Prisoners were regrouped in line with the answers each gave. As was the case before the massacre, it prevented us from re-establishing firm relations with one another. The threat of another massacre was kept in front of our noses by constant interrogations and our vulnerability was emphasised.

One post-interview journey for me went a little further than from one block to the next. In early 1990 I was put on the prison bus to Evin – an old acquaintance that I was not anxious to renew. I managed to avoid the Jihad forced labour blocks because of my ill-health. Many prisoners didn't and became slave labour.

Work would start at 8am and end around 5pm. Men were put

to work in the carpentry shop making crates for guns and ammunition; though the war was over, the regime clearly had its sights set on the next. Others made light switches in the electrical shop, and in the machine shop general repairs were handled. Lastly, there was a Jihad brigade who, with grim irony, were given the job of building more cells and blocks. All worked to a quota. If you didn't fulfil it, it was recorded and your prospects of release receded.

Most members of the Jihad block, about 400, had been in prison since their teens, some earlier, and had no experience of the work they were put to. No training was given, no protection provided. Accidents were common especially in the machine shop. Men lost fingers, even hands, with horrifying frequency.

Abbas, a Mojahedin sympathiser had been in jail for seven years since the age of 14. Now 21, he had managed to survive torture and massacre, and retained his spirit. Although unprepared to compromise with the regime, he was strongly focused on getting out and rebuilding his life. Volunteering for the Jihad block was seen by many prisoners as a way of accelerating release.

Abbas worked in the carpentry shop, on the circular machine saw, feeding in the uncut wood. One day, hurrying to meet his quota, he severed the four fingers of his right hand. He stood there, in shock, gaping at his fingers lying in the bloody sawdust.

Recovering with a bony stump where once his hand had been knocked the fight out of Abbas in a way the threats and attacks of the regime failed to. Although he put on a brave face, those close to him could see the deep pain and sorrow within. To have survived so much of the intentional brutality of the regime only to be robbed of the use of his hand by a dumb machine demoralised him profoundly. He continued, one-handed, to work in the Jihad block and was released about six months later.

The Human Rights Commission inquiries were giving Khomeini problems with international relations. The regime was visibly rattled, and wanted to bully prisoners into telling the commission how tenderly the regime catered for every need.

In the spring of 1990, a large number of prisoners were bussed under armed guard to the commission's temporary office in Tehran. These reluctant demonstrators were then forced to chant their condemnation of the commission's critical reports on the abuses that they knew they would return to later that day.

I had dodged the demonstration draft. But I had not got out of the whole thing. Soon after this prisoners' forced picket, I was taken, blindfolded, to the interrogation block. I was seated in a wooden cubicle containing a school chair with a wooden extension on which to write. I was hunched in this child-sized desk for maybe an hour, staring at a blank wall from under my blindfold. Someone entered silently and a sheaf of paper was slipped over my arm onto the writing surface.

A protracted question and answer session followed; one where no words were exchanged between me and my captors. My interrogator would write down a question. He would then leave and give me between 30 and 45 minutes to compose my answer. Then he would return, take my answer sheet and write down the next question. In this way, a short series of questions and answers managed to drag out all day.

The interrogators obviously wanted to be precise; to leave me opportunities to be sloppy and drop myself in it, and have it all in black and white for the record. Aware of this, I would sit sucking my pen for a good half-hour before committing a word to paper. I wanted to be sure my answers were watertight. The session proceeded like a chess game, with the interrogator and I each trying to lure the other into a strategic mistake; me to get off the hook, him to jam me firmly on it.

And so it started: 'There are some questions you need to answer,' said my first question sheet. 'Your release hinges on the co-operation you give us. And it must be completely confidential. Can you write in English?'

'Not very well.' Half-an-hour to write that.

'Do your best, anyway. We want you to write a confidential letter to Dr Galindo Pohl, the Human Rights Commission's chief investigator. In it you must condemn the opposition grouplets. We want you to blame the grouplets for the damage they have caused you. Tell him that they have destroyed your life, and the lives of your family. You should also explain how well you have been treated in prison by the Islamic security guards, from the time of your capture to the present.'

'Brother,' I wrote, 'if there is one thing you drummed into us during the past few years it is that a prisoner should not get involved in politics. Writing this letter is definitely a political act. How do you reconcile this with your insistence that I stay out of politics?'

My opponent frowned over this answer, and then agitatedly scribbled, 'Who told you writing a letter to Galindo Pohl is political activity? We are asking you to complain against those who have wrecked your life.'

'Condemning the opposition is political. And once I have written this letter to the commission it will be a public document. By publicly condemning these grouplets, don't I put mine and my family's lives in danger, if they are terrorists, as you say?'

Since there was no realistic way of forcing me to write their letter, and I didn't want to expose myself as openly hostile to the regime, we had to play cat and mouse with each other.

'No,' my interrogator promised, 'we will give you full protection.' The cheese in the trap.

'But these grouplets have assassinated some of the Islamic regime's leading officials. If you can't protect them, how can you protect me and my family?' The mouse is staying well inside his hole, thank you.

'You think about it,' offered the fat Islamic cat. 'Do you want to get out of here, or stay and rot? I'll leave you the pen and paper. You have two hours to write the letter. This is your last chance.'

The time passed. When he returned, there was nothing written in English. But he had another of my notes in Persian. 'Self-preservation is the individual's prime instinct. The lessons I have learned in prison, to abstain from all political activity, prevent me from writing any letter supporting or condemning any party.'

He took my answer sheet away. Then he returned, and slapped me hard on the back of my head, like a bullying school master. I rocked forward in my classroom chair with the force of the blow. He spoke for the first time. 'You dirty animal! Get lost,' this being the signal for the guards to return me to my cell.

CHAPTER 20

WOMEN'S STRUGGLE AGAINST THE ISLAMIC REGIME

Women have long faced an uphill struggle for recognition as full human beings in Iran. They have shared the prisons with us, and carried their own burden around with them everywhere: the black, voluminous chador that symbolises their imprisonment by the misogynistic doctrine of the mullahs. Throughout the century, the women of Iran have trod the long and painful road to liberation. Unfortunately, it has not been a straight one.

My grandparents' generation overthrew the old absolutist order. One of the principal gains of their constitutional revolution between 1905 and 1907 was that it weakened the stranglehold of the religious hierarchy over the educational and judicial system. Before this time, education was solely the province of the mullahs. Justice, such as it was, was down to the whim of the presiding mullah. The result of the overturning of this system was that women were, for the first time, recognised as citizens, rather than chattel of the Kajar dynasty's lowly subjects. As Iran dragged itself painfully into the 20th century, women were offered the possibility – and all too often it was to remain no more than that – of transforming themselves from property to active participants in the moulding of our country.

This was the grey tyranny that millions of women thought they were finally casting off with the 1979 revolution. In reality, we entered a chapter of our history that reversed the limited formal gains of the constitutional revolution of some 70 years earlier. Iran's feudal past hung round the necks of its women like a dead weight.

After the establishment of the Islamic regime, hundreds of thousands of women were thrown out of offices and factories throughout the country. Tens of thousands were flogged in the streets for not veiling themselves. Throughout the country, Islamic courts sentenced hundreds of women accused of adultery to death by stoning, public hanging or being hurled off a cliff. Iran was thrown back a century in its social attitudes. The 20th century, so far, has been a long detour between religious absolutism and... religious absolutism.

Today, if you travel through some of the more backward provinces of Iran you will see many women, all wearing the anonymous chador which proclaims them a non-person. But you will not see one alone. In the metropolitan centres such as Tehran a woman may walk alone – but if she walks in the company of another man, it has to be with one who is seen as having the authority to accompany her – a husband or a brother. On any excursion, documents can be demanded to prove such a link. A woman virgin up to the age of 50 cannot be married without the permission of her male guardian.

A woman can't leave the country without the authority of a male member of the family. She can't book a hotel room or anything else in her own name. She can only do it in lieu of a husband or father. A woman is at most the bearer of someone else's authority. She has none of her own. We have almost complete sexual apartheid in Iran.

But, try as they might, the mullahs can't get the genie back in the bottle. There can be no going back to the last century. The whole development of the intervening period has made women aware, and has inspired them to fight. Paradoxically, even those women who swarmed in a seething black mass of chador in support of Khomeini came into conflict with his grand design. In combining in support of the Islamic 'revolution', they subconsciously revolted against its intent to crush and consign them to the home life of their great-grandmothers.

The regime's attack on women could not have passed without meeting resistance from women who have studied in the classrooms and universities, and who have been educated in struggle en masse, in the workplaces and on the streets. Women flocked to those parties demanding the overthrow of the Islamic regime, and its replacement by a democratic form of state, as soon as the feudalistic implications of Khomeini's aims became apparent.

This process of radicalisation was met with the arrest of tens of thousands of women. They were imprisoned, interrogated and tortured. Many were shot. The policy of sexual apartheid against women meant, too, that women in prison suffered more than their male counterparts.

Women prisoners had to wear the smothering black veil, thick leggings and trousers. In stifling, sweaty prison conditions, this sealed each woman within their own personal hell in the wider hell of the jail. Those who refused to conform to this dress code were moved from the political blocks and placed in cells reserved for prostitutes.

Mothers were compelled to look after their children in the bleak cells and corridors of the prisons. A verdict against one woman would mean jail for all her young children. Even if the father was not himself imprisoned, and had no political connections to besmirch his character in the eyes of the regime, he would not be allowed to care for the children, so tender was the concern for the Islamic regime for the role of motherhood.

On the rare occasion that there was no one outside to care for the prisoner's children, the interrogators would threaten to throw the children out if their mother did not co-operate. The children became the eyes and legs for their mothers who were in darkness under a blindfold and unable to walk as a result of tortures. They also tended their mothers as best as they were able. These were enormous responsibilities for a child of maybe three or four.

In 1983, 20 cells in Evin's 209 alone had 26 children distributed between them, some four or five years old when they had the doors bolted behind them, others who were born in prison. As a result of torture, many women had lost the ability to give their children milk. This gave the torturers another lever to use against them: they would be told that if they wanted milk for their babies, they would have to give information in return.

The children's concept of the adult male was drawn entirely from what they saw of the guards and interrogators. They had no idea of the outside world. They had never seen a flower, the moon or the stars – they could not envisage a world outside their grey concrete box. Their mothers would draw them pictures in the dirt on the floor to try and convey to them some vision of a bigger, brighter and happier world. But it must have seemed like just some incredible fairy story to young minds whose only experience was of grey walls, ogres in khaki, and victimised, wounded women cloaked in black.

Young children in the jails were interrogated. As a result, they didn't play cowboys and Indians or doctors and nurses, like other children. The main prison game was prisoners and interrogators. I was told by a woman comrade about just one example from Evin in 1983. A four-year-old boy, Yavar, got 12 of his playmates to line up, facing the wall, while he went down the line, shouting at each in turn in his high-pitched voice, 'Where is your daddy?'

Women sentenced to death were systematically gang-raped by the prison guards beforehand, to ensure the victim had 'no chance of getting to heaven' – the destination of all virgins, according to Iran's clergy. Some women were raped during and after interrogation.

Pregnancy bought no pardon or delay, either from torture or the firing squad. Shahnaz Alikhani, a sympathiser of the left, was tortured and eventually executed in the last stages of pregnancy in Evin. One 209 interrogator, Ghasem, justified this by arguing, 'If an innocent stands between us and our enemy, then we must remove that innocent to kill our enemy. The scriptures give us this right.'

Nor were women shown any favours during the massacres; quite the reverse. Whereas men were told to embrace Islam or face the firing squad, the 'choice' open to women was still more horrific: take up Islam or be flogged to death. Evin, in particular, saw many women tread this slow agonising path to eternity.

Following are the results of interviews I have done with several female ex-prisoners of the regime.

Mehri was a prisoner from Kurdistan, captured in Sanandaj in September 1983. From there, she was brought to Komiteh Moshterak, along with her three-year-old daughter. Here she was held, blindfolded, sat in a corridor, facing the wall. Her daughter was placed on her lap and also made to face the wall. The corridor was lined with women in the same position, many bleeding as a result of interrogation.

She was kept there for 15 days and then transferred to Evin. As a result of beating during interrogation, Mehri bled continuously from the vagina. This did not stop for three months. Upon her arrival at Evin's block 209, she was taken straight to a women's ward in the infirmary. Ages ranged from girls of 13 to women in their 70s.

'One who was in her 60s was known by all as "Mother Mary".' The guards had arrived at her house, pretending to be friends of her son, an activist. When her son failed to show up, they arrested Mary instead. 'The skin on her soles had been flayed off through torture,' recalled Mehri. 'By the time I arrived she had already been operated on twice. But she hadn't told the guards where her son was.

'One pregnant woman had the flesh literally hanging off her feet as a result of the systematic lashing of her soles. Another woman, Leila, was the sister-in-law of the revolutionary poet Said Sultanpour, who had been arrested during his wedding ceremony and shot within the week. Leila's legs were bandaged up to the knee. Her feet had been smashed to a bloody sponge, and red smudges were left on anything her feet touched.'

Later, Mehri and her child were transferred to a cell with eight other women, two of whom were Zoroastrians from the Fedayeen Minority, two members of Peykar, two from the Communist league and two from Rahe Kargar. There was also another little girl of four in the room. 'We put the children under the sink, and the rest of us sat around the walls of the tiny cell.' To make matters worse, the two Peykar women were Tavabs. One, Lida, was a polytechnic student, and the other, Zari, was the head of the women's block in 209.

'The sanitation in 209 was unspeakable,' explained Mehri. 'We didn't have any sanitary towels and pleas for them got us nowhere. My baby and the other small girl weren't given any milk. My toddler was obviously disturbed. When I was tortured, she was brought into the room. She cried and the interrogators hoped that this would be extra pressure to make me talk. One day in 209, she blindfolded her foam doll, and then beat the little doll so vigorously that it disintegrated under the blows.

'The air in the cell was stifling, and my daughter developed a heart condition. She would hit herself and pull her hair in frustration at being unable to breathe properly. The only thing that seemed to bring her comfort was the noise of the trolley that brought us food twice a day. Years later, when people would come to our house, she would ask them to show her the soles of their feet. She wanted to see if the visitor had been through torture.

'While I was spending time in block 209, every now and then I would be taken from my cell by the guards for interrogation. My interrogator was a mullah. Many girls I met in 209 alerted me that this mullah would take me into a quiet room and would try to sexually molest me. He put me on a chair in front of him. He was sitting in a chair opposite me and he edged slowly towards me so that his knees were pressing against mine. Then he asked me, "Do you smoke?"

'"Yes." I replied.

'"We don't give any cigarettes to women."

'"A cigarette does not distinguish between the sexes," I said.

'When they brought me back from Evin to Sanandaj prison, I came across horrifying encounters between prison guards and women prisoners.

'At Sanandaj there was a prison guard who went by the name of Kadkhoda – God looking over your shoulder. He was from Azerbaijan, very tall and with extremely wide shoulders. He had two responsibilities in Sanandaj. The first and foremost was as the official flogger – any prisoner picked up in their cell for "mischief-making" or other acts of resistance would be tied face down on a bed and whipped. At these whipping sessions, each time he raised the whip above his head he would utter in a loud, deep voice, "God is great! Khomeini is our leader!"

'His other responsibility was as the official representative of the Islamic court. He would escort prisoners from one prison to another, from the Komitehs to prisons all around the country. He had the use of a large Land Rover for this purpose. This was like those used by the military, with a two-seater cabin at the front and two benches at the rear which faced each other, where the prisoners would be seated, sometimes up to ten at a time. Like a good Islamic guard, he was married with two wives and six children. His face was sunken, with a thick, black beard which fell over the top half of his chest. After the court sentenced me, I was handed over to Kadkhoda's jurisdiction.

'"I will be taking you to your house so that you can have a meeting with your family," he told me. "After that we will drive straight to Evin."

'On the journey to my house I was so appalled at the thought that someone might see me in his Land Rover that I hid my face below the level of the dashboard for the entire journey. As soon as we reached the house I saw about 50 people, all dressed in black. They came out of the house – all of them were weeping openly. I tried to ask people the reason for their sorrow. No one would answer me. Finally, my father told me that my cousin had been shot to death by the Pasdars during an attack against Kurdish guerrilla opposition forces in the mountains. So my temporary homecoming was blackened by this tragic episode.

'My father thanked Kadkhoda for bringing me to see my family at this time. Then we climbed back into the Land Rover and headed off for Tehran. It was customary, and Kadkhoda knew it, that prisoners arriving after dark would not be admitted into prison. It was obvious that Kadkhoda had detoured to my family's house precisely so that we would not arrive at Evin until after dark. He had pulled this stunt many times with other women prisoners. As we drove into Tehran, he stopped the car in the city outskirts and turned off the engine. He turned around to me and asked, "Are you sleepy?"

'"No," I said, warily.

'"Let's go into the back of the car and sleep together," he suggested, ignoring my answer.

'"No, no – I am not sleepy at all. You go ahead and have a good sleep yourself. I promise you, for the sake of my little baby girl, I will not leave the car while you sleep. If you wish, you may handcuff me to the steering wheel or the front seat if you do not trust me whilst you are asleep."

'Ignoring me, he pressed on. "Come on, let's go into the back and sleep, like brother and sister."

'"No, I have never slept in the same bed as my brother!" I retorted.

'He asked, "Aren't you a communist?" I told him that that was what I'd been charged with. "Well," he said. "I thought you reds believed in free sex. What's the problem?"

'"Where did you get that idea from?" I said, shrinking back into the seat. "Listen, blindfold me and cuff me to the steering wheel so I can't escape if you must, but there's no way I'm getting in the back of that van with you. I'm no whore." At last he seemed resigned to defeat in the matter, and I spent a cold night chained up.

'The sexual adventurism of this Pasdar was well-known amongst the women prisoners of Sanandaj. Another woman, Golnaz, was brought from the Golden Fortress prison to Sanandaj in Kurdistan by Kadkhoda. Golnaz had already passed through doomsday in the Golden Fortress. During the night of her journey to Kurdistan, Kadkhoda stopped the Land Rover and removed the handcuffs from her wrists. He then suggested they go into the back of the vehicle and sleep together.

'Golnaz shouted at him. When he saw her resistance, to save face he said, "Oh, I was only trying to see how you would react. I have no desire to consort with such an impure communist infidel. I was looking to test your resolve, your resistance."

'Two other women prisoners, transported from Esfahan, a province in central Iran, to Kurdistan were the subject of his attention. One of them, Nastaran, was just 18 years old and had been in prison since she was 14. Once again, during the late evening, Kadkhoda offered his services to her.

'Later, Nastaran confided with other women prisoners in

Sanandaj prison. Some months later, another woman, Parveen, aged 28 and a supporter of the Fedayeen Majority, told of Kadkhoda's advances on her journey to prison. He started stroking her head, telling her what beautiful hair she had.

'"You communists, of course, you have no objection to using the contraceptive pill."

'"What do you mean?" asked Parveen.

'"How much do you love your husband?"

'"That's none of your bloody business!"

'"Do you still think of your husband? Do you remember how he looks?"

'"No, not very much – why are you asking these odd questions?"

Kadkhoda was not slow to reveal his real intentions once the subtle approach failed him once again: "Let's go and sleep together in the back of the car." Again, total rebuttal.

'Another woman prisoner, this time a Tavab, related a similar story. Behieh, from the Democratic Party of Kurdistan, married with a young child, told me of her journey to Sanandaj. She was forced to sleep with Kadkhoda in his Land Rover.

'My last encounter with Kadkhoda was when he hollered at me in front of interrogators, "You should have gone to the firing squad the first time you were captured."

'I shouted back at him, "If I was to have been shot after my first arrest, then you should have been shot six times – of course not for political offences!"'

'The interrogators and the judge all heard my words but said nothing.

'Kadkhoda was not a unique character amongst the Islamic prison guards. The second time that I was captured in Sanandaj and imprisoned, the interrogator was a real sadist. He took every opportunity to make sexual advances while he and I were alone in the interrogation room. Several days after my capture, he said to me, "Take these papers, fill them out and return tomorrow."

'They next day he returned and found the papers blank

'"Listen, you have just arrived. If you don't give us all the information that you have, I swear to Imam Khomeini that when you get out of this prison you will not leave alone, you will leave with a child!" The threat of rape was therefore most apparent from the outset if I did not comply with him.

'I spoke to a fellow prisoner about this incident. Her name was Akram. I wanted help with the only way out that I could see. She reluctantly gave me a handful of Diazepam tablets that her family had brought for her. I also got some other tablets. At six o'clock the next morning, I swallowed all of these pills at once. I had decided to take my own life rather than be forced to submit to the sexual assault by this Islamic guard.

'I slipped into a drugged sleep. When I opened my eyes I was in the city general hospital. Fortunately, some of the doctors and nurses were close friends of my family. The story of my suicide attempt raced through the city. Almost all of the prisoners got to hear of this. They heard that a girl from cell 27 had attempted suicide in order to preserve her honour in the face of the barbaric Islamic prison guards.

'On the second day of my first encounter with the Islamic prison guards – during my first period of capture – I tried to slit my wrists. On my way back to prison from the hospital after my sleeping-pill suicide attempt, a 14-year-old girl, a Tavab, accompanied me back to my cell. She asked me why I tried to take my life. I replied that the interrogator had given me an ultimatum – he would rape me if I did not provide the information that they wanted, which I was not prepared to do.

'As a result of this oppressive sexual threat from the guards at Sanandaj, several suicide attempts had been made by others while I was there. The overall atmosphere of repression within the prison system in Iran led to male as well as female prisoners attempting to take their lives. In one incident, a male prisoner had attempted to kill himself by cutting the main artery in his neck with a shard of glass from the bathroom mirror. However the guards arrived at that moment and managed to stop him doing so, but he was able to cut his tongue instead. Today, Kaveh lives in exile in Western Europe with only half of his tongue. This incident occurred in the same week that I overdosed.

'In the same prison, another political prisoner, from Komoleh called Khaled – a teacher – doused himself with petrol and set fire to himself. These atrocities were not unique to Sanandaj prison. Fozi, who was imprisoned at Marivan [50km from Sanandaj] was able to tell of many similar incidents. She was captured in a small village near Marivan. She was from a well-to-do, religious family in Sanandaj. They were supporters of a well-known Sunni mullah called Moftizadeh who co-operated with the Islamic regime and the Islamic revolutionary guards at the very beginning of the uprisings in Sanandaj in 1981, in order to eliminate the resistance of the opposition forces in Kurdistan. Later on, he himself was captured and imprisoned for many years by the Islamic regime.

'Fozi intended to join the Kurdish guerrillas in the mountains of Kurdistan to fight against the regime. She was young, attractive and strong-willed. When captured, she was taken to the local headquarters of the Islamic guards. They kept her in detention in Marivan for some time until she was sent to the Islamic court in Sanandaj.

'When she arrived at the women's block there, she was no longer the same young woman who had wanted to fight in the mountains alongside the guerrillas. The pain and agony of torture had broken her psychologically and she was deranged. She was suffering from gangrene and her lower legs oozed a white and yellow pus from opened wounds. The odour from this rotten, infected flesh carried a long way. She was unable to stay in any cell within the block. Neither the Tavabs nor the intransigents nor the passives would accept her in their cell because of the stench from her wounds. As a result she was left in the corridor of the block.

'In winter, the temperature in Kurdistan would drop to between minus 10°C-20°C, but throughout Fozi was kept out in the corridor, where there was no heating. During this time, I took her to the bathroom to help her bathe herself about four or five times. No one else would help her. I helped her dress and wash her injured legs. I assisted her in feeding herself.

'Each day she would sit on the cold floor, cursing at the Tavabs. She would especially swear at a woman called Zohreh Alipour, who was the chief Tavab in the women's block at Sanandaj. She had been captured in conjunction with a man who was in the leadership of the Komoleh, in Sanandaj [his story is told in chapter five]. Fozi would sit in her corridor and holler out, "Zohreh Alipour, last night the Islamic chief judge came to your cell and slept with you! You whore!"

'Whenever I wanted to help Fozi to the shower-room, she would refuse to go, warning me of hidden cameras in the shower cubicle, installed there by the Islamic chief judge. This was, she maintained, so that he could ogle at us in the shower. Only if I accompanied her, undressed, into the shower would she agree. The treatment that she had suffered had resulted in this paranoia.

'After two months they took her to the revolutionary guards' headquarters in Sanandaj. When she returned, snow covered the ground everywhere. The harsh Kurdish winter had descended upon the land. The guard who brought her back said that she would be sent to a mental health institution in time. He ordered me to help her shower.

'"Why me?" I asked.

'"Fozi has requested that you should escort her to the shower."

'While I was washing her, I asked why she had put on so much weight. She kept repeating, over and over, that the chief judge was spying on us in the shower cubicle. She seemed extremely anxious.

'"I'm very scared. I've written a letter for you. It is in the pocket of my dress. Take that letter with you, but promise me that you will not read it until I have left here."'

'Unsure of what the letter might contain, I complied with her request. I took special care to hide the envelope from the guards. When she left the prison block, I opened the envelope and read Fozi's letter. It read as follows:

'The night I was captured I was taken to the Islamic guard headquarters in Marivan. Late at night in a solitary cell, suddenly the light went off. A guard came into my cell with a coal-miner's lantern. He clamped his hand over my mouth and raped me.

'Later on, we heard from the prison guards that on her way through to the province of Hamedan, Fozi had managed to escape from her guards and fled into the snow-covered mountains. However, she was never found, nor had she returned to her family or friends.'

Harir was captured in June 1987 when Islamic guards came to her house. Her brother was a Kurdish guerrilla in the Komoleh who had been killed by the Islamic guards in a mountain skirmish. The brother's affiliations made the family a target.

Everyone except Harir was out. The guards tore the place apart, searching for hidden guns. They dug up the floor but still found nothing, as Harir looked on.

The guards took out their disappointment on Harir. She was blindfolded, bound and dragged screaming from the house. Neighbours informed her family what had happened upon their return – there was no official notification of arrest.

For over six months the family incessantly badgered the Islamic courts as to the whereabouts of their daughter. But the courts denied that she had ever been arrested. Eventually, the courts succumbed to the family's insistent demands and acknowledged her arrest. It was claimed that this was because a gun had been found with her. They told the family that she would be hanged.

The guards had no information about any political activity by Harir. The usual method in such cases was to pile on the pressure until the prisoner falsely incriminated herself. The guards demanded she confess her association with the opposition in Kurdistan. Every day for the first six months she was strapped down to the bed frame and interrogated for between three to five hours. The soles of her feet were beaten raw and bleeding in these sessions. Her torturers would sit next to her, wearing only their undergarments, to intimidate her sexually.

At other times she would be taken, blindfolded, to the interrogation cell door to listen to the screams of others under torture. 'It would have been easier to be under torture myself, than to be forced to sit and listen to it happen to others, and be able to do nothing to help.'

She was not going to incriminate herself, as she had nothing to say. At the end of the six months, a new torturer took over, upping the stakes to force a confession. The first session was the most brutal she had experienced. At the end of this day, the interrogator told her, 'I'll give you 24 hours to confess, or I swear by Imam Khomeini, I'll rape you' – the guarantee of her violation with an oath on religious authority.

Harir spent the night confronting her bleak options. At dawn she made her final decision. She faced rape at the hands of this monster or the scaffold – perhaps both – whatever she said. She decided to go with dignity and take her own life. But her prison cell did not contain the tools for the job. All she had was a jam jar.

Harir waited for the corridor to go quiet, and smashed it against the wall. She now had a jagged edge. She slashed her left wrist. As the blood began to flow, she thought, 'This isn't quick enough', and cut into the crook of her arm with the glass shard, slippery with her own blood. It ran quickly now, warming the cold concrete floor as it formed an expanding pool around her. She slipped into unconsciousness, grateful for the release, 'feeling that I would never have to face the monster who had tortured me, and would rape me.'

Dawn was a bad time for suicide. The guard was changed and the new shift went around the cells to wake the prisoners up for prayer. Harir was discovered unconscious, the cell floor running with blood. She was rushed to the infirmary. The wounds were deep and became infected as a result of the inescapable prison filth. However, she pulled through.

Two months after her attempted suicide, with the guards still unable to force a false confession from her, she was released.

The situation of women prisoners in the Golden Fortress while I was there was every bit as vile as experienced by Mehri and Harir. If possible, it was worse than the position we male prisoners were in.

'Intransigent' women were taken to block 8 in section 3. This was the women's quarantine block, where they were crammed in the same way as the men. If any women presumed to complain at this treatment, Haji Davoud and his entourage would storm into the block and instruct the women to replace their blindfolds, don hijab and face the wall. Then they would be beaten.

Haji Davoud got a particular thrill from kicking women on the backside. The force from such a kick on a slightly built teenager from this obese bear of a man would send the victim flying through the air. This caused persistent bleeding, a common complaint among women prisoners. Injuries would receive no treatment. You had to hope that they would heal by themselves – often a vain hope in insanitary conditions that frequently led to infection.

One night in October 1983, Haji Davoud and his wrecking crew tore into block 8, beating women left and right, dragging them out of the cells to another block. They were forced to stand, blindfolded, facing the wall for 24 hours. After this, with the strength drained from their pain-racked legs, they were told to sit cross-legged. They were then divided from each other by plywood partitions which were so close they touched their shoulders. At the back of each stood a woman Tavab, watching every move. Any move meant a beating. Welcome to doomsday.

The experience of women in doomsday was similar to that of the men. It was only a few weeks for some and a few months for others before they were screaming uncontrollably, pleading for Haji Davoud to come and listen to what they had to say. Some of them would scream, calling for him to bring pens and confession paper so that they could write everything they knew. Others were both crying and laughing insanely at the same time. This is something I don't need to recount second-hand, as the guards would broadcast the women's voices through the public address system and filmed those confessing to further harass those who had not yet broken.

We were forced to sit for long hours on hard concrete floors – often from three in the morning to three in the evening – watching these innocent young girls incriminating themselves, their parents, their friends and comrades; even the very values and conditions that they had fought so hard for.

Haji Davoud was not satisfied with just political incrimination. He would ask these innocent young girls to recount their sexual misconduct. Some of them were forced, in this way, to incriminate their parents. In reality, this was the women's only way to satisfy Haji Davoud so he would release them from doomsday. Then, suddenly, the noise of many voices would arise from one end of the corridor: 'God is great, Khomeini is Imam! Down with America, down with Russia, down with Israel, down with Saddam! Down with communists and down with *Monafegh*!'

This was a sign of non-approval of the confession by the kapos – they wanted more detail, more information from the wretched girl prisoners. Many of them were captured while still sitting at their desks in their high schools. Once the echo of the Tavabs' slogans had died, these poor girls were forced to make even more abhorrent and false sexual incriminations against themselves, their parents and their comrades.

Many women who went through this experience lost the ability – or will – to speak and their powers of concentration. Some were forced to take their own lives, the only way to end the hell of doomsday which still existed in their minds. Throughout the prison the majority walked alone, ate alone, slept alone and kept to themselves. Doomsday had taught them not to communicate in any way with any other human being. It was such a harrowing and dark experience that in almost all cases this painful lesson was well learned the first time around.

Around the first week of July in 1988 in Evin, as in Gohardasht, the television was taken away. Those newspapers approved for the prisoners were stopped, all visits to the infirmary were cancelled and any official callings of prisoners ceased. All visits by relatives, usually fortnightly, were cancelled. In effect, all the blocks were put on a 'quarantine footing'. No one could enter, no one could leave.

Susan, a woman prisoner in Evin at this time, related what she and the other women were subjected to. Thirty Mojahedin women prisoners were brought into her block, identified as intransigents by the regime. 'One night during the first week of July, the prison guards started to call out their names and they were taken out in batches of five,' she recalled.

'It was said that they were to be transferred from Evin to Gohardasht. By the end of that evening, all 30 had been taken away. One of these 30 women was Maryam Golzadeh Ghafouri, the daughter of Ayatollah Golzadeh Ghafouri, a prominent religious figure who had become a Mojahedin supporter. We knew that they had been taken away for execution, as a few days before the male prisoners had told their families that a massacre was on the way, and the news had filtered back to us.

'Even though we were in this atmosphere of constant executions, we were still unable to fully comprehend the extent of the massacre itself.

'The first prisoners to be shot were Mojahedin supporters. The killing of the Mojahedin continued throughout the month. Once the Inquisition had cleansed its bloody hands after dealing with the Mojahedin it turned on the left groups.

'In these early weeks of the massacre, we had heard Ayatollah Ardebili, the head of the Islamic Judiciary, on the television. During a Friday prayer session at Tehran University, he had called for the execution of all *Monafegh* and communist prisoners who presented a danger to the regime. Thousands who had joined this prayer session dutifully chanted along with his macabre verses.

'It was clear that the decision to unleash the massacre had been taken and endorsed at the very highest levels of government and that the pulpit was used to gain support for the elimination of the jailed opposition. As this was the word of the Imam, no one could openly oppose it and expect to live.

'All of those left-wing prisoners who did not call themselves Muslim were executed. At least 200 women were executed in Evin including several women with severe disabilities as a result of the previous torture that the Islamic regime had inflicted upon them. Those who had passed through the Inquisition, those who had said they were moslems but no longer prayed, would get five doses of the lash every day – to match each of the five daily prayer sessions. This would continue until they either submitted to prayer or were slowly flogged to death. The situation was quite unclear – some accepted prayer in fear of a further session in the Inquisition resulting in their execution. Others still continued to resist.

'In addition to refusing to pray, some prisoners undertook a hunger strike in protest. One girl, Sorour Davish Kohan, died from her five-times daily lashes. Some women prisoners took their own lives because they felt that this was the only way to end their suffering. Maheen Badavi, who had become well-known as a symbol of women's resistance within the prisons – especially for surviving a prolonged period in Haji Davoud's doomsday – took this way out, such was the degree of torture inflicted on her. A number of other women committed suicide by slashing their wrists with shards of glass. Another group tried the same method, but were saved from death by emergency treatment in the infirmary. Despite these desperate protests, the authorities persisted with the lashing sessions.

'Other women tried an overdose of sleeping pills. One woman, Efat, a supporter of the Mojahedin, poisoned herself by swallowing hair-removal cream. In the Islamic religion, men and women have to clean themselves totally and even get rid of pubic hair, hence the women being given hair-removal cream. It took a full two days for her to die.

'Two girls who endured the five daily lashings undertook a 23-day hunger strike. Weakened by the strike, both slipped into unconsciousness. The extent of the regime's concern was indicated by the fact that they were brought back to consciousness by being lashed.

'Most of these lashing sessions were conducted by the prison's deputy governor a well-known torturer and murderer in Evin who had participated in all of the previous massacres there, from 1980 onwards. From being a simple guard, he had risen to the post of deputy governor at Evin; given due recognition for his consistent brutality throughout these years.'

The mother who was flogged by her own 13 year-old Tavab daughter in Evin shows the hostility of a regime that could cynically pit women against each other. I have seen many women, young and old, in prison, bleeding from the feet, others with infected legs – women who were no longer able to stand and forced to drag themselves between solitary and torture cells in block 209, crawling blindfolded while keeping their hijab in place by gripping it between teeth clenched in fear, anger and agony. I saw them myself, crawling from one end of the block corridor to the other, leaving a bloody trail smeared on the floor behind them.

Thousands of young women taken to the prisons and torture chambers of the Islamic regime received similar treatment – the same physical and mental assault faced by male prisoners, plus the semi-routine use of rape.

The regime has never denied the rape of hundreds, possibly thousands, of women held to be virgins when condemned to death. This final terror is lawful, and justified by religion as taught by the ayatollahs.

The Islamic regime is an enemy of more than half of our population. Women cannot advance their interests while this regime continues to exist. Thousands of women have been, and continue to be, held in its prisons and many more have lost their lives – all for doing no more than struggling for their rights. This is a testimony to the prominent role women play in the struggle against the Islamic regime.

Ultimately, the Islamic regime will be shattered on the rock of women's resistance, which all its terror and brutality can only strengthen. The regime is sitting on a volcano; it is just a matter of when it erupts.

Chapter 21

The Islamic Courts

When a suspect is arrested he will not be told what he is being charged with. Neither will he be allowed to consult a lawyer throughout his interrogation. Almost all suspects will be tortured, sometimes so severely that they die. During this time most prisoners will be held in solitary. They will not be allowed visits from their families before their file is completed.

The defendant will then be taken before an Islamic court. This is held in secret in the prison. It has no jury and no counsel for the defence. What is presented as evidence of guilt has been extracted under severe torture. The defendant cannot present witnesses in his or her defence. There is no right of appeal.

A prisoner is usually taken to court blindfolded. They have no idea who their accusers are, who has given evidence against them or what the prosecution case is. Court proceedings are summary – often barely five minutes. Often the presiding judge (a mullah) is also the prosecutor and court recorder. In some

243

cases, these judges have also acted as executioner. One famous mullah, Ayatollah Khalkhali, who died in 2003, was known as 'the hanging judge' and acted in exactly this way during the first years of the Islamic regime.

Another, Hadi Ghaffari, participated in the capture, torture, interrogation and execution of many prisoners in Evin between 1980 and 1984. Now he also is a sitting member of the parliament, and heads a large industrial complex which used to produce women's and men's underwear under the name of Starlight during the Shah's reign. This lucrative business, now the Al-Hadi Foundation, was given to him by a decree of Ayatollah Khomeini, designating it a non-profit making organisation under Hadi Ghaffari's care.

The only others present at these Islamic court trials are security guards. The judge will invariably accuse the defendant of being an enemy of God, the people, Islam and the Imam Khomeini, a paid stooge of imperialism, Israel and Saddam Hussein and variations on these themes. These rantings constitute the reading of the charges, the presentation of the prosecution case and the summing-up, all in one. It is the nearest the accused gets to the proprieties of a trial.

Over the past 15 years, hundreds of thousands of political prisoners have gone to these courts subjected to a barrage of accusations, sentenced and thrown back to the cells – all in less time than it takes to make a cup of tea. Tens of thousands have been summarily executed, others have been flogged and tortured before being shot.

Custodial sentences begin from the day of the trial, not from the day of arrest. I spent a year and a half in prison before my trial; others spent two or three years. All this is time served in addition to the sentence handed down by the court.

The prisoner will be held on remand until something can be unearthed about him for trial. One trial may not be the end of it. At any time during a sentence, prisoners can be brought before another court for retrial. Many of my own comrades were retried in this manner and their sentences increased – some were summarily executed.

Sentences included public hanging, the firing squad or worse. Ali Shokouhi, the general secretary of Rahe Kargar, was given 500 lashes before being shot, for the crime of defending Marxism at his trial. Manijeh Hodayi, a female member of Peykar, was given the same sentence, again for openly defending her revolutionary activities against the Islamic regime.

These are not isolated cases. Many others, most nameless and undocumented, suffered the same brutal end for standing by their principles.

Evin's Islamic courts, where I was tried, are located in a central building, also housing branches of the Islamic prosecutor's office. Here, too, was the office responsible for the transfer of prisoners from one jail to another, throughout the country. It was also a holding centre for those awaiting trial.

Interrogations take place on the ground floor of the courthouse. A prisoner due for interrogation will be taken from his block to a corridor in the central building, and wait to be dragged to the interrogation cell. Whenever I was here, I could hear the rhythmic thwack of the interrogators' sticks and the screams and cries of the tortured. Prisoners going to the infirmary came through this building, the central nervous system for the prison through which we would pass en route from one horror to the next.

Paradoxically, I always looked forward to my visits because it brought together prisoners from all over the prison and further afield – it gave us a chance to find out what was happening outside our own little corner. If I were lucky enough to sit next to a recently arrested prisoner, I might pick up bits and pieces about what was happening outside.

Curiosity had its dangers, however. The person sitting next to mc could bc a Tavab or even an interrogator, trying to trap me into giving information or encouraging you to break prison rules – a common tactic used by the guards. Even if the new companion was all right, you could be caught murmuring fragments of prison news by one of the many guards who constantly patrolled back and forth.

Early one morning, 18 months after my arrest, I was taken from my cell to Evin's central building. I was put amongst about 50 others who sat facing the wall, blindfolded. None of us knew where we were headed for. As I sat there, I heard my first name, then my father's, called out several times by a guard. I hesitantly raised my hand. The guard yanked on my sleeve and ordered me to follow him up a flight of stone steps. Then he ordered me to sit in a corridor and I was on my own.

About three hours passed before another guard arrived and called out my name again. I raised my hand and was led to the next port of call. As I walked in his wake, I tried to watch him from below my blindfold. With a start, I realised that his head only came up to my chest – he could not have been more than 14 years old, striding along with an oversized Kalashnikov slung over his shoulder.

I was taken down a narrow corridor to a room on the left. My young guard went behind a desk. There were two other desks in the room. The one on the right had a man of 50 to 60 years old behind it. I later found out that he was called Mirfendereski, a legal expert in the Ministry of Justice and the court recorder. Facing him was a young, stocky mullah with a light complexion. Now I knew that this must be the Islamic court. I warned myself to be careful. My life would depend on the answers I gave to their questions.

The mullah told me to take off my blindfold. He was flicking through a thick file in a jerky nervous manner, his thick beard nearly brushing the pages as he turned them. Years later I found out his name was Haji Mobasheri, a man responsible for executing thousands. He asked me my name, my father's name and my occupation, all the time leafing through my file. Then he asked, 'Is there a gun involved in your case?'

'No,' I replied.

He then began to ask the same questions that I had been asked so many times before. The older man opposite, who was also flicking through a file, lifted his eyes to me and asked, 'Are you sure there is no gun involved in this case?' It was obvious that they had not even attempted to properly review the paperwork for my case.

'No,' I said. 'I've never even touched a gun. I wouldn't know how to use one.'

The questioning was interrupted by a shout from Haji Mobasheri: 'All you counter-revolutionaries have taken up arms against the Islamic Republic. If a donkey is caught in heavy traffic, it will stop and wait for it to clear before it moves again. You communists haven't even got that amount of sense. You tried to move against our revolution at its height, without waiting for things to settle. That's why we have killed you by the tens of thousands.'

'Sir, I swear on Imam Khomeini's head that I have had nothing to do with guns.'

Neither had read the case notes. They were just hoping that I would confess to having a gun. If I did that, it would be a short journey from the court to the firing squad. There was no way I was going to plead guilty to charges that I had spent a year and a half on the torture rack denying.

'Shut up,' snapped the mullah. 'Until you come up with the information that you are holding back, you will be sent back to 209 – till you rot, if necessary.'

So that was my trial – I could have written it down in full on the back of a cigarette packet.

My file was forwarded to Section 6 of the Islamic prosecutor's office – 'repeat interrogations'. I went back to 209, to go through the mill, again. The chief interrogator, Masoud, told me to sign a statement, that read: 'Having refused to accept the charges at my first trial, I give the right to the court to hand down the death penalty if the interrogators are able to find any new information incriminating me.'

I signed this, telling them, 'You can't get any incriminating evidence on me, anyway.' It took the interrogators nine more months to get enough new material to warrant another trial. This time, when I was taken back to Evin's central block, I noticed that there was another person sitting in the middle of the court room. When Haji Mobasheri, the judge, told me to take off my blindfold, I saw this person was a heavily-veiled woman. When she spoke, I knew she was Mariam, Farhad's wife. She was there to give evidence against me. From the hesitation in her voice, and what she said, it was obvious she had been through a tremendous ordeal.

Mariam asked the judge if she could say, 'Hello' to me. She said that after her husband's execution, she had changed her mind about politics and the Islamic regime. She said that she had been sentenced to death but was hoping to have this commuted. I showed no reaction, but Farhad's execution had come as a shock. The last time I had seen him was when we were separated soon after our arrival in Evin. I had heard nothing since. The little he had said had obviously been too much.

'Brother Masoud, the chief interrogator, wanted me to come to the court to give further evidence about you. First I refused, as I didn't want to incriminate you. I'm sorry that it's me who is responsible for destroying your life. But lots of other information has been given about you by other prisoners. You shouldn't insist on denying it all. Accept some, and the judge will have a freer hand to pass sentence.'

As they did on Farhad, I thought bitterly.

I said, 'Most of this information has been given by you, and those arrested with you. No one else has incriminated me. Why should I accept your statements?'

Mobasheri turned to her and asked, 'Was this man a member of your organisation?'

'I have no information that would support that claim,' replied Mariam. 'Only my husband had that information, but he never told me.'

The judge then asked me, 'Did you have a cadre name within your organisation?'

'I have a pen name I write under,' I answered, 'but you couldn't call it a cadre name. I was using it ten years before the Islamic revolution. I have evidence to prove this at home.'

Then the judge went through the charges. I even got the donkey fable again. He probably trotted out this tired little tale to everyone who came through the doors and had forgotten I'd already heard it. The court ended at this point, and I was returned to my cell.

When I looked back at what had taken place in court, I realised that Mariam had played her hand with great skill. Even though under the shadow of the executioner, she had withheld extremely valuable information, any bit of which could have sent me to the firing squad. Rather than incriminate me, she had protected me. She had also told me that her husband was dead, that she too was under sentence of death and that her appearance was no act of wilful betrayal, but under of the pressure from the chief interrogator of Section 6.

The Islamic court is nothing more than the continuation of the interrogation procedures, with the difference that in 209 the information is extracted through torture, whereas in court, judges such as Gilani and Mobasheri force prisoners to incriminate themselves through the threat of the firing squad. The aim is to squeeze out the last piece of information. This not only incriminates the man in the dock, but anyone else.

The morning of my move to the Golden Fortress in autumn

1983 was the only indication I had that I had been sentenced. This happened three months after the trial. But it was another six months before I found out what the sentence was – 15 years.

When a woman was hauled up before the courts, she would first be asked whether she was married or not. Then the judge would generally remark that the accused was involved in politics to get a husband. If she was married then she was judged to be successful in it, if she was single, then she was obviously still trying. Older women were told, 'You should be ashamed of yourself, chasing men at your age. Why, you're older than my sister, and she has three grandchildren!' If the accused had children, she too was told to hang her head in shame – running about with big ideas in her head when she should be at home looking after the family. That a woman could be political because she believed in what she was fighting for was incomprehensible to the Islamic judiciary.

Shohreh's story follows here, as told to a woman who shared some of her time in jail. Shohreh had a father who became a candidate for the Mojahedin in the first Islamic election in 1980. It did not take him long to realise that he should flee the country before the Islamic courts sent him to the next world. Young Shohreh, aged 14 at the time, was brought into Evin prison by the Islamic guards. She was told that she was a hostage for her father. Until her father came to Evin in person, she would not be released.

Shohreh underwent intense torture. When the interrogators in Evin were disappointed with the results, namely their lack of success at extracting her father's location, they accused her of being a member of Rahe Kargar, of being a Fedayeen Minority supporter and of having responsibility for issuing propaganda for the east Tehran section of Rahe Kargar. If this was not enough subversive activity for anyone, she was accused of having responsibility for the provisions committee for the west

Tehran section of the Rahe Kargar organisation. Imagine, a 14–year-old girl, controlling the intricate planning operations over whole cities of not one but two large political groups.

Under these pretexts, she was taken off to the so-called Islamic courts of justice. There, the court was presented with signed confessions for this so-called criminal conduct. These signed confessions could have only been obtained under torture. The court branded her a *mohareb*, a non-believer who had taken up arms against Islam. This is what she told her comrades after just ten minutes in the court: 'The judge, after asking me my name and my father's name, asked the prosecutor, "Is she to be shot?" The prosecutor [the same person who interrogated her in the torture room] replied, "Yes, Haji." Then the judge said to me, "Get lost! We won't see you anymore!"' She was returned to her cell to collect her belongings and took the opportunity to recount the brief court appearance to her cellmates. Then she was shot.

Harir, who we have already met, recounts her brief visit to the courthouse in Sanandaj in 1990: 'Five and a half months after my arrest, one day around ten in the morning, a security guard opened the door to my solitary cell. He said to me, "You can take a shower today and wash your clothes." Two months had passed since I had last been permitted to do so.

'As I had no other clothes with me in the cell, after my shower and laundry I had to return to my cell wearing the wet clothes. Back in my cell, I had to remove my washed clothing to allow it to dry. Dry or not, I had to put them back on fairly quickly. I did not want to be seen naked by the lecherous eyes of the guards. Luckily, none of them came by before my clothes had dried.

'Later, a guard returned, saying, "Pick up your bag. We are leaving." I was led out of the solitary block. I could see his distinct military uniform from underneath my blindfold. I guessed the

251

trip must be one that would take me outside of this prison. One guard came up to me and handcuffed my wrists. I started to argue with him. "Who do you think I am, a criminal?"

'The young guard told me in a quiet murmur, "Don't be angry. Today these cuffs are on your wrists, tomorrow they will be on mine."

'Then a deep, loud voice bellowed out, "Brothers, are you ready?" A number of voices replied. "Yes, we are ready." Then again, "How about your cartridges?" "They are ready too, brother," came the reply, repeated by all the guards around me. "Get ready to fire, God be with you!" roared the deep voice one more time.

'I was very shaken. I wondered whether they would be taking me to Evin, perhaps to complete the court proceedings against me. But the car that I had been bundled into stopped somewhere in the middle of the city. The guards with me told me to take my blindfold off. I was taken into a building, which I recognised as the central headquarters of the police during the Shah's regime.

'They took me to the second floor, where I was led to the Islamic revolutionary court department. There were two rectangular tables full of papers and files relating to prisoners in the court. The judge sat behind one table and the court recorder behind the other.

'The recorder had a thick beard, but was wearing no Islamic robe or turban. He looked around 40–45 years old. The judge was a young man, only about 30. He too had neither cassock nor turban. He was wearing what looked like house pyjamas, made of a very fine white cloth – cotton or silk. His trouser legs had ridden up to his knee so I could see the lower half of his leg from where I was sitting. On his desk, in addition to many fat prisoners' files, there was also a large aluminium tray full of melon peel. By one corner of this table, close to where he was sitting, stood a black-and-white lamb. Every so often, the lamb would bleat and the judge would pick up a couple of pieces of melon peel and fed the lamb with them. I was expecting to see the common features of the Islamic court, not a judge in pyjamas with his trousers rolled up to his knees playing nursemaid to a lamb.

'The recorder told me to take a seat, one of several in the middle of the floor which faced the judge and the recorder. I took a seat and as soon as I sat down the court recorder started to read out the charges made against me by the interrogators: "Armed uprising against the Islamic state. Composing poetry of an anti-Islamic nature. Inciting the community and school-children to oppose the Islamic regime. Reading and distributing anti-Islamic government propaganda."

'As I was listening to this list of fabrications and falsehoods, the judge interrupted. "Are you Harir? You should have been put in front of the firing squad the last time that you were here! Go to Hell!"' He didn't take his eyes off the lamb as he spoke, stroking its haunches and feeding it from the palm of his hand. Upon his curt dismissal, the court recorder dragged me out of the room and handed me back to the guards who had driven me from prison that morning.

'Back in the jail, I was taken from a solitary cell to a normal block, occupied by many women inmates. I thought that I would definitely be set free, that the judge had exonerated me – in his own peculiar way – as there was no incriminating evidence against me whatsoever. Only my brother had been an active supporter of one of the opposition groups, Komoleh.

'Five days later, a guard came to see me and told me again to collect my plastic bag of possessions and follow him. Again I was taken from the prison to the old police headquarters building. This time I thought that I would be set free. There, they made me sign a piece of paper acknowledging the final judgement on my case. I was so excited that I could hardly stop myself from weeping with joy and relief.

'Just as I picked up the pen to sign the document, I saw that, to my horror, it was not one for my release, but for imprisonment for eight more years. I refused to sign, but the guards told me that if I did not then the judge could easily get angry and change his decision from eight years to life. Reluctantly, sobbing away, I signed the wretched document.'

CHAPTER 22

ESCAPE

I n mid-1990 a thaw began. We were allowed family visits in
Gohardasht. Restrictions on books and other literature
were relaxed. Medical treatment was made more readily
available. And forced communal prayer was abandoned. Around
200 prisoners who had completed their sentences but had
refused to make televised confessions were finally paroled, often
up to five years after their proper release date. Another 500
prisoners received pardons. Others, many of whom had spent
eight to ten years in jail, were given leave of absence for a
month or so, to stay with their families. I was one of these.

My family had been campaigning hard for my release, going
from one government agency and department to the next to put
my case. One mullah asked for one million Touman (about
£90,000) for my freedom. My wife and father talked to me about
this on a prison visit but I made it clear that this was unacceptable,
even if the cash could be raised. But to discuss this, we had to
resort to gestures and allusions because we were separated by

screens in the visiting area. If someone from the prison authorities found out that someone else from another department was going to get his palm greased, then they would blow the whistle – not out of any honest reaction to corruption, but from pique that someone else was making money and not them.

Eventually, a prison middle man managed to extort 200,000 Touman from a cousin of mine who was naive enough to take his vague promises of release as good coin. He'd been had, as my name was already listed for a month's home leave.

Brought before Haji Nasirian in his office in late 1990, I was told that the arrangement was my family had provided the deeds to a cousin's house as security against me fleeing the country once outside the prison gates. Thoughts flooded into my head, but one raged through like a torrent, sweeping all else aside: Once I'm out, I'm never going back! How do I do it? How do I get out and stay out?' I wasn't going to be satisfied by a peek under the blindfold at freedom. I was determined that the blindfold was going to come off for good.

Two years earlier, I would not have accepted such a compromise. But the massacres had made it plain that we were not only prisoners, but hostages. The regime would not hesitate to kill every one of us whenever it considered it expedient. Momentarily, they had left the door ajar. We needed to push it and run before it slammed shut forever.

This had to be done without a compromise of principle. Freedom at the expense of a confession, of a renunciation of beliefs, or of disclosing the names of others would have been too high a price. But, just for the moment, it was possible to walk through the jail's heavy iron gates without such a toll being demanded.

About half the 200 men on my block had already visited their families and returned. They were eagerly quizzed about their impressions. The answers seemed encouraging: the prisoners had been well received, even welcomed, by those outside. This was in contrast to the early 1980s, when there was no wide support for the opposition and neighbours who you had known for years would inform on you to the Islamic committees. This identification with the regime had evaporated, leaving behind sullen resentment of it, and an increasingly open respect for those who had fought back and paid the price.

About a week after my interview with Haji Nasirian, I was called to a visit from my family at about 10am, along with the other nine men in my visiting batch. My family had been waiting at the prison since 5am, filling in forms and the like, as had many other families on this standard visiting day. Most families wanted to get in and out of the prison as swiftly as possible. Visits were often harrowing experiences, and Evin wasn't a place you wanted to hang around.

In the visitors' waiting room, women hugging framed photographs of their sons and daughters to their chest under their chador showed these pictures to other families, explaining that this loved one had been shot or hanged. They were there to find out where the bodies of their murdered kin had been hidden. Macabre though this was, it was the main way information about the massacre spread, helping families to gauge its extent.

As usual, I was taken through the prison, but instead of going to a visiting booth, I was led to the main office. I had no idea what was happening, but dared not ask my guards.

Before me stood a prison official. 'Your family is here to take you home for your month's visit. Remember, we will be watching you constantly – whatever you do, wherever you go. Whether or not you will be released hinges on how you behave.'

No one had referred to my release since my interview with Haji Naserian, and no prospective date given at the time. The idea was to catch each prisoner unawares, so no arrangements could be made between prisoners. This meant that I was not primed with messages from cellmates for those outside.

The official motioned a guard to take me to an adjoining room. My clothes, shoes and body were searched for messages. I was led out into the courtyard, and sat in the back of a Jeep, with one armed guard next to me. I remained blindfolded.

The guard beside me asked, 'How do you feel now? You were very sick last time I saw you.'

'I'm still not well,' I replied, 'Maybe I can get some medical treatment while I'm on leave. But where do you know me from?' He said he recognised me from a particularly brutal beating I received in the 'jogging protest' at Gohardasht. By this time we were almost at the big main gate. The guards at the security post checked my papers and removed my blindfold.

The gates swung open with the screech of iron on iron and the hum of electrical motors. Before me stood my wife, three sisters and father, bathed in the early afternoon of a bright sunny day. You have no idea what a beautiful sight that is.

Upon seeing me one of my sisters fainted. We had to carry her 250 metres across waste ground to where the rest of my family waited: about 20 of them, with several cars and a minibus. With them waited many friends I had not seen for long, long years. None of this seemed real. I had not seen a world without walls for so long that it now seemed strange and wonderful beyond belief. I was surrounded by sun, sky, family and friends. I could see children returning from school; experiences I had been robbed of for years.

It was odd. I was having difficulty walking, not just because I was so weak, though that was true, but because I had been confined for so long that, out in the open, I just couldn't get my bearings. There was no wall before me to adjust my perspective to. Gloriously disorientated, feeling a sense of agoraphobia, I reeled around like a drunkard. Friends clasped me from either side and steered me towards our transport. We clambered joyously into the vehicles: me in the back of a car, along with my wife.

On arriving home, the celebrations began. The family had splashed out on a live lamb, which was ceremonially slaughtered and cooked. This is a traditional form of welcome. Beasts as large as camels are sometimes bought live and feasted on in this way – though we wouldn't have got one in our oven. The lamb was divided up, making sure that those neighbours hardest hit by the times got their share first. The party got into full swing. Groups of two, four, ten friends arrived in a steady stream, bearing flowers, cakes and drinks. My oldest daughter made sure that everyone was made welcome.

As people finished eating, I unconsciously went straight into my prison routine. I went around the house picking up dishes. In automatic pilot, as the partygoers looked on curiously, I carried the stack of crockery into kitchen and began washing up. My eldest daughter followed on my heels.

'Dad, what are you doing? Stop and go back into the party. Please!'

I insisted that I was going to do the dishes, that I felt guilty about leaving them around. Male friends of the family who had followed me in were horrified: it just isn't done for a man to do such jobs in Iran. 'For God's sake stop! If you carry on like this, you'll have our wives expecting us to wash up too!'

But the more they pleaded, the more I dug my heels in.

Doubt was nagging at me as I milled around the party. As the night drew on and people left I became more jittery. Why? Ten years of bromide, beatings and isolation are not good for a man. 'I hope my wife won't be disappointed with me' I thought, 'There's no way I'm going to be able to perform as expected of a husband – especially after an absence of ten years.'

I was anxious about what sort of relationship would be possible with my children. They had grown up without me. I watched them throughout the night: they seemed like strangers. My 14-year-old girl was now a woman. My daughter was a teenager. And my son was now a gangly 13-year-old, as tall as his father. How was it possible, given all this time and all that the whole family had been through, for me to take up the mantle of father?

That night, I dreamed I was still in prison. I was hiding in my cell and the guards were looking for me. I was in for a beating. I was shaken awake by my wife, horrified at the way I thrashed about and screamed in my sleep. It was as if my subconscious refused to accept that I really was free.

Every night, I would stay up while the family slept, hunched over the radio. I moved the dial over from World Service, Voice of America and Radio Moscow to the underground Iranian opposition stations and back again. I absorbed news like a sponge.

My difficulty with being outdoors persisted. The blue dome of the sky wheeled and lurched every time I poked my head outdoors as if I was drunk. I couldn't judge perspective, distances or speeds. Crossing the road seemed more hazardous for me than for a hedgehog. I couldn't judge the speed of approaching cars. Had I not been constantly watched and helped by patient family and friends, I would surely have bounced off someone's front bumper. Indeed, one time I was knocked to the ground as I stepped into the path of a moving vehicle. Fortunately I was only grazed and bruised. Better still, the concerned driver was behind the wheel of an ambulance.

For two weeks people came visiting: friends and relatives from the provinces, even Islamic associates of my father came with flowers. How things had changed since my arrest, when no one in the family dared to say that I had been arrested for fear of reprisals.

I saw a series of medical specialists, who examined each of my many ailments. After ten years of harsh jail life, this meant a considerable number of doctors. The gratifying thing was knowing that each one had pushed me up their long waiting lists as soon as they found out I was being temporarily released, and what my condition was. Some had year-long

queues. Perhaps more surprisingly they refused to accept a fee
– this at a time in Iran when money was the determining
factor in relationships.

My pleasure wasn't entirely personal. It was inspiring to know
that those of us who had held out against the regime in prison
had not been forgotten, but had won respect and admiration.
The welcome seemed to validate our whole struggle.

But I constantly reminded myself of the need to be watchful.
I had to be very circumspect on the phone or in gatherings. All
the people I spoke to I trusted, but words filter through. I also
needed to prepare to leave the country. This needed careful
planning, and from the second week onwards I devoted all my
time to preparations.

Using the pretext of medical treatment, I called a halt to
social visits. In Iran the tradition is that if someone visits you,
you repay them with a return visit. If I'd done that, I would have
been too busy seeing family and friends to even think of
skipping the country. My excuses made, I established contact
with comrades in my organisation.

I explained the urgency of getting out of the country.
Messages were left for me with a third person, so that there
would be no direct link with our house, which was
undoubtedly being watched. In this way, I got details of when
and where to meet someone who would take me the 1,000 or
so kilometres from Tehran to a town on the Turkish border, and
from there over into Turkey. I arranged to meet him in the
border town itself, so minimising my contact with others, who
might have to face heavy flack once I was safely away.

No one else knew about these plans, not even my wife. I
could not afford to have anyone give anything away, by even so
much as a change in behaviour, that might provoke suspicion.

I had already asked a relative to let us borrow a car for day
trips to visit provincial branches of the family. A sister lived
halfway between Tehran and the border, and this was our

ostensible weekend destination. As we loaded our things into the car for a supposed two-day trip, my family didn't know that this was not the final destination.

We arrived at her house at about 10pm, where we spent two or three hours with her family. At about 2am, I announced we were leaving for a wedding the next morning, between 400 and 500 kilometres further on – and conveniently near the border. Our car left, with a male friend driving, two sisters, two small children, my wife and myself – a natural-looking family outing, even if at an odd hour. I had grown a beard, my friend usually wore one and the women had covered their faces with all due propriety, so we even looked respectably Islamic.

It was not the best time to travel. Iran today is like a garrison. As you travel through it, you come across countless checkpoints along the road. Most are manned by Basij, the youth wing of the Islamic Guard. Some are in dugouts with the guard sitting behind a heavy machine gun, finger on the trigger, as if they are expecting the entire tank battalions of Iraq to come rumbling along their little country road, rather than just the casual traveller. After dark, such military readiness intensifies.

We were stopped leaving the city where my sister lived, waved down at a guards' kiosk at the roadside. A sandbag wall ran in front of it, over which poked the threatening muzzle of a heavy automatic. Three or four young khaki-clad men kept the gun company in its sandbag nest. Out came another guard, with a pistol at his side. He ordered our driver out of the car, asked to see identification, and then walked to the back of the car with him, to go through the boot. Satisfied that our family car was not the advanced guard of an Iraqi invasion, we were ordered on our way.

I was not too disturbed by this, as in the two weeks I had been out, such checks around Tehran had become familiar. Those outside Evin and Gohardasht just lived in a bigger prison, and the border of Iran was its perimeter wall.

As we drew nearer to the border, security checks became more frequent and rigorous. Now we were all ordered out, questioned – children included – and the whole car searched. Each checkpoint was more thorough than the last. At the town nearest the border, the last was the worst. It was a large brick building, sitting right in the middle of the road, at the centre of a roundabout. Guards armed with Kalashnikovs stood at each junction, stopping every car. Sandbagged machine-gun nests looked down every road.

We were all ordered out. One young guard checked the car, took up the back seats, and looked underneath the car. Another went through our bags, strewing their contents over the road in the search for guns, subversive literature or who knew what else. Anyway, whatever it was, he didn't find it.

We were asked the purpose of our journey. 'Where are you going, Haji Aghah?' one asked, his use of the deferential title thankfully indicating that I looked suitably religious and respectable. I showed our invitations: 'We're off to a wedding, brother.' They always like you more when you call them brother (I hoped).

My stomach was knotted and tense at this last hurdle. Anything could go wrong. I knew from bitter experience that we could be derailed if a guard took exception to the look of one of us. The 15-minute search crept slowly on before we were told to pack up our stuff and be on our way. Even then guards still watched from the windows. We took our time, not wanting to seem nervous or hurried in case we were pulled back for further questioning. No one did, and in another ten minutes we were on the road again and heading towards the border town.

It had been a long drive, with frequent interruptions, so by now it was almost midday. We were all hungry, thirsty and tired. The family stopped off at a village cafe. 'Eat whatever you like,' I announced. 'I'm picking up the tab for us all.'

I left with one of the small children, who was about six or

seven, telling the rest of our group that I was going to buy him a toy, and would meet them later. We wandered through the bazaar together, where we bought what caught the boy's eye. I was keeping a sharp eye, meanwhile, on those around me, to make sure we were not being watched or followed. Being a border town, security was very tight.

Satisfied that things were all right, we walked to a busy street corner, where people queued for a number of telephone booths. The queue inched slowly forward. I eventually got to a booth and tried to look busy; dialling, redialling, putting more money in and talking to no one on the other end, waiting for someone to approach me, as had been arranged.

No one came and eventually I had to put the phone down and leave, in case the length of my apparent calls attracted suspicion. We went to a nearby cafe for a tea, with sweets for my nephew. We then took another wander through the bazaar, buying souvenirs, and then returned, loaded with unwanted handmade crafts, to the booths to try my luck again.

Again I queued, and again eventually wound up in a booth, pretending to make phone calls. Again, no one came. I left, complaining to those around me that I could not get my connection, so that it would not be thought suspicious if I turned up later.

So, to another cafe, more sweets, more tea. My nephew was having a whale of a time. 'Let's go and buy some souvenirs', I said.

'But Uncle,' he said, 'you've just bought a lot. How many do you want?'

'Well, I think you need some too,' I said, trying to sound enthusiastic. 'Let's go and see what we can find.' And off we went again. We must have been the bazaar's best customers that day.

By now it was nearly 3.30pm, and my rendezvous had been set for 1pm. I was beginning to get very edgy. Thoughts elbowed their way, uninvited, into my mind, like drunken gatecrashers. What if this was a trap? Even if it wasn't, I might be picked up for behaving so suspiciously and sent back to Evin.

I had not seen my family for nearly three hours. They would want to know where I was, so I would soon have to get back to them. So back we went, me and the boy laden with souvenirs. We ran across one another, as the rest of the family was driving slowly through the streets looking for us. I told them that I was expecting to meet someone, but that he hadn't turned up. I said that I would go and look for him again, and if he couldn't be found we would begin to make our way to the wedding. They were quite surprised, as I had not mentioned a word of this before.

This would be my last run round the town. It was getting too dangerous to keep going over my tracks. If I did not find my contact, I would return with the family to Tehran. It was not wise to attempt to get over the border by myself. The freelance middle men who could be contacted to get you over the border could just as well lead you into a trap. Your journey over the border could turn out to be a walk into Evin. I had met enough of these unfortunate victims in prison.

So off we went once more. Through the bazaar, collecting more souvenirs, and again by a winding, hopefully leisurely looking, route to the phone booths. By now I was despondent and nervous. It felt like all eyes were on me. Hopefully anyone on the lookout would now understand my plight in failing to connect with my fictional party on the other end of the line, or shifts had changed, and I would be a new face to the next lot.

Kept going on hope, I queued, and again went into a booth. I wasn't looking at what I was dialling, but instead my eyes travelled around the area, searching for someone who looked like they might be looking for me. But there was no one, and after a fruitless 10 minutes, I left the booth with the heaviest of hearts.

For the last time, I took a slow walk round the 20 booths, telling myself if no one showed up, I would go straight back to Tehran.

The circuit of the booths was almost complete, and I began to head off with my, by now, very frustrated young nephew in tow. He knew something unusual was going on, but couldn't figure it out. As I passed the last phone booth, looking for some sign of recognition from the man inside, someone tapped me on the back. I felt sick. The security forces! How could I lie my way out of this? I turned.

The man before me smiled and asked, 'Have you finished your shopping yet?'

A wave of relief lifted me. This was my contact's introduction. But I had to make sure: 'What do you mean, my shopping?'

'I know I'm late', he said apologetically, 'I was supposed to be here at one o'clock. We don't have much time, I'll explain it all later.' He told me to take my nephew back to the family and make my excuses one more time, in such a way that none of my family would become suspicious.

This done, I was told to walk down the right-hand side of the main street, where I would be picked up by car. I handed back my confused nephew to my family – along with armfuls of bric-a-brac – and told them that I had run into an old friend, and that I was stopping with him for a few days.

'Go home, and I'll see you in Tehran soon.'

We said 'Goodbye' briefly and by now the family had become suspicious. Our driver wanted to know why I was rushing off with barely a word. 'Sorry,' I said. 'No time to explain. But you'd better leave soon.' Which, again, did little to quieten them.

I waved off the family car, crossed the road and walked down the right-hand side of the road. About a hundred metres down, a car pulled up, the door opened and I jumped in, turning to find myself sitting next to Ali, with whom I had made the arrangements in Tehran. I knew I was in safe hands. Still, they could see that I was tense and upset. I complained at the nerve-racking delay and the laxity of their security arrangements. Ali explained that the man who was supposed to contact me had also had to drive in and he'd had a flat tyre on the way to the rendezvous. He had been stuck without a spare and was towed back to his starting point.

All in all, it had cost three hours of wasted time and a near-nervous breakdown for me.

We drove to a village nearer the border, where I was taken to a house. This turned out to be that of Ali's family, and we were given a good welcome: provided with food, tea and some friendly chat. I was introduced to a rather frail looking Kurdish man with three children of four, five and seven; two girls and a boy in between. The guides were going to take me and this family across into Turkey. The man's wife, he told me, had made it to Sweden, and he and the children were trying to join her. The children already had United Nations refugee status, but there was no official way to get them out of the country.

After finishing our meal of country bread, yoghurt and other village produce, Ali told us to dress warmly, as it would get very cold in the mountains at night. The children had barely anything to wear. Their plastic sandals with no socks would not do to traverse the Kurdish mountains, and the rest of their clothing was not much better. I gave them my spare socks, so both the girls had on two outsize pairs, and the boy one. Ali maintained that the journey would be impossible for them in their sandals, so their father gave one of the other men in the house enough money to go to the village and buy three pairs of wellington boots. This meant a further half an hour's wait while we hung around for his return.

Looking at these children, with their new boots, huge socks and thin, threadbare clothing, I had real doubts. It was going to be a long trek over the rugged Kurdish mountains which were covered in snow and swept by the November winds. We had an enemy this side of the border, while the Turkish state security forces on the other side would hardly welcome us with open arms. Yet here we were, with a four, five and seven-year-old, as if we were about to go on a country picnic.

I raised my doubts with their father. 'Don't worry', he told me. 'These kids have been on the run from the Islamic regime through the mountains since they can remember. They've had to escape from one village to the next away from ground troop attacks and air raids. It's second nature to them. We're Kurds: we're used to these mountains. You just worry about yourself.'

Dusk was descending when we left the house. We clambered into a WWII covered Jeep, the transportees squashed in the back, with Ali driving and a relative of his, Kalan, acting as a guard in the passenger seat. He cradled a sniper's rifle in the crook of his arm. Kalan was in his mid-20s, tall and strongly built. He didn't really look like he needed the rifle. He sat hunched against the door, ready to fire, should the need arise. Once more we drove towards the border, this time on our final leg.

As we headed upland, the only signs of life were children driving flocks of sheep in the opposite direction. The occasional farmer's Jeep would pass us going the other way, its occupants waving as they went. As we went on, even these encounters became rarer. The track was now so rough and steep that any less hardy form of vehicle would have ground to a halt. The drive continued in silence. We surveyed the bleak slopes around us, scanning them for people – particularly troops. It was a stop-start journey. When we approached the crown of each mountain, we would stop and Kalan would get out, run to the other side, and look for danger. He would sweep the way ahead with his binoculars, gun by his side. If he wasn't happy that the way was clear, then we would wait down the far slope until it was considered safe. Then we would drive along until we reached the next mountain peak, where the same security ritual would be repeated.

Some of the route was too much even for the Jeep. At the bottom of the valleys we would face a stream. Ali would follow it downstream until a suitable place to ford could be found. All but Ali would get out so that our Jeep was not too weighed down. We splashed after it, wading through the icy waters.

On the mountain tops we had a similar problem. Often it was too icy, too steep or both for the Jeep to get over with us in it, so we would follow on behind, bags slung over our shoulders. By now four or five hours had passed. It was the middle of the night, and we were in one small Jeep, surrounded by the huge sentinels of the Kurdish mountains. The midnight cold dug its nails into us. Kalan and Ali were used to it, as was the old man. I had the clothes for it, but the children were freezing and miserable. They had on their single items of clothing, thin and so worn and dirty you couldn't tell what the colour used to be. I dug into my sack and handed out the clothes I had. Two got a pullover each, the elder girl my jacket, the arms falling down past her knees. The two smallest got a hat each. You could hardly see them under the rolled up clothing and pulled-down hats.

Finally, we pulled up at a small, dried-mud hut, right on a peak. The moon illuminated the mountains as far as we could see, stretching out in every direction. Here we met our other guide: old, tall, with a face as craggy as the country in which he lived. He was called Raíse: a name for a tribal chief. He and a young couple were waiting in the hut for us. This desolate outpost was where they lived.

Inside, sheltered from the piercing wind and snow, we relaxed. In the centre of the hut's floor was a hollow in which a fire was built up, where they baked bread. We sat, surrounding the fire, toes stretched and waggling, blissfully defrosting. The floor was covered with woollen army blankets and where the chief usually sat, a kilim, woven with Kurdish designs. He offered this prime position to all of us, and wouldn't sit until one of us had occupied it; the old man and his three children sat there, as they were so cold.

We were served from a teapot, heated over the fire, freshly baked bread, and cheese made with milk from their sheep. There was no lavatory. If you felt nature's call, you answered it by melting the snow outside.

Raíse had to make the decision as to whether it was safe to continue. After eating, he went outside with a pack of cigarettes and his binoculars to scan the mountains; looking east for the Islamic guards, and west for the Turkish border patrols. Every now and then, he would come in and report movements. He finally decided that it would be safe enough between 2am and 3am; a rising mist concealing our progress from unfriendly eyes.

Now that we were leaving Iran behind, we handed over our Iranian currency to the couple in the hut, who could make better use of it than us. We also gave them some American dollars out of gratitude for the good food and company, dollars being more stable than Touman.

The children were asleep within minutes of getting into the warm and they took some waking when we were ready to leave. We said our goodbyes to Ali and Kalan, who told us they would meet us a few days later in Turkey, all being well. Then it was out of the warm glow of the little hut into the black of the mountain night, once more to feel the icy fingers of the wind pull at our thin clothing. We now had to contend with intermittent mountain snowfall without the shelter of our Jeep – soon to be sorely missed. The last ten miles would be made on foot.

At 2am we headed off down the mountain slope, in single file behind Raíse. The young man from the hut, Hamad, acted as scout way out in front. Both had binoculars round their necks and a rifle slung over their backs.

The older girl was fiercely independent, trying to show that she didn't need any help. But every now and then she would miss her step and would have to be pulled back to her feet. The four-year-old needed a lot of help, but would only trust her father. I held the little boy's hand tightly, helping to pull him up the slopes and guiding him down, steering him away from the many sheer drops we had to skirt round and along. The older girl chose to divide her time between Hamad and Raíse, so all of us took care of the children. They cried from fear, cold and fatigue over the roughest ground, but there was no time to stop. Our little group had to cover far too much ground before morning if we were to reach anything like safety by daybreak.

At dawn, we found ourselves on a slope looking down on the Turkish border. The earth had been turned over by a bulldozer in one unbroken line, so that if anyone crossed the border they would leave footprints. Over we went, leaving our mark.

A large, grey concrete barracks stood on the horizon, overlooking the valleys. It was surrounded by high walls and barbed wire. The Turkish troop build-up had been as a result of the Gulf war, but was also employed to crush the Kurdish resistance in the area. Both of these conflicts made our crossing that much more hazardous, and life for the Kurdish people of the area uncertain and dangerous.

The sun now struck the mountainside, preventing further progress. Any movement forward would have cast our shadows on the mountain in a way that could be seen from the Turkish barracks.

We headed towards a nearby village, where we would be safe for the day. The villagers told our guides they had been raided that night by Turkish forces looking for guerrillas of the Kurdish Workers' Party (PKK). Many houses had been pulled apart in searches and three or four had been razed to the ground.

The area was thick with Turkish forces. They swarmed through the local villages like a plague of rats. We moved from hut to hut throughout the day so that the locals would not get an idea who we were. The villagers were understandably wary of helping out strangers because the Turkish forces came down hard on Kurds thought to be sympathetic to the uprising. They would destroy crops and carry out random arrests and even summary executions.

By nightfall we were eager to move on. We were introduced to a new guide, a middle-aged, well respected local named Rasheed. He took us by car down the mountain lanes to the nearest border town. It was a hazardous journey. At every twist in the road we would stop and Rashid would survey the road through his binoculars. If the way wasn't clear, we would be hurried out of the car and into the roadside ditch, up would come the bonnet of the car and Rashid and the driver would pretend to be getting their old banger started again. We would lie in the ditch below the level of the window, hardly daring to breathe, until the danger passed.

The children seemed to be old hands at this, as if it was as natural as a game of hide-and-seek. But this wasn't an extension of their games, more a skill they had been forced to learn to survive the war and repression of their homeland. Each time we got through one of these interruptions, I felt I had got over one more hurdle that stood between me and freedom. Three or four hours passed in this manner before we reached the town.

We were taken to a village on the outskirts, where we stayed for nearly a week. The couple who put us up had a large young family and a sizeable house, plus a number of smaller buildings around the yard. We were treated as part of the family, eating with them, being entertained by their music. Kurdish music was banned, so they were careful to keep the noise down. My fellow refugee had his own songs, and would give his own performance, sometimes accompanied by his three children.

Well looked-after though we were, we could not leave the house. There was a great danger that we would be stopped and questioned by Turkish Jandarma, leading to our deportation back to Iran and our hosts' arrest. As long as we stayed here, all our lives were in danger.

Though both the family I escaped with and the one we stayed with were Kurdish, their languages were different, as were their customs. It was not always easy to communicate. We got by with gestures during the days we spent there.

Rasheed would come over once or twice a day to ensure that everything was all right, as did our original guide, Ali. Rasheed said that he was finalising arrangements for the next leg of the trip. One morning, he arrived in a taxi. He explained that this was going to take us to the capital city, Ankara, about 700 miles away. This would get us out of heavily militarised and policed Turkish Kurdistan. We piled in and set off once more, with Rasheed sitting alongside the driver.

Before we left the town, our driver pulled in at a petrol station to fill up. As he was doing so, an armoured troop carrier pulled up on the opposite side of the street. Two soldiers in full combat gear crossed, carrying semi-automatics, and demanded to see our driver's identification. They questioned Rasheed. One walked round to the back of the car to take a look at us. The children stared back at him. The old man looked Kurdish, but could have been Iranian, Iraqi or Turkish. As many of the older Kurdish people could not speak Turkish, the soldier didn't bother to question him. I had on a woollen hat of a local style, trying to look native. I was playing sick, and Rasheed told the soldier that they were taking me to the nearest town for medical treatment. I hoped I appeared ill enough not to be questioned.

The boot was searched, and nothing suspicious was discovered. I was so scared I really didn't need to pretend I was ill, as my hands trembled and my body was bathed in a cold sweat. Our group must have been their patrol's 'first customer', so we were treated to a more thorough search than was normal. After they had poked, prodded and questioned until they were bored, they returned to the troop carrier and we were on our way.

While we passed through Kurdistan Rasheed maintained his habit of stopping at bends to check ahead. When we passed through towns, our driver was careful to keep to the back roads, avoiding any check points. We didn't stop off anywhere, instead eating food we bought along the way, taking our meals while on the move. Rasheed would stop at friendly shops for food and ask the shopkeeper if there were any security checks in front of us. The whole long journey was one incessant worry.

As we continued, the country became flatter. All the land around us was under cultivation. Although the ground was icy, many people from the villages we passed through were still working on the soil.

The car passed through the outskirts of Ankara at about 8pm. This gave us about three hours to kill until the next leg, from Ankara to Istanbul, by bus. We went to the central bus terminal and sat around while Rasheed arranged our tickets. Drivers stood by their coaches, competing for trade, shouting 'Istanbul! Istanbul!', along with their price. We stretched our legs around the bus terminal, taking in the sights before the next long drive. I cleaned up in the public toilets and grabbed myself a bite to eat at a nearby cafe.

At 11pm we clambered into our coach, Rasheed still with us. It would be another 12 to 16 hours on the road, depending on the bus' reliability. After an uncomfortable night's sleep curled up on a bus seat, we pulled into Istanbul at noon. As we stretched out our aches and pains, Rasheed hailed a taxi and took us to a hotel, where we registered under false names. He then passed us over to our next contact, Omar, who was responsible for forged passports and visas.

We were permanently on edge. The whole operation was fraught with risk, both for us and our contacts. There seemed to be a million and one ways in which the whole thing could fall through, even at this late stage. We shared the hotel with other refugees from Iran and Iraq. From them, we heard of others who had been turned back when reaching their destination; some who were arrested while boarding their plane, and others who were ripped off by those who had promised to get them out, leaving them high, dry and broke. A few were apprehended by the security forces and handed back to Iran. As if this was not enough, the Islamic regime had its own killers at work in Turkey, hunting down and murdering refugees. Fear hung over us while we sat around in this refugees' limbo.

After three weeks, when it seemed clear that there was no chance of an immediate transfer to a third country, we decided that it was best to register with the United Nations High Commission on Refugees in Ankara. That, we thought, would make the Turkish authorities less keen to hand us back. Omar made arrangements for the trip to Ankara, once more by overnight bus. We found ourselves a place in the queue at the UN's refugee office, as others who shared our plight milled around, filled in and flourished papers, and harangued officials. This bureaucratic limbo thronged with diverse people and a babble of Turkish, Kurdish, Arabic and Persian tongues. All there seemed to share a peculiar lost, desolate look that characterises so many refugees. There wasn't one of us who knew where we would be next week, and there wasn't one who didn't fear deportation back to where they had escaped from at so much cost.

We queued all day. Towards the evening we were taken to a booth and photographed. Each of us was subject to an individual, probing interview. It felt more like being charged at a police station than being helped to freedom and safety. By nightfall we were given a paper which confirmed our registration with the UN as refugees. At last we had some legal status.

It was a frustrating time. Any thoughts we might have had of a quick passage through Turkey to another country had been banished as we sat in our Istanbul hotel rooms, sinking further into depression as time passed. Each day was just like the last. It was on just such an evening that Turkish police raided the hotel. They forced their way into rooms. The word went round and the 'illegal' refugees got out quick. Even though I was legal, I had already checked out exits less orthodox than the front door. I knew the ways down the fire escape and the windows it was safe to jump from.

It seemed safest not to hang around and explain my legally established status to the police. It is not unknown for the Turkish state to hand legal refugees back to Iran and worry about the paperwork later. I was not registered under my real name and it didn't seem wise to wait to see if the police would choose to make anything out of this irregularity. So down the fire escape I went, and along a narrow alleyway. I got on the main road, frantically hailed a taxi and shouted, 'Bus terminal!', in my broken Turkish. Once I was at the terminal I phoned comrades in Istanbul, explaining what had happened, and then others in Ankara, arranging to be picked up at the station when I arrived the next day.

Noon the next day saw me waiting for my contacts in Ankara. I was picked up by two comrades and taken to a small flat where two families and two individual refugees stayed. The rent was extortionate, and everything was so expensive that everyone was living off a communal vat of beans, supplemented occasionally by butter and potatoes. The water supply was cut off between 8am and 12 midnight in this part of the city so we had to save water to wash dishes and clothes. There was only enough hot water for two or three people a day to shower. It was like being back in prison.

Each family received 500,000 Turkish lira per month, which at the time was about £45. Most went on rent, even though so many people were lodged in one apartment. There was no chance of a refugee finding work, and those who kept their heads above absolute poverty were able to do so only if they had families in the West to help them. Those who had escaped repression in their own countries had to apply to the UN's Refugee Council for official status. If they were denied twice, that was it. They had no legal standing or protection in the country.

The Refugee Council was not only bureaucratic, it was prone to leaks. Often information given to the council would wind up back in the hands of the Islamic regime, generally through one or two of the translators, who had a nice little sideline working for the government we had fled. This put the refugees' lives in danger from the regime's assassins who seemed to operate with impunity, and left our families in Iran open to reprisals. Although the UN was our best way out of Turkey, it was also our greatest danger. The horror stories I heard from other refugees made me keep my distance from the council.

While I was in Turkey, there were two major demonstrations of Iranian refugees outside the UN building in Ankara. The Iranian regime had rented an adjoining apartment so the demonstrators were forced to make their protest with faces covered. Overt co-operation between the Turkish and Iranian governments has aggravated the situation for the refugees caught in the middle. Lists of refugees have been handed back to Iran and, worse, as have refugees in exchange for Kurdish separatists wanted by the Turkish state.

As late as June 1994, a group of Iranian political refugees, some of whom even had acceptance from Denmark, Canada and other countries were arrested. This was as a result of information passed from the UN High Commission for Refugees office in Ankara to the Islamic regime. Another group of Iranian refugees who had seen what had occurred got in the way as the police tried to load the political refugees onto a bus for a border exchange. In the confusion a refugee named Susan Gourjisefat – who had spent eight years in an Islamic jail for her membership of Rahe Kargar – managed to escape. Her husband

and son were held by police demanding she give herself up. Only a worldwide campaign won their release. Nevertheless, at the time of writing, the Turkish state still refuses to allow them to leave Turkey for Denmark, where they have been accepted. In short, Turkey was not a place where Iranian refugees wanted to linger.

A month passed while I lived in this crowded Ankara apartment. During this whole time, it was not possible for me to phone my family and tell them where I was, or even that I was still alive. At this precarious stage, I could afford no footprints. But I did receive a call from a contact in Germany, telling me that he had made arrangements for me to move there. Though my situation in Turkey was not good, this didn't seem an attractive prospect. This was at a time of frequent riots outside refugee hostels in Germany instigated by the far right, and petrol-bombing of immigrants' houses. Germany wasn't exactly rolling out the welcome mat. I didn't want to escape political persecution in Iran only to swap it for racial persecution in Germany.

I neither spoke nor understood the language and realised through my experience in Turkey how isolated that would make me. After much hesitancy, I decided to hold out for an English-speaking country. So, the night before I was due to go to Germany, I phoned my contact there and explained my decision.

He was not best pleased, especially so late in the day. He expressed concern that I was ducking the political issues, as Germany was at this time the European centre of political opposition to the Islamic regime. I said that the opposite was the case. I wanted to be somewhere I could communicate.

He asked if it was the US I wanted. I replied, 'No'. I'd lived in the States for quite some time before, and knew that the political scene was pretty dead, especially within the refugee community. The affluent monarchists liked it, to the extent that the Beverly

Hills area of Los Angeles became known as downtown Iran-geles. They even have their own round-the-clock radio and cable stations. The radical Iranian political refugees were spread so thin that you couldn't really call them a community in the US. Furthermore, America's distance from Europe left it totally cut off from the main focus of Iranian exile protest. As far as refugee politics went, it was a backwater. Canada and Australia were out of the question for the same reason.

I wanted to get to Britain. I asked Omar, my contact in Ankara, to try to get the documentation that would make this possible. It turned out that this would prove more costly and time-consuming. Britain would take another month. I waited until one of my Turkish contacts turned up with a forged Spanish passport and other travel documents, to make it possible for me to get out of Turkey, through Germany and to Britain. I was to leave that day.

Three hours before I was due to go to the airport, I took a look at my passport. My hair colour was apparently 'light brown'. There was no way that this passport was going to get me through, unless the immigration control in Turkey, Germany and Britain all happened to be colour blind. I told Omar that I was not going to risk travelling with these documents. 'No problem', he said. 'I've dealt with worse cases than this. Just be glad it's not the colour of your eyes that's wrong', he said with a smirk. Off we drove, looking for a hairdresser with light-brown dye to spare.

'Quick,' Omar explained to the bemused hairdressers as we burst through the door, 'this man's getting married in an hour-and-a-half. As you can see, he needs emergency treatment!' (Thanks for the compliment, I thought). They went to work, dying my hair, moustache and eyebrows light brown. I walked out of the shop with a new head of lustrous locks, hoping that the colour definition on my passport photo was poor enough to let me get away with it.

With no time to spare, we drove like fury to Ankara airport. Omar had his foot to the floor, fist constantly thumping the car horn at anything that came anywhere near our path. We got to passport control with minutes to spare. Hot and flustered with nervous tension, I stood in front of the passport booth as the policeman stared at me and my photo. I just hoped the sweat wouldn't make the dye run. But he nodded me through and I was soon on the plane. The flight transfer in Germany went smoothly – almost blissfully at this stage – as did my clearance through customs at Heathrow ten hours after leaving Ankara.

I was just a bit disappointed that nobody remarked how nice my hair looked.

CHAPTER 23

PRISON HISTORY AND POLITICAL TRENDS

Before I was arrested I had become accustomed to standing in queues for bread, meat and rice, fat, soap and practically every other essential of life. All of these became scarce and only found on the black market for 20 to 30 times more than the official price. One would not expect to experience the same queues in prison. But in the Islamic regime's prisons, I had to queue to get in, queue for the toilet, for the infirmary, for food, queue to be tortured. There was even a queue for the firing squad.

This was a reflection of what was going on in Iranian society as a result of the war with Iraq: queues for bread and water, for trains and buses, in the towns and in the cities; queues in battle to go to the frontline, queues for burial plots for the victims of the war and the victims of torture and repression.

The policies pursued in the prisons were symptomatic of the wider political aims of the government, as developments inside paralleled the wider perspectives of the regime.

281

What we were subjected to within the prison walls was a microcosm of Iran, illustrating how the regime viewed the society it ruled.

Our experiences showed the inability of the regime to understand the reciprocal and dynamic relationship between the individual and society. The mullahs' outlook could not countenance change in either the individual or society. For the religious authorities, the world was immutable, governed by divine laws which they saw themselves as bound to guard and implement. In a very real sense, all of Iran is one huge jail; the prison regulations being religious dogma.

A general characteristic of the Islamic regime is that it constantly distorts the reality of its own existence and of those under it. It paints human rights as wrong, clerical reaction as progress and democracy, counter-revolution as the only true revolution.

Look at the name 'Islamic Republic'. It is a contradiction in terms. A republic is governed by its people, whereas the Islamic regime is ostensibly the rule of God, through a fraction of the religious hierarchy. The leader has full and ultimate power over the judicial, executive and legislative spheres of the state. He is the commander-in-chief of all armed forces. Society is run by the interpretation of the Koran by one – unelected – man. He has jurisdiction over your whole life, private and public: how you conduct yourself, who you marry.

The structures of a republic, whereby a government would be checked and guided by the populace, are absent. This individual gets his instructions from God; his job is to enforce these on earth, and there can be no interference in this. All this and more constitutes what is called the Vali-Faghih – the absolute rule of the prime religious authority. In 1979 we overthrew a secular monarch and were rewarded with the imposition of a clerical one.

There is no clearer example of this theocracy's disdain for the people than that which we lived out in prison. Guards, interrogators, torturers and state prosecutors are not called by these names. The prisoner is forced to call her rapist, mutilator and butcher 'brother'. The places in which all this takes place are not called prisons. No: I spent three years at the 'Islamic University of Evin'.

Conditions in prison changed according to the political priorities of the regime. When it felt threatened, as in the summer of 1988, we paid a terrific price. But this was preceded by a period of relative liberalisation as Ayatollah Montazeri emphasised the need for religious indoctrination rather than terror. Below is a breakdown of these distinct periods:

- February 1979 to September 1980: from the revolution to the start of the Iran–Iraq war.
- September 1980 to June 1981: The period to the Mojahedin's failed coup.
- June 1981 to 1985: The Islamic regime destroys all organised political opposition.
- Consolidation of the regime up to the end of the Iran–Iraq war. A period of relative liberalisation.
- Late 1987 to early 1989: Internal oppression in response to the reaction to Iran's military defeat. The prison counterpart is the massive wave of executions.
- Spring 1989 to 1991: The regime seeks Western economic support and greater integration into the world market. It normalises conditions in prisons. Some prisoners are given early release dates.

FEBRUARY 1979 TO SEPTEMBER 1980

This was the honeymoon period. Most prison officials had spent years in the jails under the Shah – two examples well known to Iranians being the first governor of Evin under Khomeini, Haji Kasha, and his successor, Haji Lajiverdi. Most political prisoners were officials of the old regime: Savak torturers, royalist army brass, deposed ministers and the like.

Some left-wing and Mojahedin prisoners were jailed, in particular from areas where struggle continued after the revolution along emerging class or national lines, as in Kurdistan or Turkmensahra, where the peasants seized the land and organised peasant shoras under the leadership of the Fedayeen. Workers' shoras that seized control of factories and refused to concede power to the Islamic regime also found their militants being arrested.

Censorship had not been tightened yet, and prisoners could still freely obtain literature within the jails, whether Marx's works or the papers of the left organisations. Such practices as blindfolding had yet to be introduced and were derided as 'Israeli' by prison officials. Relations between political prisoners and guards was cordial and those I knew in prison at the time went so far as to describe prison food as excellent.

This was a time when political discussions not only took place between prisoners, but between prisoners and guards. The honeymoon, however, proved to be short-lived.

SEPTEMBER 1980 TO JUNE 1981

The regime began to attack democratic freedoms systematically: women's rights, workers' organisations, Kurdish national rights – the list became ever longer. It was inevitable that those who stood against this tide and defended the gains won through the overthrow of the Shah would be swept into prison.

All freedom of expression was crushed under the weight of Khomeini's interpretation of Islamic orthodoxy – just six months after we had swept away the Shah's censorship. Khomeini gave the order to 'break the pens of the ungodly writers into pieces'. Those who had given voice to the revolutionary sentiments of February 1979 were denied access to the media and often jailed. Many papers were closed down, from communist to liberal. Newspaper offices were razed to the ground by mobs of Hezbollah. And, in the hallmark of totalitarian regimes, mass book burnings were organised. Huge bonfires of critical works appeared where once had stood bookstalls. The biggest were piled up in front of the University of Tehran. In the lowest pit of Hell, Hitler must have danced with glee.

The regime was preparing the ground for a frontal assault on the left and all opposition. It needed a pretext, and this was provided by the Mojahedin's poorly-prepared putsch. After they blew up the headquarters of the Islamic Republican Party, killing around 120 leaders of the regime, and the second bomb attack on the prime minister and president, the mullahs gave the green light to wipe out the opposition. People were killed indiscriminately. The regime declared martial law and closed down every road entering every city. Groups of Hezbollah rampaged throughout the country, interning thousands of innocent people.

Hundreds and thousands were killed in these clashes. The Hezbollah would assemble in the city centres, block all surrounding roads and round up all the people in the streets. Sometimes they would round up even more people later that day, at other times they would move to other areas of the cities. People were manhandled into police vans or other vehicles commandeered by the Hezbollah, including buses stopped and emptied mid-journey, and driven to local headquarters of the Hezbollah. Here, captives would be interrogated and despatched to Islamic revolutionary guard prisons or Islamic Komitehs. Few were released after interrogation.

The first member of Rahe Kargar to be killed in these events was a young student arrested near Tehran University as she tried to make her way to a street protest. Taken to Evin, she was tortured and summarily shot with a copy of *Rahe Kargar* as evidence. It took us three years to find out for certain what had happened to her, as the only thing she gave under torture was a false name. Like so many others, she lies in an anonymous grave somewhere in Tehran.

The Prosecutor General, Mousavi Tabrizi, said that those wounded in these street clashes should not be taken to hospitals. He echoed the views of Khomeini, who believed these events constituted a threat against Islam, God and the Islamic regime. According to him, such wounded were at war with Allah and 'the Imam of the epoch', Khomeini. As a result, the law decreed their lives were worthless, or 'dangerous on earth' and so they should be killed whenever they were found. Although no official figures are available, unofficial estimates put the number of wounded who were summarily killed at several hundred in Tehran alone. You can imagine, if this was the regime's way of working in the open arena of the cities, how atrocious life was hidden behind the walls of the prisons.

JUNE 1981 TO 1985

Contact between political groups was minimal. The groups in prison focused on day-to-day survival, leaving no space for political discussion with others. Even within a particular organisation, discussion was brought to a standstill, especially within Evin and the Golden Fortress. Any kind of interpersonal contact was dangerous and each individual fought desperately to save himself and his comrades.

Tudeh and the Fedayeen Majority were the smallest of the groups within the prisons because their support for the regime had temporarily shielded them from its assault. But this also cut off their prisoners from the rest of the left in the jails. In 1983 the number of inmates from Tudeh and the Fedayeen Majority in the Golden Fortress was only about 40. Haji Davoud concentrated them in section 3, Mujaradi block 3. Their behaviour was not uniform and their relations with others varied according to the individuals. Some were active Tavabs, working closely with the prison officials. Others just wanted to keep their heads down, survive from one day to the next and get out as soon as possible, while some would actively resist. Some prisoners toed the leadership line, that the regime was 'popular, anti-imperialist and progressive', and that the war with Iraq was for 'the defence of the homeland'. Others would in practice break with this line by working with those their leaders called 'counter-revolutionary' in defence of prisoners' rights and conditions. For them, this exposed the contradiction between their organisations' line and their own experiences. Unfortunately, they made up only a small percentage of the Tudeh and Majority prisoners as yet. But the number and the outlook of these prisoners was to change radically from 1984 on, after the arrest of hundreds of leading cadres.

The Mojahedin had most members behind bars and was singled out for special treatment, as it had a very young and inexperienced rank and file. About 80 per cent were under 18. The regime put them under extreme pressure in an attempt to break as many as possible and create an army of Tavab youth in the prisons. The regime was encouraged in this policy by the forced defection of many prominent militia activists in the Mojahedin's failed rising of 1981.

One successful militia leader, Mehran Asdaghi, became a Tavab, and a focal point for the recruitment of many other young Tavabs from the same background. In the Golden Fortress he organised a Tavab 'flying column' that would maraud from block to block, leaving a trail of blood and broken bodies after it.

The prison officials tried to attract the youth and so isolate the intransigent Mojahed. By creating a strong pole of Tavab attraction in this way, the regime wanted to win over the passive majority and destroy the core of the Mojahedin. Most Mojahedin who did not capitulate, attempted to defend themselves by feigning passivity, or becoming tactical Tavabs.

287

Having accepted this fetid swamp for expediency's sake, some were soon submerged in it. Haji Davoud relied on his ability to attract young people – 'Good Islamic kids who have been fooled by the counter-revolutionaries'. The Tavabs were his way of 'helping them to save their souls'. Those Mojahedin who resisted went through quarantine, doomsday, solitary and were often executed.

The ranks of the left-wing organisations were peppered with Tavabs, but not to the same extent as the Mojahedin. Often they took on the role of advisors to Hajis Lajiverdi and Davoud, and executed their own comrades.

After the Mojahedin, the left-wing organisations made up the largest prison body. Although much smaller than the Mojahedin, they resisted the pressures much better. The mainstay of the intransigents was the left, which provided the greatest proportion of its overall numbers to prison resistance than any other category.

Conditions at this time fomented distrust between one prisoner and the next. Contacts between the left and the Mojahedin were minimal. The Mojahedin's leaders within the jails were keen to limit their members' links with the left in order to preserve their Islamic credentials in the eyes of an increasingly murderous regime. They also sought to limit the influence of the left on their young and inexperienced members.

As a result of all this, the left, Tudeh and Majority and the Mojahedin, ignored each other. This was the period of the greatest hostility and least co-operation between organisations in the whole history of prison in Iran. This played into the hands of the regime, which was eager to foster alienation and mutual mistrust. If prisoners did not trust each other, it was impossible for them to organise together, and the work of the prison authorities became much easier. It was probably the only way that the massive influx into the prisons at the time could have been handled without an explosion.

These conditions encouraged the emergence of Tavabiat, as many prisoners were overwhelmed by an entirely new situation that they did not know how to confront.

1985 TO 1987

International human rights organisations focused on the Islamic regime's prison record, as news of the show trials, summary executions, doomsday and quarantine filtered through to the outside world. This was stimulated by the emerging organisation of the prisoners' families, demanding to know what was being done to their incarcerated relatives. Khomeini's heir apparent, Ayatollah Montazeri, was particularly sensitive to such pressure, as he made great play of listening to the opinions of the people. (This proved to be his Achilles heel: after the prison massacres of 1988–89, Montazeri wrote to Khomeini criticising this butchery as 'un-Islamic'. Such outspoken opinions were not well received and Montazeri found himself supplanted by the more pliant Khameini, a student of Montazeri who didn't then even hold the religious rank of ayatollah.)

The war was ebbing and the regime was not challenged by internal opposition. Consequently, it felt able to make concessions to the prisoners' families and human rights organisations. Figures associated with the recent prison regime, such as Haji Davoud and Haji Lajiverdi, were quietly shunted sideways. A new prison leadership associated with Montazeri was installed. The institution of Tavabism was discredited and prisoners were given limited freedom of movement and organisation, although no right of political expression was conceded.

Political organisations within the prisons attempted to utilise these opportunities not only to organise within themselves, but to coordinate essential actions with other groupings. This included not just political resistance within the blocks but sporting activities. The new atmosphere also began to encourage political discussion among individuals and groups. This level of co-operation is unique in Iranian prison life under both the Shah and the Islamic regime. The effects of this were not entirely beneficial. With the lifting of the intense pressure, some groupings which had been forced to co-operate by the previous conditions again became openly hostile.

By this time, most of the Tudeh and Fedayeen Majority prisoners had become integrated within the prison resistance, as most had now been in jail for four or five years, and had dropped any support for the regime.

The main forces of the left – Fedayeen Minority, Rahe Kargar, Komoleh and the remnants of Peykar – formed the core of resistance. Alliances were forged with Mojahedin prisoners when possible. The relationship with the Tudeh and Majority proved more rocky, as the left in some prisons refused to associate with organisations that had previously given full support to the Islamic regime.

Structured discussions began to take place on the reasons for the defeat of the revolution, the nature of the Islamic regime and the like.

The Mojahedin leadership attempted to insulate its rank and file from political discussion which threatened to undermine their organisation, as its membership was younger and far more politically inexperienced on average than that of the left. Instead, they attempted to fill their time with handicrafts, physical exercise and the like. In addition, their members were kept on the boil by being told that the regime's collapse was imminent. Optimism substituted for balanced political judgement as they waited for their tank battalions to roll in from Iraq.

The resistance which was successfully organised through this period would not have been possible without the wide scale co-operation between the diverse political organisations throughout the prisons of Iran.

LATE 1987 TO EARLY 1989

Prison authorities attempted to clamp down on the freedoms won during the previous period. This led to the systematic elimination of those considered to represent a threat to the Islamic regime – especially if they ever saw the outside of a prison compound again.

Unified prisoners' organisations were attacked and the prison authorities refused to recognise prisoners' representatives. A process of identifying activists began. Collective actions were forcibly smashed. Individual prisoners were screened through weekly interrogation. Questions and answers were all recorded in writing. Those identified as troublemakers were removed from their blocks and put into solitary. All prisoners were under permanent 24-hour a day lockup – the effective reintroduction of quarantine.

In early 1988, there was huge prison reorganisation on the basis of the information gathered. Great care was taken to separate the Islamic from the prisoners of the left. Once begun, this reshuffling went on for four months. It had the effect of dispersing the prison activists, destroying their organisations.

The regime then embarked on the mass execution of political prisoners. As a result of the constant moving of prisoners, news of the massacres was slow to spread, as the prison grapevine was destroyed. Most reports estimate that between 10,000 and 12,000 prisoners were executed at this time. The Mojahedin was the hardest hit by these massacres and, for the first time, the Tudeh party also lost the majority of their leaders and cadres to execution.

The massacres had the obvious effect of forcing prisoners back into themselves – having prison contacts once more carried the death penalty.

SPRING 1989 TO 1991

The regime denied any massacre, trying to force prisoners to write declarations that no such event took place. Pressure from prisoners' families built up, understandably as they were worried at not seeing their sons and daughters for months. Political exiles bought news of the massacres to world attention.

The regime screened its remaining prisoners to see if it was possible to allow some out on a short-term discharge to alleviate the accusations.

The massacres brutally illustrated to those in the hands of the Islamic regime's prison authorities that they were no more than hostages to be used in bargaining when possible, slaughtered when not. The immediate effect of this was to further limit prison activity – aware that they can be shot at any time, the priority for each individual was not to attract attention. The cohesion between political groupings was consequently not rebuilt.

CHAPTER 24

A CENTURY
OF PRISONS

The modern prison system in Iran came into existence with the establishment of the centralised state after the 1907 constitutional revolution. Before this, each feudal fiefdom throughout Persia would run its own system. Justice was administered by the Islamic sharia courts, overseen by mullahs. There was no standard and unified legal code, and each judge dispensed judgement in accordance with their own interpretation of the Koran and other Islamic authorities.

A basic demand of the 1907 revolution was the removal of the sharia courts and the enactment of a centralised judicial system similar to the Napoleonic code of France. But in 1922, Reza Shah established a one man dictatorship: the Pahlavi dynasty. This arrested the development of the wider potential of civil society, while maintaining the concept of a unified judicial code. The establishment of Soviet power in northern regions of the country in the wake of the 1917 Russian revolution was met with repression from the Shah, to try to prevent Iranian people from sympathising with the Russians after their revolution, and, in 1931, the anti-Communist act was passed. The maximum penalty for violating this act was death.

In 1936 the 'Group of 53', led by Dr Taghi Arani, were arrested, charged with conspiracy to overthrow the government through a 'Bolshevik revolution'. Substantive evidence included circulating and translating proscribed books, plus contributing to the illegal theoretical magazine, *The World*. One defendant was accused of sending money to aid the Republican side in the Spanish civil war. The group, made up of academics and professionals, had no wide support, so Reza Shah had a free hand to dispense with them as he wished.

During their trial, each defendant was provided with a book detailing the court proceedings, and how they could enact their own defence, should they wish to do so. Each was provided with their own defence lawyer by the Ministry of Justice. Arani commented that some of these defence lawyers inflicted more harm on the accused than the prosecution. This was not universally the case. One lawyer in particular, Dr Aghayan, put forward a strong and courageous defence of his client. Every defendant was allowed to address the court. The trial took place in open court, with each side allowed to call witnesses. Representatives of the national and international press were present, and the case was widely reported.

According to one of the imprisoned 53, Bozorg Alavi, (considered the founder of modern Iranian literature), fresh eggs, cigarettes and even opium were allowed into the prison of Komiteh Moshterak. The prisoners were given daily deliveries of hot food. Dirty washing was handed to the prisoners' families, who returned it clean. The guards were most amenable to bribery and, if the price was right, acted as couriers for the prisoners.

There was an exercise period each day, which the 53 were

allowed to organise as a group, without interference from prison officials.

Arani, the leader of the 53, said to visualise a bayonet point under your chin during interrogation. If you nod your head, you stab yourself; if you shake your head, you remain unscathed. In other words, admit to nothing. He attempted to organise a hunger strike and, as punishment for this, was sentenced to 300 lashes. As a response, over 100 prisoners took up the hunger strike.

CHAPTER 25

PARADISE LOST... OR REGAINED? A LOOK TO THE FUTURE

The major industrial city of Ghazvin is just over 150 kilometres northwest of Tehran. In late October 1994 it erupted. The population took to the streets en masse, arming themselves as their numbers grew. Crowds were drawn to the headquarters of the Islamic guard. The building was attacked and the demonstrators rebuffed under heavy fire. Undeterred, they attacked again – and again, like waves against a rock until, suffering great losses, they were at last successful in seizing the building. It was ransacked and put to the torch, after which the crowds moved their attention to other buildings belonging to the security forces.

With the initial victory over the Islamic guard to encourage them, other offices fell and the streets were stripped of billboards bearing pictures of Khomeini and Islamic slogans. Once the security forces had been driven out, attention was turned to the banks, who had their funds redistributed, and municipal buildings, which were occupied by the demonstrators and became organising centres for what had become a city-wide uprising.

A citizens' defence militia was organised, and brigades of between one to two hundred people secured the major roads into the city. Vehicles were only admitted through the checkpoints if they bore banners with slogans such as 'Down with the Islamic regime!' on them. The city was cleansed of the regime's paraphernalia. The citizens were in control of their own city.

Local armed forces were deployed against the population. However, after a couple of initial clashes, these forces in effect mutinied: they refused to be deployed against civilians. The government had to resort to deploying its crack troops from Tehran and other cities further afield.

After three days of bloody fighting, in which Ghazvin's defenders were strafed from helicopter gunships, the Islamic regime won back the city. But its troops had been forced to fight for every street, every house, as the citizens' militia fought bitterly for their city. House-to-house searches and arrests continued for over a month throughout Ghazvin. As a direct response, three brigadiers and a colonel representing opinion from the armed forces and Islamic guard submitted a letter to the regime, deploring their use against those who 'have committed no crime except to speak out the common demands of the people'.

Ghazvin was no isolated event. In 1993–94 alone there were massive, spontaneous uprisings in the cities of Mashad, Arak, Tabriz, Zahedan and Shiraz. Six revolts, all in provincial capitals, in two years. The frequency with which they were occurring was increasing, as was the number of people involved.

All these revolts were important. But I have dwelt on events in Ghazvin because at the time it bore the closest resemblance to the revolutionary upheavals which precipitated the over-throw of the Shah in 1979. In Ghazvin, the masses were at their most determined, the most conscious of their goal – the overthrow of the regime. Undoubtedly, the experience of those who participated in the earlier revolution was well-employed to prepare the ground for a new one.

When I, and many others, were jailed, we were told that we were nothing more than isolated intellectuals, infested with Western corruption. The regime believed that by physically eliminating us, it eliminated the 'cancer' of dissent and dissatisfaction. The events of the mid-1990s show what a hopeless project this was.

No one protested when I was arrested. Yet when I was released, I was bowled over by the welcome from those same neighbours who had been glad to see the back of the troublemaker ten years before. Our whole country learned painfully – through unemployment, poverty, repression and war – exactly what Khomeini's promise of the kingdom of God on earth meant. And they were angry – red with rage – at how they have been lied to, and the millions of lives this lie has cost.

Khomeini's promises of 1979 did not square with the reality. The gulf between Islamic utopia and reality filled up with more corpses by the day. And when the dead number your mother or brother, when you can be the next in the war zone where years later we were still finding the dead, you cannot ignore it. In fact, you cannot live with it: this grotesque Islamic behemoth threatens your life at every turn and lurch. Eventually, your very survival demands that it goes or you do. Until the fundamentalist regime is consigned to the dustbin of history, all our lives in Iran are threatened.

So forcefully have the dictates of survival impressed themselves on the minds of millions now, that they are prepared to risk their lives in uprisings like those of Ghazvin, Mashad, Arak, Tabriz, Zahedan and Shiraz.

And so we come to the present day and little seems to have changed but that doesn't mean that things can't change.

First of all, let's make clear just who is President Mahmoud Ahmadinejad. He is nothing more than a puppet in the hands of the leader of the Islamic regime, Ayatollah Seyed Ali Hoseyni Khamenei, who has been Supreme Leader of Iran since June 1989 and who claims to run the country on the basis of God's law. His whole structure of government is based on ministers from the counter-revolutionary force of Islamic Jihadists who have fought in Afghanistan, Iraq and Lebanon.

At the moment most of the ministers are former generals in the army whose only present fight is to see who can get the lion's share of property, oil and revenues in Iran. The whole structure is based on fascism, much like the Nazis, with black-shirted forces in the streets running around and arresting everyone from workers to intellectuals and students. Workers are still being killed because they want the simple things their counterparts in the West take for granted – the right to organise, bargain, and if needs be, strike.

Apart from the Shia hierarchy, of which Khamenei is the head, and Ahmedinajad's government, there is a third segment– the security arm which is responsible for international terrorism, drug smuggling and trading in arms and ammunition to African states.

The present regime faced its most important challenge with the protests following the 2009 presidential election. Protests have erupted ever since, again in February 2011 concurrent with the Arab Spring and it is my belief that as the people overthrew the Shah in 1979 they can overthrow this present regime. It won't come with an attack from the West because I don't believe the people, and there are nearly 80 million of them, are in favour of foreign military intervention. We have seen the chaos that resulted in Iraq and Afghanistan and the damage done in Libya. If the West really wants to help smash this regime then they should firstly stop buying any Iranian oil and then more importantly stop selling refined products like petrol back to them. If these two things happened the regime would be finished within months. It may sound simple but if millions and millions of Iranians suddenly found themselves without any petrol for their cars the protests of 2009 would seem tame by comparison.

And finally the question I am asked probably more than any other: Is Iran really building a nuclear bomb? When I was a professor of economics at Tehran University right at the beginning of this story I was arguing for a non-nuclear Iran. Why should a country which has the second largest gas supplies in the world and the third or fourth biggest oil reserves suddenly need nuclear power? There was no economic justification for it then and there is none now, unless of course the aim is for more than simply nuclear power. So my answer is yes, they are trying to create nuclear bombs.

Were we right to stand up and oppose the regime when we did? Did we achieve anything as a result of all the sacrifice? History will be the judge of that, not the mullahs who passed death sentences on innumerable women and men who wanted no more than a better world. But history fights no battles, creates nothing, destroys nothing. History is no more or less than the sum of the efforts of real women and men. Judgement will be informed by those who experienced the regime at its worst: the many thousands who survived the prison system and helped form the backbone to opposition.

I have tried to write a testimony to all those who resisted the Islamic regime in its foul prisons; a tribute to all those who died, like my friend and comrade Firooz Alvandi. But this will not be the tribute... though it is coming. The only tribute worthy of the fallen is the realisation of the sort of society they gave their lives in the struggle to build: pluralistic, democratic and just.

In 1979, our people made the mistake of overthrowing one ruler, only to hand power to another. The result was a tragedy. If that tragedy is not to be repeated, then the power that the workers take must be held for themselves, in the bodies they create. Only the masses can guarantee the rights of the masses: rights for workers, women, nationalities and all the others that have been denied for so long.

EPILOGUE

Unfortunately Dr. Ghaffari's amazing escape to the UK was no immediate cause for celebration because his wife, who was still in Tehran, had no idea where her husband was and his children had lost their father.

'The night before I decided to leave I told my wife I was going but not where I was going,' he explains. 'She had no idea. But still I pleaded with her not to tell anyone else, none of the family or friends, no one. I feared if anyone else knew pressure could be put on them. This way my wife could honestly say she had never been involved in any of my political activities and now I was gone she did not know where I was.'

Dr. Ghaffari had already been to court and given over everything to his wife so the Islamic Regime could not get their hands on his apartment in Tehran when he disappeared. Before leaving he kissed his children and told them to be good and said he was going to visit their aunt who lived in a town near Tabriz. In fact he did contact his sister, but it was not until a week after he arrived in the UK. He phoned her and told her to get in touch with his wife, tell her the news that he was in the UK, and ask the family to prepare to leave for Turkey immediately because at the time no visas were needed to pass across the border with Iran and Turkey.

When his wife and children arrived in the Turkish capital Ankara they had little money but stayed with 'comrades' of Dr. Ghaffari who also had relations in prison in Iran. Although there was 10 to 15 people living in two rooms his wife and children were relatively safe. It was cold that winter but they stayed there for three months.

'I didn't know exactly where they were,' he says. 'But they were in a safe place and that's when I contacted Amnesty International in London.'

Amnesty International knew immediately who Dr. Ghaffari was because he was listed as a prisoner of conscience and a person whose life was in danger. They quickly contacted the Home Office to help sort out Dr. Ghaffari's legal status in the UK. Once that was completed and his family's whereabouts established it took about a month for Amnesty International to send airline tickets to his wife and children in Ankara so they could all be re-united in London.

Dr. Ghaffari still lives in London with his wife. Two of his children are also in the UK with his eldest daughter living in Sweden.

The tortures and beatings that Dr. Ghaffari suffered during his years of incarceration have left a toll on his health. He has a broken back and suffers from the neurological disorder Huntington's Disease. He has to go to hospital every month and is treated as an in-patient about every six months.

But he is unswervingly grateful to the British people. He says: 'I would like to thank everyone including your wonderful health service for everything you have done for me and my family.'

GLOSSARY

Baha'ists: religious followers of Baha'u'llah whom they believe is a messenger from God similar to Abraham, Zoroaster, Moses, Buddha, Jesus and Muhammed.

Bazaari: name given to merchants and workers in bazaars, the traditional marketplaces of Iran.

Chador: an open cloak worn as an outer garment by Iranian women and female teenagers with a head hole at the top. It is tossed over the head and then held closed in the front.

Evin: a prison in north-western Tehran. Due to the number of intellectuals held there, it was nicknamed Evin University.

Fatwah: a juristic ruling concerning Islamic law issued by an Islamic scholar. In popular terms it is seen to be a death sentence imposed upon a person. This is one possibility but is rarely used. It came to prominence over Salman Rushdie's allegedly profane book *The Satanic Verses*.

Fedais: non-disciplined guerrilla fighters, usually associated with opposition to the Islamic regime, but some supported Khomeini and fought on the side of the regime.

Fedayeen: a Marxist-leaning activist group. Operating between 1971 and 1983, the Fedayeen carried out a number of political assassinations in the course of the struggle against the Shah, after which the group was suppressed. In 1979, the Iranian People's Fedâi Guerrillas split from the Organization of Iranian People's Fedaian (Majority).

Ghapani: a form of torture in which victims are hung up like lamb carcasses.

Ghazvin: at an altitude of 1800 metres and 165 kilometres north of Tehran, the climate is cold but dry. It is the capital and largest city of the Province of Qazvin and has a population approaching 500,000 people.

Ghezel Hesar: Iran's biggest prison and known as the 'Golden Fortress'.

Iran–Iraq war: it lasted from September 1980 to August 1988, making it the longest conventional war of the 20th century. It began with Iraq invading Iran and resulted in more than 500,000 deaths and many more injured. There was such large-scale trench warfare that it is often compared to World War I.

Gohardshast: a prison 20 km west of Tehran, where there were systematic executions and interrogation of monarchists, students and Marxists after the 1979 revolution.

Hejab: (or Hijab) refers to the head covering traditionally worn by Muslim women.

Hezbollahi: members of the Party of God (Hezbollah), formed at the time of the 1979 Iranian revolution to assist Ayatollah Ruhollah Khomeini and his forces in consolidating power.

Imam: an Islamic leader for the Muslim community and often worship leader at a mosque.

Jandarma: paramilitary force with responsibility for security throughout the countryside and specific border sectors.

Kilim: flat tapestry-woven carpet or rug.

Komiteh Moshterak: a security prison in Tehran, which literally means 'joint committee' first used by the Shah.

Majles: Iranian Parliament or People's House – national legislative body of Iran.

Mohareb: perpetrator of a crime under Islamic law. Literally means 'enemy of God'.

Pasdar: a Revolutionary Guard (or Army of the Guardians of the Islamic Revolution to give them their correct title), belonging to a branch of Iran's military founded after the Iranian revolution of 1979.

Peykar: also known as the 'Maxist Mojahedin' and a splinter group of the People's Mujahedin of Iran (PMol). Founded in 1975, by the mid-Eighties it was no longer considered active.

Rahe Kargar: a Marxist Iranian political organisation founded in 1980 calling for social justice, human rights and revolution in Iran.

SAVAK: the secret police, domestic security and intelligence service established by Shah Reza Mohammed on the recommendation of the British Government. It lasted from 1957 until the Pahlavi dynasty overthrow of 1979.

Shoras: workers' councils.

Tavabiat: system of using 'tavabs' or collaborators to spy and report on prisoners in jail.

Tudeh: an Iranian communist party formed in 1941. It still exists in a much weakened form because it was banned following mass arrests by the Islamic regime in 1982 and mass executions in 1988.